Murder on the Rails

The True Story of the Detective Who Unlocked the
Shocking Secrets of the Boxcar Serial Killer

Lt. William G. Palmini, Jr.
and
Tanya Chalupa

New Horizon Press
Far Hills, New Jersey

New Horizon Press
P.O. Box 669
Far Hills, NJ 07931

Palmini, Jr., William G. and Tanya Chalupa:
Murder on the Rails:
The True Story of the Detective Who Unlocked the Shocking Secrets of the
Boxcar Serial Killer

Cover Design: Wendy Bass
Interior Design: Susan M. Sanderson

Library of Congress Control Number: 200410801

ISBN: 0-88282-243-8
New Horizon Press

Manufactured in the U.S.A.

2008   2007   2006   2005   2004   /   5   4   3   2   1

Table of Contents

Acknowledgments

This book could not have been written without the help and guidance of many individuals. First, the authors would like to thank our agent Jake Elwell for his faith and direction.

In the research for this book, our special thanks go to the following individuals for their assistance and input: Sergeant Mike Allison of the Roseville Police Department, California, Detective Bill Summers of the Placer County Sheriff's Office, California, and Detective Mike Quakenbush, Salem Police Department, Oregon. The authors also thank and acknowledge the following law enforcement officers for their contributions: Sergeant Wade Harper, Emeryville Police Department; retired Sergeant Douglas Bera, Woodland Police Department; Officer Keith Libby, Barstow Police Department; Detective Jack Underhill, Colton Police Department; Detective Jim Rider, Big Spring Police Department; Sergeant Donna Brown and Sergeant Jeff Johnson, Tallahassee Police Department; Detective Guy Yoshikawa, Salt Lake City Police Department; Special Agent Bruce Mellor, Kansas Bureau of Investigation; Agent Barry Galloway, California Department of Justice and Detective Kevin Horn, formerly with the Albany Police Department now serving as International Police Advisor in Iraq.

We are also grateful to Mary Silveria for her generosity in sharing so much of her life with Robert Joseph Silveria Jr., and to Naomi Correia for her lively accounts of life on the edge. Also, many thanks to the members of the FTRA who allowed us into their world.

Introduction

Robert Silveria Jr. was not the only killer I dealt with in my thirty-six years in law enforcement. I investigated scores of high profile crime cases before he came along. What made him different when we finally came face to face was his ability to make me forget, for at least a few moments, that I was dealing with a brutal killer with a long and bloody trail who had committed heinous crimes against fellow human beings.

Silveria pulled me into his world not once, not twice but three times, until I finally stopped to take a good look at what was happening. I used to buy into all the classic textbook explanations about serial killers. Silveria made me realize that not all serial killers are from the same mold and neither are all cops. And while all investigations into murders should be judged equally important, the fact is, they're not. We live in a strange world, where what appears simple can be incredibly complex. Nothing points this out better than the elusive, entangled case of the Boxcar Serial Murderer. His was the kind of case that comes only once in a cop's career, if ever.

As time passed and I combined the clues and insights that came from the investigation, as well as from talks with members of his family, friends and other members of his group, with what I personally saw and learned from Silveria, I recognized that Silveria's early years were filled with classic signs of what was to come. At an

1

early age, he was using drugs, robbing homes and doing poorly in school. Though he grew up in a comfortable, middle-class home, these attributes contain many of the characteristics of a serial killer. One of these is that the killer tends to be a white male with destructive behavior evident in his early years, from a middle-class or upper-middle-class background.

✓ Serial killers usually don't stand out in a crowd. They tend to blend in with their environment. They can be married with children, successful at work and even admired by the community while carrying out a pattern of murders. When they are finally caught, neighbors, friends, and family members are usually astounded by the revelation. ʼ

It is in the way they view others that the classic psychopathic tendencies are shown. Serial killers view their victims and other people as inanimate objects. They feel no remorse for their victims. Finally, serial killers usually have a good intellect, which helps them avert attention and makes them capable of selecting perfect victims. These psychopaths are usually caught by accident and tend to think that no human being can be as clever or as bright as they are.

There is no certainty as to whether serial killers are made or born or if they can be changed. It's believed that the personalities of future serial killers are formed at the end of the first year of infancy. From an early age they show violent and/or antisocial tendencies. If they are let out of confinement, the history of some shows they will kill again and again. Nevertheless, Silveria's life, while he appears to share much with the classic definitions of serial killers, raises interesting questions.

Eventually, I came to understand that Silveria's madness had a purpose to it that went beyond the rage guiding it. He drew attention to the group of which he was a part, a violent sub-culture the American public wasn't even aware existed, the Freight Train Riders of America (FTRA). I learned that the organization was made up of an "invisible" population of train hoppers who survive on the forgotten edge of society, where men give up their original names for monikers that fellow train-hoppers choose for them. The group is loosely structured, a shadow segment of society boasting a membership estimated to be in the thousands. As in the old days of the Wild West, they live by their own code of honor and, most of all, silence. They can be spotted in every town a railroad passes through, rarely wandering outside their self-imposed boundaries of rescue missions and rail yards. Many are fugitives shying away from the law. As a member of the vicious FTRA execution squad, Silveria was a man trapped in his own worst nightmare. He spun a deadly web around the fate of others, earning himself the dubious honor of becoming the first known rail riding serial killer in more than a hundred years of railroad history.

What I didn't know when we first met was the long and strange history I would have with Silveria, returning not only to the case within my jurisdiction but his convoluted and violent history long after the books on him were closed, until finally, the pieces of the puzzle fit and I came to understand the whole untold story.

My involvement with Silveria was ignited by the brutal murder of a homeless Vietnam veteran in the city of Albany, California, where I worked as a detective and was called in on the investigation on July 22, 1995. When we finally met, Silveria described the killing to me in detail. If I close my eyes and lean back in the chair in my den on a lazy Saturday afternoon, surrounded by memorabilia from his investigation, I still can picture him.

1

Cops and Serial Killers

*"I am the leader of my nation. I could have
tortured others of your world, but I chose to
torture my world, because I prey on the weak."*
Robert Joseph Silveria, Jr.

Chances are that Robert Joseph Silveria, Jr. wasn't planning to
kill anyone that summer evening. He headed north, towards
a place that would give him privacy from prying eyes, walking past
the point where the Berkeley city line ends and the city of Albany,
California begins, going northeast in the direction of Albany's El
Cerrito — little hill in Spanish. The hill is a mass of soil and rock
that towers like some giant, solitary mushroom over freeways and
tall buildings, overgrown with thick patches of trees and single-
family homes. Right behind the hill is the town of El Cerrito, adja-
cent to Albany. The jurisdictions merge into one seemingly
unending metropolis, where the larger cities in the San Francisco
East Bay, like Oakland, Richmond and Berkeley, blend in with

their smaller neighbors of Albany, Emeryville and El Cerrito. They are all united by one road, San Pablo Avenue, and form part of the I-80 corridor that runs up to Sacramento, the state capital.

To those who might have seen him, Silveria looked like any free-spirited transient in his thirties as he walked up a dirt road by the rail tracks under the canopy of a panoramic vista. There was no madness reflected in his bright-blue eyes that matched the sky to his east. His face was scrubbed, but his hair and clothes were unwashed. His lean, muscular body, accustomed to jumping in and out of boxcars, moved with ease despite the backpack roll over his shoulders that contained all his belongings in the world. He stepped almost effortlessly over unpaved ground littered with debris and pebbles. Tattoos on his arms of mythical birds, flowers, Viking figures and menacing skulls barely disguised the needle marks. His hands and fingernails were covered in grease and soot that was difficult to wash out, no matter how hard he tried. His knuckles, which easily formed into fists, showed old bruises.

The blue denim jacket with cut-off sleeves that he wore was scrawled with monikers and symbols in different people's handwriting. There were doodles drawn next to names like Desert Rat, Catfish, California Spud, Rooster, Fast Freddie and Deadline Dixie. Hovering above these was a huge, cracked skull that Silveria skillfully drew himself. Around his neck a silver concho, more commonly worn on bolo ties, held together the ends of a black bandanna that barely covered the word "Freedom" tattooed in flowing letters on the left side of his neck. Sewn on the bandanna was a shark tooth and a button with the word "Flashback." Hanging below this was a black leather Indian medicine pouch that contained momentos from friends and trophies from victims. The button and his concho were the only two items that linked him to four other killers in the FTRA — Freight Train Riders of America.

Silveria's well-chiseled features were appealing, except for some light scars that were remnants of the time he was attacked by some men while sleeping under a bridge in Spokane, Washington. At that point Silveria wasn't yet an FTRA member. The men assaulted him with oak sticks, like the clubs FTRA adherents carry, discarded axe handles used to drive spikes down on railroad tracks. It wasn't the first time that Silveria had been beaten up, but since then he'd been on a mission to kill people like those who had attacked him. The only problem was he became one of them — a full-fledged member of the FTRA. A light mustache and a hint of a beard covered the lower part of his face. To another transient or train hopper, he would have appeared totally approachable and non-threatening, unlike the occasional speeding Southern Pacific train passing by that day, intruding on the peacefulness of the remote neighborhood with its high-pitched shrieks of warning.

Silveria's black bandanna and silver concho were articles of clothing that represented his membership in the northern faction of the Freight Train Riders of America. Other factions of the group include the enforcement groups: the Wrecking Crew in the north and the Goon Squad in the south. Robert Silveria was recruited into an FTRA group in 1991 that went beyond administrating enforcement — a practice that basically consisted of a group of men clobbering victims with oak goon sticks. He was recruited into an extremely violent faction of the FTRA, an execution squad, or a death squad, as cops would eventually come to describe it. The small band of FTRA killers he was indoctrinated into typically loaded their intended victim up on liquor and fed him drugs until he passed out.

The group knew the trains' schedules and would place the unconscious victim on the tracks to be run over. Sometimes the inebriated individual was simply led to the tracks where they cut his throat or cracked his skull open. Sometimes they "executed" the victim with a machete, an ax or a sharp buck knife. They carried his body to the middle of the rail tracks. An engineer of a freight train carrying even a light load would not be able to stop in time when he realized that what appeared from the distance to be common debris was in fact a human body.

A body dropped on the tracks and hit by a passing freight train receives extensive trauma that most likely would include dismemberment of body parts. Police, and especially the coroner, would not have much to go on. The deceased, of course, would be tested for alcohol and drugs. This was part of the critical plan when the killing was carried out, to lead the coroner and the police to draw the conclusion that the person was so out of it that he fell down in the middle of the tracks and was accidentally run over or perhaps committed suicide. In fact, it was homicide —— nothing short of murder.

When Silveria walked by the tracks in Albany that day in July, he didn't have to worry about exposing his FTRA dress code and revealing his membership in the organization to outsiders, especially to any police officers he might encounter along the way. It's a big continent. Two thousand or so guys riding the rails with different colored bandannas tied around their neck to signify the railway routes they traveled was something the rail crews might pick up on, but unless they shared the information, local cops would most likely not notice it, especially if they didn't have a major rail exchange in their town. In my case, I didn't know at the time that the FTRA even existed.

Silveria had every reason to feel safe as he continued heading toward the concrete bridge by East Shore Highway, which runs parallel to I-80 near the Albany Hill. He paused when he noticed a familiar campsite on the opposite side of the tracks, partially hidden behind thick layers of foliage and located midway between the Berkeley shelter and the bridge he was headed towards. It was about twenty-five yards from a chain-link fence that separated the undeveloped area, where the homeless resided, and the railroad property from businesses located along the highway. Crossing the tracks, Silveria walked over small planks lined up to serve as a footbridge to the main entrance to the campsite. To an untrained eye, at first glance, the place might have looked like a mini-landfill piled with discarded junk. It was trashed, littered with bottles, garbage and items discarded by others only to find a new home here. But on closer examination, a newcomer to this secluded hooch might discern that, despite its hodgepodge look, the placement of the objects followed a logical sequence. Sections of tree limbs covered in plastic tarp, clothing, old rugs and blankets formed an entryway at each end of the camp. There was a living room area designated by a bulky upholstered chair and some mattresses, beach chairs, an old plush dining chair and a metal folding chair. A makeshift kitchen included an odd-shaped, green, wood-burning stove with a stove pipe and a black teapot. Kindling was stored nearby in a blue plastic laundry basket. At least half a dozen broken bicycles littered the ground among crates and other debris. Squatters typically discard bicycles after a flat tire or because the bike simply wears down. Money is tight so it's easier for them to steal a new bike or pick one up at a rummage sale for a few bucks. But some find it hard to part with the few possessions they do have, even if the objects appear meaningless, like a bicycle that will never be ridden again or a cracked, antique flower vase that will never hold another fragrant bouquet. It was a typical messy transient's hooch, filled with circling flies and permeated with smells of decay and human feces, but minus its inhabitant.

Silveria turned around and walked out of the camp to continue heading towards the bridge where he would have a clear view of the towering Berkeley hills or, if he faced west, he could watch the distant San Francisco skyline fade into the night behind lights looped over the Bay Bridge. He could also see Golden Gate Fields, a race track on the other side of the freeway where over the years celebrities like Joe DiMaggio, Telly Savallas, Albert Finney and the buxom Carol Doda watched horse racing with the hoi polloi. They were folks I met in passing, sort of a fringe benefit that comes with working for a police department in the same town as a popular race track. A special treat for me was when Carol Doda and I exchanged phone numbers. She later sent me a signed photo of herself, inviting me to visit her and catch her strip tease act in North Beach, the old Italian section of San Francisco. But of course, Silveria's mind that day wasn't on celebrities or going on top of the freeway ramp for the views. He was wanted to go under the structure, where tall, cylindrical, concrete posts cast shadows across the ground — a good place for a man to hide.

Silveria had arrived in the area on a freight train earlier that day. His travels that month started in Vancouver, Washington, where he and other FTRA members pooled their money to buy enough booze to celebrate the Fourth of July for ten days. The Fourth of July party lasted through the 13th, the group's "special" number. They had a lot with which to celebrate that year, because of a large amount of methamphetamine Silveria brought with him after ripping off a drug dealer in Arizona a month earlier. After leaving Vancouver, Silveria hopped a train to Pasco, Washington, where he picked up food stamps under one of his aliases before heading down to the East Bay and then making his way across to San Francisco. There, he picked up another $119 worth of food stamps under another assumed name at a check cashing kiosk on Mission Street. Immediately selling the food stamps and using the money to buy drugs by Fisherman's Wharf, he got a ball of heroin and a bag of needles. Then he headed back to the Berkeley mission in East Bay. By July 17 he was in El Paso, Texas. Six days later he jumped off a train in Richmond and headed first to Berkeley to pick up his drugs and check for any messages and then to Albany to shoot dope. He had time to waste before August rolled around, with the opportunity to collect assistance under another assumed name.

Silveria and his buddies frequented the home where the legendary Catfish lived in a house owned by his girlfriend. Catfish was one of the original FTRA members qualified to have a gold concho and qualified to wear both black and red bandannas, which signified the routes train hoppers traveled: the black denoted the northern train routes and the red represented the southern rail routes. Those that traveled the routes in eastern states wore blue bandannas, but regardless of the color of their scarves, they all formed one brotherhood of rail riders. Silveria later told me he rode trains in an excess of one million miles.

"That makes you qualify for a gold concho?" I said, surprised.

Silveria looked away for a few seconds. Locked behind bars, he wasn't going anywhere, but he grinned nevertheless, "Yeah, I guess it does."

Catfish's girlfriend's property was also an FTRA safehouse, screened from the street by pine trees in a neighborhood of low-income houses and apartments. On the side of the garage doors, written in chalk, was, "If you value your life as much as I value my house, don't fuck with it." Neighbors told reporters that after Catfish got himself into trouble for fatally stabbing a man in front of the house during a drunken brawl over his girlfriend, police were frequently called in to settle disturbances and the female resident was always inviting "bums" to stay there.

The pattern of Robert Silveria's life echoed a typical FTRA existence, a life regulated by assistance checks and food stamps collected with phony ID cards. The multiple identities the members assume usually cover addresses in multiple cities and states, so the FTRA frequently move from state to state, not in the comfort of train cabins and dining cars, but in box cars and flat beds, vulnerable to the elements, sleeping on dirty floorboards and eating whatever food had been stashed in a knapsack. Sometimes meals are cooked over a Coleman stove inside a boxcar, but one must be careful that the steam or smoke from cooking doesn't attract notice from a rail security agent, or "bull," as the train hoppers call them. Typically, however, the food is cooked in "jungles" — campsites where train hoppers congregate before they "catch out" to their next destination. They also frequent rescue mission shelters in each of their stops to reconnect with old acquaintances, post messages and clean up. Sometimes they stand on corners or at freeway entrances with signs asking for work or money. Any money they acquire, they spend as soon as they get it. In Silveria's case it was usually spent on alcohol, marijuana and the poison of poisons, heroin. As for the phony identifications he carried? Well, most of them belonged to his murdered victims — train hoppers like himself.

Violence and drugs are another pattern typical of the FTRA existence and involve frequent drunken brawls. It's hard to find an FTRA rail rider who hasn't thrown a man out of a moving train. Of course, they'll usually tell you it was in self-defense and maybe it's even true in most cases. In Silveria's case, the drugs brought out a rage in him and he admitted to pushing men off boxcars because they pissed him off by challenging him. The "soft core" FTRA riders, the majority of the members, however, are only interested in hopping trains and getting drunk or high.

That day in Albany, California, Silveria's heroin habit needed feeding. He focused on the concrete, raised freeway ramp, beneath which he could shoot up dope undisturbed. He knew that afterwards he would be hoping for a victim to come along. He knew the routine well and so far it had worked. That day his hopes panned out.

The campsite Silveria had wandered into earlier belonged to James McLean, a down-on-his-luck, fifty-year-old Vietnam veteran, whom transients living in the area preferred to call J.C., as opposed to the new name he gave himself when he settled in the area — Jesus Christ McLean. McLean, born in the city of Richmond in California, had once been a rail rider, hopping freight trains back and forth along the West Coast before settling in the Bay Area among the urban homeless and close to the invisible border where Albany ends and Richmond begins.

At the time Silveria was walking through McLean's hooch, McLean was seen with another homeless man, Hippie, and a couple of teens, a boy and a girl, both extraordinarily blonde and both new to the area. McLean soon left the trio, hopping on his ten-speed bike to head back to his camp, stopping at times to pick up aluminum cans and to rummage through trash bins behind industrial buildings located by the concrete bridge. McLean's dog, a black Labrador mix named Blue, followed close behind, sniffing and marking territory. From a distance, McLean's receding hairline, thick grayish locks and heavy beard gave him a wolf-like appearance. An old leg wound where the bone never healed properly caused him to limp in spite of the military styled boots he wore with a double heel attached to one of them. He spotted Silveria sitting under the concrete bridge. He knew Silveria by his train-hopping moniker, "Sidetrack," and shouted it out. The two were well acquainted, having met some time ago in Roseville, where the largest switching yard in the west is located approximately ninety miles northeast of Albany. Silveria recalled the guy as having a cantankerous personality, but at that moment he was very friendly and appeared genuinely happy to see Silveria.

"Come on, have a beer with me at my camp," he called, then he switched and suggested a stronger form of chemical enhancement. "What are you shooting? I know this meth dealer where we can score. Let's go to my camp just down the road here. You're welcome to stay for the night." Silveria, noticing McLean's boots, which looked to be in good condition from where he was sitting, accepted the invitation. He rose and followed McLean less than a quarter of a mile down a trail that ran parallel to the railroad tracks. McLean pulled his ten-speed bike along side of him while Blue ran up ahead. The sky was growing darker. A couple of black transients were walking ahead of them along the tracks towards a campfire rising from behind thick shrubbery in the distance. They started to cross the tracks then turned and noticed McLean behind them walking with Silveria.

"Hey, Pops," one of them called out to McLean, "you got any change to spare?"

"Fuck off. Go get a job," McLean fired back. He turned to Silveria and snickered, "Fucking niggers." Even an outsider like Silveria, who by then was high on junk, could spot that McLean and the two black men were very familiar with each other. He heard echoes of laughter before the two men disappeared behind the trees. Silveria and McLean moved away from the tracks too, crossing over a short wooden plank that led to the inner sanctum of McLean's hooch.

"Just drop your gear here. It'll be safe," McLean said, pointing to a spot on the ground. Silveria dropped his roll and backpack, allowing it to thump against the earth. Then the two men headed out, with McLean pulling his bike alongside of him as they crossed the tracks to walk the seven blocks to a small market with an outside public phone. Occasionally, McLean rode his bike and waited at the end of the block for Silveria to catch up. When the two reached the first part of their destination, McLean opened his wallet and pulled out the phone number of the methamphetamine dealer he had told Silveria about earlier. Silveria's razor-sharp-blues fell on a thick pile of bills sticking out of McLean's billfold. Silveria realized his hopes were once again panning out. He had found his next victim.

There appeared to be enough money sticking out of McLean's wallet for Silveria to buy a balloon of heroin. There was only one minor problem for Silveria. He had to figure out how he was going to rob Mclean to get to the cash. He could only act out if he went into a state of rage. Without his rage, Silveria did not have the guts to rob or murder — he had only the desire. He depended on his victims to fire up his rage and now he needed McLean's cooperation.

Silveria and McLean crossed more streets to reach the dealer who would sell them crank. McLean warned Silveria of the bad neighborhood they were passing through and how dangerous it was because of all the thugs and lowlifes living there. Little did he know that the instrument of his own death was at that moment by his side.

After scoring, McLean and Silveria headed back to the hooch. As they were reentering the transient's campsite, Silveria mentioned to McLean he had a bag of rigs, needles he picked up in San Francisco. The aging vet perked up. He hinted that he would like to have a few. Silveria ignored McLean's hints and came right out and said he would sell him a couple for five bucks. McLean shook his head. "Hey, come on...can't you just give me some? Look, I'm letting you stay the night here. I'm sharing my stuff with you. You should have just offered me some without my asking."

Inside the hooch, McLean continued pressing Silveria to hand over a couple of needles, but Silveria wouldn't budge. "I might need a bit of cash later on. Look, I'm willing to sell you a couple. Take it or leave it," he shrugged.

McLean turned livid. "All right, here's your goddamned

money." McLean pulled out his wallet and handed Silveria a five dollar bill. Silveria took the money, picked up his back pack and pulled out a bag of needles.

After he and Silveria made the needle exchange, McLean ordered, "Now get the hell out of my camp."

"I'll go," Silveria said calmly, but now the fiery rage inside him was bursting, ready to explode. No one spoke to Silveria like that and lived to talk about it. If word got out along the rails that McLean kicked him out of his hooch, Silveria would lose his power and influence in the group. His reputation for toughness would be damaged. The next thing that could happen might be that someone would try to cut his bandanna off his neck and brag that he had Sidetrack's rag. In his group, this was a stigma equal to castration. The rage inside Silveria was primed.

But McLean had his own tough veneer to maintain. He cursed Silveria, then turned around limping towards the deeper end of his hooch, to get as far away from his ungracious guest as he could. With McLean's back turned to him, Silveria seized the moment to reach inside his backpack and pull out his axe handle — a goon stick. With long, rapid steps, he dashed forward until he was right behind the unsuspecting McLean. He swung his arm back. Just then, McLean, hearing something behind him, turned around in time to catch the full force of the goon stick on his forehead. Blood poured from the wound. The might of Silveria's axe handle forced J.C. to buckle and fall to the ground.

McLean's dog rushed at Silveria, growling and barking. Silveria dropped the ax handle and pulled out a ten-inch knife from a sheath attached to the side of his belt and stabbed the creature. Blue howled in pain and fell down limp on the ground, whimpering, with blood running from his wound. McLean remained on the ground, too. The crack of the axe handle against his skull left him dazed. He tried pulling himself up, but Silveria was too quick for him. Silveria leaned down over his victim and, like a Roman soldier from long, long ago, thrust his knife into the lower right chest of Jesus Christ McLean. He twisted and turned it before pulling the knife out. Under the dim light of a city night sky lit by distant street lamps and neon signs, he watched McLean grimace in pain, his open mouth and wide eyes etched in a frozen stare as he gasped his last breath.

There were other campsites near McLean's den. A forty-three-year-old female transient known as K.C. was in one of them that day, along with three companions, a woman who was a Hell's Angels affiliate, her brother and Charlie, a drifter who had been staying with K.C. in her camp for the past ten days. K.C. sat up when she heard McLean shouting to someone to get out of his camp. She heard McLean's dog, Blue, barking in the distance. Then, there was an eerie cry that sounded like some animal being struck by a car and after that, silence. The sound of the animal disturbed her, but then she decided it was probably nothing. "It was just like J.C.," she would later tell us, referring to McLean, "to throw people out of his camp." He had a reputation as a temperamental recluse among other transients and his family. The terms crabby, belligerent and cantankerous were often used to describe him. But that night, his irritable personality ceased to exist. K.C. and her group of companions were totally unaware that less than twenty yards away a murder had just occurred.

After stabbing McLean, Silveria took a metal folding chair that had been leaning against some crates and placed it on top of McLean's head. He hated seeing the open eyes of his dead victims, staring at some distant space as if asking, *Why? Why me?* Those eyes had a way of haunting him. Covering them up freed him to concentrate on more practical matters. He removed

McLean's wallet and the plastic bag of crack he had in his pants
pockets. Next, he began to remove the dead man's boots. He saw
that one of them had an extra heel attached to compensate for the
deformity in the leg. Silveria untied both boots and pulled them
off before shoving them inside the green backpack to join his
other belongings. Later, when I headed the investigation, the
other detectives and officers in the department, Will Leggett,
Kevin Horn, Sgt. Bob Christianson, Ted Allen and Barry Galloway and I wondered about the missing boots, but none of us
knew this piece of information about the extra heel being attached
to one of McLean's boots. Only his killer and those very close to
McLean knew that he wore an extra heel to even out his stance.
None of the witnesses we interviewed volunteered this piece of
information when we questioned them about the missing boots.
Had we known about the extra heel, we would have used it as
hold-out information, but instead we kept the story about his dog
out of the press.

Silveria walked out of McLean's hooch with brisk
steps. He paused only once and briefly right outside its entrance
to examine the dead man's wallet under the glow from distant
street lamps. There was a blue veteran's medical card in it. Silveria had no use for it. He threw it to the side where it fell on
the ground among weeds and bushes. He made his way
towards the nearby Richmond rail yard and hopped a piggy-
back, also called a double stacker, hiding above the back trailer
wheels or axle, something he could do only when traveling at
night. Piggybacks are high priority trains, much faster than any
of the other freight trains, and by dawn he was more than a
thousand miles away.

Hippie, who was seen by witnesses earlier in the day
with McLean, was unaware of the deadly scene in McLean's
encampment when he decided to go over there and pay him a
visit. Like his friend McLean, Hippie parted in the late after-

noon from the two blond teens that he and J.C. had hung out with that day. It was later that night, around 10 P.M., when he decided to go to a local McDonald's to buy four hamburgers, two for himself and two for J.C. as a repayment for two hamburgers he ate at McLean's camp a couple of weeks earlier. Coming out of the fast food chain, Hippie spotted the two light-haired teens laughing as they ran across San Pablo Avenue towards a bus stop. Hippie wondered if they were brother and sister, their hair was so much alike, but then he recalled that the boy introduced the girl as his old lady when he stated that they were both from Arizona.

Hippie made his way towards McLean's camp carrying the hamburgers. Approaching the campsite, he was surprised that it looked dark and empty. When he crossed the wooden plank leading into the interior of the hooch, he noticed that McLean's bike was parked by the entrance. In the twenty years that he had known him, Hippie never knew McLean to go any long distance without his bike because of his bad leg. He figured McLean couldn't be far away, but Hippie couldn't see much else in the camp since it was so dark in there. Then he noticed flashlights some distance away in other encampments and decided that J.C. had probably left and was visiting someone. Hippie didn't want to intrude or disturb anyone so he decided to go to the camp where he had been staying temporarily while its regular occupant was away, locked up in jail.

The following morning Hippie returned to look for J.C. again. Looking around in the morning light, he came upon McLean. It was not unusual for Hippie to find McLean passed out on drugs or alcohol, lying unconscious on the ground like he was dead. But this time there was something different. Hippie couldn't quite pinpoint it, but something about McLean did not look right. Hippie called out his friend's name, "J.C.," again and again. There was no response. McLean lay there hunched over in a fetal position, partially hidden under a folded metal chair. Hippie stepped back, staring down at his buddy. Something was different about him. Something was wrong. He turned around and went first to the encampment of a woman with whom J.C. partied Friday night after throwing everyone else out of his camp. She was still asleep. Hippie woke her up and told her he was worried about McLean, but she just mumbled something under her breath and rolled over, turning her back to him. Hippie felt he was losing time. He walked briskly, at times breaking into a run, in order to quickly reach the camp of the transient known as Caveman. Caveman had done time in the late 1970s with McLean at the Santa Rita jail, where the two first met. At the time, McLean was known as Ragmop, before he changed his name to Jesus Christ McLean. Caveman didn't show any more interest in J.C. than the woman did. He reminded Hippie that being in a stupor was McLean's usual state in the morning and said, "There's nothing to get excited about."

Hippie decided to go to K.C.'s camp. On his way there he encountered T.J. Fleishman, who was going to McLean's to ask him if he was interested in going with him to a flea market. Hippie told Fleishman his concerns and Fleishman readily accompanied him back to McLean's camp. When Fleishman arrived with Hippie in McLean's hooch, he too didn't like what he saw. Both men kept calling out to McLean, but there was no response. Then they noticed McLean did not have his boots on, only his grey wool socks. They still thought that McLean might be fast asleep, passed out from a night of partying. Hippie picked up the chair covering McLean's head and placed it to the side, unwittingly removing a major clue the killer left behind. Looking down at McLean's frozen face and his blood-soaked thermal shirt the two men came face to face with the horror of their unspoken fears.

The viciousness of a murderous attack looks more brutal in the daylight. Blood was splattered on McLean's body and
around his den, on the ground and on clothing hanging from
nearby tree limbs. It had poured out of his nostrils and mouth
onto his beard and shirt. The victim's eyes and mouth were
wide open; rigor mortis already had set in. Blue was lying
nearby, seriously wounded, but still alive. Leaving Hippie
behind to stand guard, Fleishman ran out of the campsite
screaming for K.C. He brought her back with him to McLean's
hooch. Still unable to comprehend that his friend was gone, he
looked at K.C. and said, "Maybe he's asleep."

"No," K.C. shook her head. "He's dead. You better go, run
to the phone booth and call the police, right now," she ordered.

Finnegan stood there immobilized. "I don't have any
change," he finally stammered.

K.C.'s voice rose an octave, "Fuck, you don't need any. Just
dial 9-1-1. Go quickly. Now!"

"Come with me," Hippie stuttered and the two men ran to
the phone booth.

2

Elvis and the Lawmen

"Are you that Elvis cop?"
Robert Joseph Silveria, Jr.

When McLean and Silveria were together, I was at a karaoke bar in Petaluma. It was one of my rare weekends off and I was set on enjoying it to the max. Although I was also rehearsing on my own time, which was part of my job, it felt more like play than work. Besides being the lead investigator in my department, I was also a spokesperson for a nationally acclaimed program, Chief Operator, funded by a grant, in which I was the only cop in the world paid by the government to do Elvis impersonations to promote traffic safety among California teens and their families. My call name was "Elvis & the Lawmen." Although the Lawmen backing me during performances fluctuated over the years and at

one time included my son, Will, I remained a constant in the program, employing the legend of Elvis Presley and the love that
audiences hold for him to save lives and prevent injuries through
the traffic safety campaign. Over time, I have conducted more
than 600 school and community performances in fifteen states
and Canada. Some organizations had me back several times. It was
gratifying to learn that California Highway Patrol data revealed a
dramatic drop in combined injuries and deaths among teens after
we first piloted the Elvis & the Lawmen program in our San Francisco target area.

    The following day, I was in my dune buggy with the top
down, wearing shorts, my tank top tossed under the side seat,
soaking up the sun and wandering through the Napa wine
country back roads. I was smoking a Montechristo cigar and, in
between puffs, singing along to a tape I was scheduled to
record soon with the attorney general of California, Dan Lungren, who was a huge Elvis fan himself. I had the tape deck
blasting. The music cascaded through the canyons and over the
hills. Then my pager went off.

    Pulling over to the side of the road, I checked the trans-
mitted numbers and saw it was the cop shop calling me. Right
there my sense told me that my play time was in danger of end-
ing prematurely. My premonition proved right. I phoned the
station and the police dispatcher at the other end told me, "You
need to come in. We've got a dead body for you to investigate."
The victim, I learned, was found by the railroad tracks.

    "Contact the Southern Pacific Railroad," I told the dis-
patcher. I knew they owned the property in the area. I also asked
for the I.D. Officer, Barry Galloway, to be contacted and sent to
the scene. Next, I phoned the sergeant who was the watch commander on duty and gave him instructions to secure the area, separate any possible witnesses and get their statements. After I
finished, I pulled my car out onto the road again and made a

U-turn. Before heading to the police department I had to go home, park the dune buggy in my garage and climb into my white Lincoln, which was better suited to handle high speeds on freeways. But first, I figured, I'd need to change my attire to something more conservative, although anything I wore at the station never seemed to be conservative enough for the chief and the guys on my staff. My personal tastes are for the flamboyant, from zoot suits to decorative leather jackets, cowboy hats and boots. Glancing in my review mirror, I saw that my naturally curly hair was completely disheveled by the wind, making me look like a Neanderthal. My eyes looked puffy and bloodshot from overstaying at the karaoke bar. My cheeks sported one-day-old stubble, which I knew I wouldn't have time to shave off. Once home, I quickly changed into a black tee shirt and jeans, flattened my hair down with a heavy dose of hair spray and then headed out to investigate a possible homicide.

When I arrived at the crime scene, there were several black and whites parked in the area. I drove towards them, over the rail tracks. Getting out of my car, I learned that the first to arrive on the scene were the Berkeley Police Department and the Berkeley Fire Department. Once it was confirmed that McLean's encampment was in Albany's jurisdiction, our dispatcher was notified and the Berkeley cops pulled out.

I saw McLean's poor wounded dog and immediately had him taken to the nearest veterinarian. He later confirmed that the animal had been stabbed. Blue was treated and eventually given to one of the homeless living near McLean's encampment.

During the next several days, the investigation into McLean's death revealed a lot about the victim's lifestyle, but nothing about his killer. Interviewing the homeless was a real challenge for me and the other Albany detectives in my division. It was especially difficult trying to pinpoint time-frames and the sequence of events. Many of the homeless spent much of their time so drugged-out or boozed-up that the days just blended into one another. I finally determined that most of McLean's neighbors had seen him alive on Friday, July 21, partying on beer and speed all day. The woman who spent the night with McLean told one of my detectives she last saw McLean the following morning at 9 A.M. when he told her he was heading out to Emeryville. Another female transient living nearby, K.C., had also had a relationship with the victim at one time. She told me she knew McLean for about seven years and that he collected a Supplemental Security Income (SSI) check each month from the government. It was her impression that he used his SSI check to purchase an eight ball, about one-eighth of an ounce of speed, for around $200 for Friday's party. She also told me that McLean had a sexual appetite for bondage, but it was common knowledge around the camps that he would not participate in any sexual act against anyone's will or consent. All those questioned who knew McLean personally, repeatedly used the same term to describe him — cantankerous. He could be curt and obnoxious, even to family members. His uncle complained to us during the investigation that McLean once made a pass at the uncle's girlfriend right there in front of him. McLean could turn on anybody, he said. No one we interviewed appeared surprised that McLean might have gone too far, touched someone's nerve endings and got himself killed, but there was no hint of who might have killed the veteran or why, for that matter. Everyone who knew him said that his "bark was bigger than his bite."

Following all the usual police procedures didn't shed any light on the case. Feeling frustrated, I decided to send out my informant to live among the homeless in the area where McLean's hooch had once been. His friends and acquaintances in the area called him Lincoln. He once had lived in penthouses, driven fancy convertibles and squired some of the most gorgeous gals in town.

He had lived a player's dream life. Unfortunately, it was financed by dope: he was a high powered drug dealer. Finally, a Drug Enforcement Agency hook reeled him in and he testified about a prominent judge's son.

Thereafter, a contract went out on Lincoln. One day, walking out of a restaurant with his girlfriend, he was greeted by a hail of bullets. Lincoln's girlfriend was fatally struck, but he survived a head wound. When he got out of the hospital with a steel plate in his skull, he made his escape by moving to California. The DEA was still after him. They wanted him back as an informant. But Lincoln didn't want to go down that road again. He chose instead to live in a broken-down trailer that was parked in a run-down, industrial part of Berkeley, picking up money from different police departments working as an informant on local, small-time drug deals. Meanwhile, he was also doing and selling drugs on a small scale himself. When his trailer got impounded, he moved to the Berkeley Marina in an area inhabited by another homeless population, hidden from the public's view by tall and thick foliage.

I grew quite fond of Lincoln and was fascinated by his stories from the past, even though it's against police rule-books to get too chummy with informants. A police officer endangers himself or herself by becoming close with snitches. This allows the power balance to shift and the informant can get the upper hand. Also, informants tend to be talkers. No secret is sacred with them and everything is up for sale. They can just as easily go to another police department or dealer and brag that they have this cop by the balls. But I didn't give a damn. I broke the rules and went out drinking with Lincoln a number of times.

Somehow, crazy Lincoln got to me. His wiry physique and tattered, unwashed clothes made him an obvious choice to go live in the campsites by the Albany railroad tracks and pick up any gossip or stories circulating about McLean's murder.

When he came by the station early one afternoon, I told Lincoln to meet me at Brennan's in Berkeley around 6 P.M. Some of the guys at the station frequented Brennan's for lunch, because they made one of the best corned beef and pastrami sandwiches in the area. It was rare for me to encounter anyone I knew there in the evenings. When I arrived at Brennan's, which had a long bar that looped around a central wall lined with bottles in the middle of a large hall filled with cafeteria-style tables and chairs, Lincoln was already waiting for me. We settled on a couple of stools at the far end of the bar. I ordered a beer for myself and a Hennessey on the rocks for Lincoln, who only drank the good stuff when he was with me. After taking a sip of beer from my bottle, I turned to face Lincoln.

"Listen, I got something I need you to do and it's high priority," I said, studying his face closely. "We had a murder down along the railway tracks in an area containing a number of camps and I need you to go down there and find out what they're talking about and what they're doing down there."

"Yeah, sure," Lincoln nodded, then he took a long gulp of his drink.

"Don't ask any questions at first. Just listen," I continued. "After a while you might start asking something like, 'What's this I hear that a guy was murdered around here?' and see what you get back."

"I got it," Lincoln grinned and nodded. Then he took another long gulp of his drink. Usually, Lincoln was talkative. I noticed he was quite thirsty, because there was only ice left in his glass. I signaled to the bartender for another order. I figured I might be there for a while. I was ready to relax myself. "Ever have their pastrami on rye?" I didn't wait for him to answer. "If not, you're in for a treat. On me," I said and grinned at Lincoln.

Lincoln lived in the Albany homeless camps for about a week. There he learned that McLean was an old, feisty crank user. Whoever murdered him was probably someone J.C. had met before, because McLean never invited anyone into his den unless he knew the person. That was the general consensus among McLean's neighbors and it matched what we learned in the department from interviewing McLean's relatives and neighbors. When I asked Lincoln who murdered McLean, there was silence. Complete silence. Not a single rumor surfaced to point to a name or an individual living in the area, indicating to me that the killer was an outsider whom McLean knew. However, there was something Lincoln uncovered. He found out that Albany youths frequented the area of the homeless camps to buy drugs, endangering themselves to HIV and AIDS and other lifelong problems. Because of this discovery, Lincoln was "wired up" with a concealed wireless microphone three times during the following couple of months and each time we conducted a drug bust in the transient camp, arresting some of the people living there who were selling dope to the kids.

When Lincoln revealed the information about the Albany teens buying drugs in the area, the focus in the department shifted from looking for McLean's killer to eliminating the concerns "created" by the homeless. Suddenly, no one really gave a damn about the victim anymore. Since McLean was rumored to have sold drugs to the kids too, the attitude became one of "good riddance" to the loser. The city now had a strong vested interest in the case, not because it involved a murder victim, but because it affected the town's youth. They jumped on the bandwagon to eliminate the problem by getting rid of the encampments by the rail tracks. The Health Department was the loudest about the unsanitary and unhealthy conditions found at the campsites on Albany property by the rails, but it was the Southern Pacific Railroad Company, since then purchased by Union Pacific Company, that led the charge to clean up and flatten the area.

Southern Pacific held a couple of meetings in their Oakland office with the agencies involved in the bulldozing of the area between the Albany tracks and East Shore Highway. I attended the meetings with Kevin Horn, a young detective I had finished training about a year earlier. Kevin was one of the guys in the department who I liked to hang out with on occasion after work. His taste for western-style boots and attire matched mine, of which our chief, who favored fine Italian suits, disapproved. At these two meetings there were also representatives from CalTrans, the Department of Health and the California Highway Patrol. The discussions centered on *when*, *how*, and *who* would do *what*. But there were also justifications laid out for the bulldozing. It was generally agreed that clearing out the area could prevent future crimes and removing the debris would eliminate what had become a breeding ground for mosquitoes and other pests. I learned later that the policy of bulldozing was typical of the way many railroad companies approached the problem when murder was committed on or near their property.

I was getting ready to invite Lincoln to my home for Christmas when he met with disaster. Witnesses said Lincoln was crossing the underground tracks at the El Cerrito BART (Bay Area Rapid Transit) station and did not hear an approaching train because he was wearing earphones listening to music. But who knows the real story? Maybe he just didn't want to live anymore. I was annoyed when the following day a couple of female dispatchers at the station sang "Lincoln got run over by a BART train," to the tune of "Grandma Got Run Over by a Reindeer," every time I passed by. It bothered me, although I tried not to show it. When I think of Lincoln now, I wish he was still around.

Ironically, while McLean's murder was on city land, it was the railroad company's entire property that also got cleaned up because of the killing. The murder of McLean, I believe, stemmed from the rails. At the time of the murder, I immediately notified the Southern Pacific Railroad Company, but they never offered me or any of the detectives in my division the information we needed. First of all, I wanted to know if they were the ones to investigate the homicide. Their agent came down to look over the scene that afternoon. But the response was that their jurisdiction extends only thirty feet on each side beyond the tracks in that particular site. Never was there any mention of the FTRA. The murder, I was informed, was on Albany property.

Though their office was not far from us in Oakland, the company's security department never responded to my tele-type. I suppose a dead body here and a dead body there is a price the rail companies pay to exist. Trespassers have haunted the tracks since the beginning of railroad history. All the meet-ings, the planning, the telephoning back and forth among the key groups from the private and the public sector took several months before the bulldozing of McLean's former camp, along with those belonging to his neighbors, finally was carried out.

During this period other things kept me busy, in addition to the occasional petty crimes in town. I recorded a traffic safety song in Sacramento with Attorney General Dan Lungren and per-formed for his group in Palm Springs. I also performed, for the first time, before an audience of over 100,000 at the New Mexico International Balloon Fiesta with Police Chief Larry Murdo, a very talented musician who stepped in on occasion as one of the Lawmen. Holding up my police badge, while dressed in a Las Vegas style Elvis white jumpsuit that glittered with jewels, I asked the following question at each performance, "How many of you think police officers should be doing this?" Whether at a school, a community event or a county fair, I always received a resounding cheer accompanied by loud applause. As Larry liked to remind critics, we were doing police work, only of a different kind. Dur-ing this period we also traveled to Philadelphia, as well as doing a series of performances around Northern California. The out-of-state gigs were all funded by the local communities inviting us to perform in their state. But I didn't forget about McLean. I kept the case open. I had a feeling in the back of my mind that sooner or later, something was going to hit.

It wasn't until almost a year later that I learned about the existence of the Freight Train Riders of America. My investigators and I were not unique in our ignorance. The Southern Pacific Railroad Company's silence about the serious problems stemming from organized groups of train hoppers kept cops like me in the San Francisco East Bay and other areas across the country from linking the crimes in their communities to the invisible train hopping population. Prior to this, I had nothing to show to the administration in Albany as to how and why I could pursue McLean's murder further. Most of us cops simply followed the dictates of the community, in particular the city administrator and the elected city council members. Like the communities in which we worked, we believed in the false safety net that bulldozing promised. Little did we realize that bulldozing couldn't bury the evil and the madness moving in all directions along the tracks. No one in the Albany Police Department involved in investigating McLean's death realized the significance of the movement of murder along the rails and that removing the smelly, infested camps of the transients would not prevent it from happening again somewhere else. Razing the camps was sold to us as the only reasonable and expedient thing to do. And so, with the mutual cooperation of the Albany Police Department, the California Highway Patrol, CalTrans, the Southern Pacific Railroad and the Alameda County Health Department, the area was "shaved" and the homeless, like Hippie, Tina, Caveman and K.C., pushed out of the campsites that for years had offered them a refuge, as primitive and bug-and-rat infested as it was.

After the murder, I had sent out teletypes to law enforcement agencies in the western region, but never received any responses. Teletypes have their limitations. Sometimes the teletype is routed to the wrong person or thrown away by the dispatcher. Some police departments are so inundated with problems or have such a shortage of help that a teletype concerning someone else's problem is completely disregarded unless it contains information matching a case on which they are currently working. In some departments, like in mine at the time, the decision to pass the teletype to me for review lay with the administrative staff. The best control we ever had in handling the constant flow of incoming teletypes was when we had Captain Mel Boyd in the department. He has since retired. I recall that he made sure that each day everyone read and initialed each teletype that came into the department.

It began to appear more and more that McLean's murder might have been a solitary incident, perhaps the result of a robbery gone wrong. McLean's wallet was missing and he was believed to have had at least $200 on him that day. The isolated killing of a bitter, homeless Vietnam veteran did not create a public outcry. After the bulldozing, I moved on to other investigations. But the case was open and still in the back of my mind. Yet at that point I was unaware of its relationship to other murders along the rails and the impact those killings and the man who committed them would have on my life.

3

A Rail-hopping Serial Killer

> *"In my heart, no matter where I was, I knew I was free."*
>
> Robert Joseph Silveria, Jr.

Word spread among law enforcement officers across the country with the speed of a hot-shot freight train that an elusive, rail-hopping serial killer had been arrested in Roseville, California on the evening of March 2, 1996. The detectives telephoned counterparts whom they barely knew in other cities in order to pass on the information.

Through the phone line, I learned about the arrest of the suspect, Robert Joseph Silveria, Jr. That Friday I was looking forward to doing nothing over the weekend but catching up on my sleep. The night before, I had been up late writing an affidavit for a search warrant for a sexual deviant case on which

I had been working intensely during the week. The sicko dad was directing his twelve-year-old daughter and a friend's fourteen year-old son on touching and having sexual contact with each other, after boozing them up to break down their resistance and inhibitions. The father, in his early forties, was shooting photos of them in the act, which he kept hidden in the trunk of his car. Of course, his wife would not believe this when we confronted her with the information. She was totally in denial, so I had to move fast, traveling ninety miles to Sacramento to visit and interview the teenage boy who was staying in a group home to pull all the facts and details together.

Glancing up at my "Elvis & the Lawmen" clock hanging high on a wall near my doorway, which was a promotional gift, I saw that it was past two o'clock in the morning. "Damn," I murmured to myself, "it doesn't pay to leave the station. I'll only have to be back in less than four hours." Just driving back and forth between my home in Marin County and the department in Alameda County would cost me well over an hour of my time. I pulled out a pillow and a blanket from my office closet, which I kept for such occasions, and threw them on the couch standing against the wall facing my desk. This wasn't like a murder case where the first seventy-two hours were most crucial in getting the evidence before the clues turned cold, but I wanted that scumbag dad behind bars, away from his daughter and the other kid as soon as possible, before he did any more damage.

Next morning I was up at the first sign of dawn. I showered and changed into the extra clothes I kept in my locker. By the time Kevin Horn arrived, I was munching on a cinnamon roll I picked up half a block from the station and drinking black coffee at my desk, reviewing the material I compiled the night before. It wasn't the world's greatest manifesto, but it was good enough to get the job done.

Kevin walked in, followed by Barry Galloway. It amused me that Barry had such a difficult time entering my office in the department. He always shook his head and glanced up on the main wall behind the couch, which was lined with photos of me in an Elvis outfit posing with baseball greats and some of the leading national and state politicians. Each time he referred to it as my "wall of shame," I chuckled. He wasn't the only cop in the department who gave me a hard time about my so-called mini-celebrity status. At least Barry was consistent, unlike the others, who mumbled about my publicity pictures, but when they wanted to impress others, they brought them into my office, pointed out the photos and talked about the stories behind them. Numerous times I had to stop doing whatever I was working on because a cop wanted to give a one-room tour of my office to local community members. Sometimes they brought in school teachers and whole classrooms of kids. I have to admit I enjoyed those visits.

We went through the usual quick exchange of pleas-antries, then Kevin and Barry sat down on the couch with their legs stretched out, each holding a coffee mug filled with freshly brewed coffee they'd poured themselves in the Xerox room alcove. Dispatchers working different shifts typically made sure there was a pot of coffee on hand. Although Kevin and Barry usually left to go home well before me, they worked pretty late and very intensely. We started to discuss strategy and the final moves on clamping down on the porno dad. I handed Kevin the affidavit and search warrant to take down to the Berkeley courthouse and find a judge to sign the papers. During business hours this usually wasn't a problem. It's basically a routine pro-cedure. All an officer had to do was ask around in the court-house for a judge who was not in session, have him or her look over the documents and then sign them, but I've had cases that involved finding a judge in the middle of the night and this meant tracking him or her down at home. In these cases, an officer would be well advised to have a higher up backing him up before he wakes up any judge.

After they left I sat there, waiting for Kevin to get back from the courthouse, when the dispatcher notified me there was a call from Detective Wade Harper with the Emeryville Police Department.

By the poor connection, I immediately could tell that Harper was calling me on his cell phone. I asked myself why he had not waited until he got back to his department and knew this in itself indicated a sense of urgency. Wade Harper and I had known each other for about seven years. I met him when he first became a detective in Emeryville. Because of the close proximity between our jurisdictions and the fact that we share fragments of the San Pablo Road and the I-80 Corridor, Emeryville and Albany Police maintained close working relations in conducting joint safety belt and DUI check points on San Pablo Road, where I often donned an Elvis jumpsuit and gave out traffic safety brochures to passing motorists. Most motorists like to avoid check points, but to our amusement, we recognized several cars coming back a second time after circling around the block. It also attracted the media to our cause.

"I'm in Auburn at the Placer County Jail and just finished speaking to Robert Silveria, who's in custody for killing a bunch of people on freight trains," Wade said in a rush. Then he threw out the punch line. "Silveria himself brought up that McLean murder in Albany and about stabbing the victim's dog. Bill, you better come up and interview this guy while he's still talkative."

Startled, I sat straight up in my chair. Pressing the phone closer to my ear with my shoulder, I pulled out a yellow pad and pen and began jotting down some of the information Wade

told me. "How did you get this?" I asked. He said a police officer he barely knew, who worked on the outskirts of Sacramento
for the city of Elk Grove, had seen a teletype that a suspect was
being held in Auburn who committed murders along the rail
lines. The officer recalled the homicide of a twenty-year-old
college student, Michael Garfinkle, in Emeryville. Why or how
the Elk Grove cop remembered this beats me, but he phoned
Harper and told him to contact a Salem, Oregon detective,
Mike Quakenbush, for more information. Quakenbush had
been following Silveria's trail for more than three months
before his capture, to ask him questions about two murders in
Oregon. I can imagine the intensity Mike applied to his investigation, not just because I got to know him later on, but
because one of the FTRA rail riders, TNT, told me years later
how he was in a camp in Vancouver, Washington by a creek
with Silveria and other FTRA rail riders when Quakenbush,
accompanied by other detectives, showed up looking for Silveria. Silveria's rail name was Sidetrack and Quakenbush and
other cops involved in the search thought they were looking for
two different men: Robert Silveria and Sidetrack.

"Robert always went to great care to look neat. He washed
and shaved. So when the cops asked him about Sidetrack or Silveria, he gave them a false ID. He looked presentable and they
believed him," TNT said shaking his head, standing on a corner
near a mission in Roseville. I couldn't help but notice that TNT
was one of the few FTRA train hoppers that still flaunt their rag
and concho. Most stopped since Silveria's arrest.

I mentioned TNT's account to both Quakenbush and
Silveria at a later date and both recalled the incident. The cops
got into a short, friendly discussion with the rail riders, including Silveria, the killer they were looking for. They discussed
train hopping, different lingo rail-riders use and their knowl-

edge of trains. Quakenbush was impressed that these guys, simply by observing a crew change, knew when and where the train was heading. But no one in the group that day admitted to the police to being a member of the FTRA or alluded that the Brotherhood existed or that the suspect the cops were looking for was right there in their midst, shooting the breeze with them. Like me at the time, Quakenbush was unaware of the existence of the FTRA and the significance of rail names. Wade Harper didn't know about the group either. Most cops didn't know about the organization. This was no harmless little group of people we were in the dark about. These guys not only knew about murders, but how to derail trains.

It took Wade and his partner, Detective Kevin Goodman, three hours to filter through the morning commute up to Auburn. At the county jail he was greeted by Detective Bill Summers, who suddenly found that he was working a ninety-hour-a-week shift after Silveria's capture, coordinating all the law enforcement investigators popping in and out. Summers warned Harper and Goodman that Emeryville P.D. might only be able to have half an hour for a preliminary interview with the suspect, because another agency was already scheduled for a 9:30 A.M. interview.

Emeryville and Albany are a stone's throw from each other, but at the same time, we might as well be thousands of miles apart. In many ways, all the little towns that are a part of the greater San Francisco metropolis are very provincial and self-contained, which carries over into the police departments. Wade Harper knew nothing about McLean's murder in Albany or about the details of the case and I didn't know anything about Michael Garfinkle's death in Emeryville, even though our agencies are only about eight miles apart. There was no media hoopla over the two deaths. Michael Garfinkle was from Tarzana, a suburb in Los Angeles County. Had he been a local youth, his death probably would have attracted greater press. His parents tried hard to push to find the killer of their son by offering a $10,000 reward, which apparently and unfortunately had no impact.

Harper wanted to ask Silveria about the murder of Garfinkle, a recent graduate of Pierce College in Los Angeles. The young man was an outstanding craftsman who liked working with his hands whether it involved woodwork, fixing cars or welding. According to his parents, one of his engineering instructors wrote "Top Gun" on Michael's last report card. A very social individual, he was also a spiritual one, studying eastern philosophy and religion. He also loved freight hopping. The long hours of waiting for one's train to come along allows the rider time to meditate. Box cars are very noisy when the train is moving; holding conversations is extremely difficult. This gave the young man another opportunity to read and to meditate on the changing scenery views outside the opened boxcar door. Michael set off with a friend and two books, one on world religions and the other on Taoism. When Michael and his friend reached Roseville, his friend wanted to take a bus back home. He didn't share the same enthusiasm for freight trains that Michael had. Garfinkle, however, wanted to continue riding the boxcar and reading his books. The pair parted and agreed to meet up at some point later. Michael got off the train at Emeryville, hung out during the early evening with some people he knew there and then joined other riders in a camp near the railroad tracks. He never made it through the night. Wade Harper was called in to investigate the body of a white male found bludgeoned to death by the Emeryville rail tracks.

Wade started his interview by determining if Silveria even knew where Emeryville, California was. Once it was established that Silveria did know the area, Harper asked him if he was involved in any fights or altercations in Emeryville. Their conversation wasn't tape recorded for a number of reasons, among which was that Harper and Goodman weren't sure they were going to get to talk to Silveria that day, because they were told that too many cops wanted to get in and speak to him. But he came anyway and took the chance that he might luck out and get to interview the prisoner at least briefly. He and Goodman were also rushed. They had other suspects and crimes with which to deal in Emeryville. In detective work, you have to turn every possible corner until you hit the jackpot.

Harper's meeting with Silveria lasted no more than thirty minutes, but it left him satisfied that he had enough information to request a longer interview with the prisoner. During the half hour he and Goodman spent with Silveria, the suspect readily admitted to an encounter by a bridge near Oakland. When Harper showed him a photograph of the area, he remembered the dramatic graffiti on the wall near the transient campground. He recalled that his victim had a black backpack, which is what Garfinkle had. He said Garfinkle had an elf-like face with pierced ears and a goatee, which fit the victim's description and that he left the victim lying on his stomach, his body covered in an old cloth and a sleeping bag. He recalled the victim's bag had an additional bag sewn into it and that the shoes he wore had waffle-stomper bottoms.

Silveria later recounted how he walked into a camp, where Garfinkle and three other riders told him he was trespassing, that it was their camp. Silveria said, "I go wherever I like." Michael should have run for his life then, but instead he and his companions pulled out and brandished axe handles, challenging the intruder. Silveria pulled out a 9 millimeter handgun. Michael Garfinkle was the nearest to Silveria. The others in the group were behind him and quickly scattered, running for their lives. Michael made a move to run too, but he tripped. By then Silveria's rage was in full control. He put away his gun, but he was still going to teach him a lesson. Pulling out his goon stick, Silveria moved to stand over the young student before he could rise back to his feet and said, "Welcome to the last day of your life." Then Silveria's fury lashed out as he pounded Garfinkle with the axe handle.

Harper pulled out other photographs of the area from a folder and showed it to Silveria. Silveria paused and then said, "I stabbed an old vet in that area living along the tracks with a dog." Silveria pointed to a spot in Albany. "I stabbed the dog too."

A few moments later, Silveria's mother phoned, pushing back the scheduled interview that was set to follow Harper. Bill Summers invited Harper to stick around. Harper did, eavesdropping on the phone conversation between Silveria and his mother. Others were listening in too. Loss of privacy is just another downside to being incarcerated. Harper told me that his impression was that Silveria's mother on the other side of the line was very upset and crying and that Silveria tried to soothe her. "At least now, Mom, people won't be getting hurt because of me," he said.

After Silveria's conversation with his mother ended, Wade scheduled another appointment to interview Silveria officially. As soon as he left the building and got into his car to head back with Goodman, he called me on his cell phone to tell me about Silveria admitting to killing McLean and stabbing his dog. The latter fact, that the victim had a dog that also was stabbed, had been kept out of the media as our hold-out information. In cases of murder police keep pieces of information involving the crime scene out of the press. It involves something unique that most likely only the murderer and the police would know. It helps to eliminate false confessions and at the same time adds credence to a confession in which information is revealed that only the killer and the police would know.

Within minutes after I finished talking to Wade Harper and hung up the phone, Barry Galloway strode into my office, the stern expression of a macho cop on his face. After taking another sip of strong black coffee, I looked up at him and grinned. "We have a road trip."

When I explained to Barry the action, he was like a kid in a candy store. I felt my own adrenaline jump up a notch or two. In a short while I'd have this lowlife dad behind bars and actually meet McLean's killer — all in one day. When Kevin returned with the arrest warrant, I announced it was time to "rock 'n' roll and give the sickest-dad-of-year award to the scumbag," only I used stronger language — the kind that could get me kicked out of some bars.

I chose Barry to head up with me to Placer County, because he was the department's identification officer and familiar with McLean's case. Official procedures requires two officers to conduct these types of interviews. This is for a number of reasons, which include the second person serving as an extra witness. In addition, the first cop's job is to be the interviewer and the second cop's role is that of a note taker. Further, it is the job of the second cop to relieve the interviewer from worrying about fidgeting with the tape recorder and other interferences that may come up. Some prisoners, like Silveria for example, frequently request to talk off the tape. The second person also serves as a support partner, in case violence occurs.

Albany is a small town with a population that seems to have gotten stuck permanently under 18,000. We didn't travel far to find the home of the man I was after. When we showed his wife the photos and the search warrant, she finally came to her senses and believed us. Returning to our office from the search, I let Kevin Horn and Barry Galloway finish up the details on the case, while I gathered up the old case files on McLean. Afterward I packed a camera, tapes, a tape recorder, pads, pens, my personal gear, which I kept on hand for long days and nights and, most importantly, a credit card.

Friday afternoon is never the best time to travel up north on I-80 from the San Francisco Bay Area. Traffic congestion doubles and sometimes triples when there's a crash on the road. In spite of my years of experience in police work, I was feeling apprehensive about interviewing Silveria. You always worry about screwing up, especially when the case has high visibility and may be closely watched in the department and by the media. Screwing up an interview is a driving fear that most investigators have. One false move and the killer walks while you look like an incompetent jerk. In spite of this neurosis, Barry and I were excited about finally meeting Robert Silveria.

4

Face to Face with a Serial Killer

"Well, are you going to sing me a song?"
Robert Joseph Silveria, Jr.

An oversized monument of an awkward-looking gold miner leaning on one knee with a gold pan in his hands is one of the first sights to greet visitors entering the city of Auburn, thirty minutes north of Sacramento. There is a noticeable change in the terrain as you get closer to the town. It moves from the muted tones and the panoramic flatness of California's San Joaquin Valley to bright, copper-red soil that shoots out beneath a hilly landscape marked with deep green pines and scattered Victorian houses. On a clear day you can spot the blue silhouette of the snow-capped Sierras in the distance. Each time I pass through this area, I am reminded of the Gold Rush era by the architecture in the town center and the high sidewalks made of wooden boards. In many ways, Auburn is characteristic of the towns in the area, which wear their histories like charms to lure tourists. The streets in the historical section typically are lined with specialty shops and antique stores. There are a couple of old bars downtown that have a long history of their own, too.

As we drove there, Barry and I talked about visiting several of them. We were bent on exploring the night life after we finished our meeting with Silveria — regardless how tired we might be.

Driving past the giant statue of the forty-niner and making a quick turn onto Highway 49, then immediately exiting, Galloway and I arrived at the Placer County Sheriff's Office, a white brick building with teal blue accents. We pulled in just as Mike Quakenbush looked like he was getting ready to leave, for he had on a down jacket over a shirt and jeans. He was standing outside the doorway to the building talking to Bill Summers. We exchanged brief introductions. I already had heard of Mike Quakenbush from Wade Harper and Bill Summers before I telephoned the Placer County Sheriff's Office to make arrangements to talk to Silveria. Quakenbush had that young cop, no-nonsense quality about him. The thing that struck me about Bill Summers was that he projected that police command quality, which so many cops I know unsuccessfully try to cultivate. Even Summers' voice resonated with authority. But what stuck in my mind was the unique situation Barry and I were in. Here we were, more than 150 miles away from our department, talking to a detective from Salem, Oregon and one from Placer County about the same prisoner.

Summers told us to wait while he went back inside the building. He returned in minutes with a copy of the Auburn newspaper containing a large color photo of Silveria on the front page. This made an even greater impact on Barry and me as we looked up at one another and nodded, speechless.

It was already pushing close to seven o'clock in the evening when Quakenbush took off for the night. Summers climbed into his vehicle, telling us to follow him in our car to the Placer County Jail, which we did. Arriving at the county jail, we parked our cars and he led us inside the building to the holding cell. Silveria had been moved, just a short while before we arrived, back to his cell for his meal and rest.

Silveria was held in a state-of-the-art holding facility. The echo of a slamming electronically controlled door rang in my ears as Barry Galloway and I entered the holding cell unarmed. It was a small room with bare walls. The only pieces of furniture were a steel table and three chairs. Shortly after we walked in, we saw Silveria being led in by heavily armed officers. Summers introduced us and gave Barry and me a police radio, which he told us earlier we were to use to call for help or to notify the deputies when we were ready to leave. Then he said, "So long," and walked out of the cell.

Standing there facing a serial killer that everyone was talking about felt a bit eerie. By then I had a good bit of information on him — Harper, Quakenbush and Summers had let me know that he wasn't your run-of- the-mill criminal. On the drive up to Auburn, Barry and I had mused about what it would be like talking to Silveria. Now the moment we had anxiously awaited had arrived. When Silveria walked in I was taken aback. He was nothing like I'd imagined. He looked too normal. I studied Silveria's face under the fluorescent light. *This guy's a serial killer*? I wondered. His features were regular and even and his complexion smooth. He appeared somewhat drawn, a bit tired, but not at all the tough monster I expected to find. Actually, he appeared rather easygoing and non-threatening. He was close to my over six-foot frame, but I thought that if I ever met him somewhere and he tried to pull anything on me, I wouldn't have any problem taking him down. This misperception was corrected, as I came to spend time talking to him: first on that Friday evening and then the following morning. I realized it was not what he looked like, but how he thought that made the difference between us. If you wandered into Silveria's arena, where his rules apply, it wouldn't matter how tough or big you were, he'd find a way to bring you down. Guys like him rely on the element of surprise when attacking their victims and they have no compunction about doing you in first. What I didn't know about Silveria then was that he also possessed extraordinary strength. An FTRA buddy of his, Angel, or Crazy Angel, as he was called in some circles, told me later how he watched Silveria pull a 300 pound coiled copper spool up a hill like it was nothing. "Now, I'm pretty strong, but Sidetrack — he's amazing," Angel grinned.

As Barry and I stood there sizing him up and vice versa, I sensed tension and awkwardness. "Why don't you sit down?" I said, pointing to one end of the steel table. I sat close to him, no more than two feet away at the other end of the corner of the table. Barry Galloway pulled up a chair and sat about six feet away from both of us, watching in case Silveria made any sudden moves to attack, thereby freeing me to concentrate on Silveria and not worry if he should suddenly become violent. Barry had a hand recorder to tape the interview and sometimes took notes, too.

Serial killers present a special challenge for investigators. Some of them exude charm and warmth that attracts sympathy with the force of a magnet, but it's the same charm and outgoing personality they frequently use to lure in victims. But as a cop, your profession requires you to keep an emotional distance. At the same time, you are required to probe deeply into their psyches, to gain their trust in the hope of getting a confession. It becomes an acting job. You pretend camaraderie even though images of their victims may flash through your mind. It can be tough at times. For example, another case I worked on involved a serial killer, Charles Jackson, who sodomized his female victims, stabbing them repeatedly while he was raping them. He finished off his sexual acts by slitting the victim's throats and ejaculating into their mouths. Now how does a cop smile and make small talk with a vermin like that? How do you shake the thought of what their victims went through when you're trying to establish personal contact and get them to talk? Frankly, I didn't want to be in a room with a low-life like Jackson. I solved that case through a DNA sample, but the gross piece of human dung was locked up in a state prison on a similar charge and died in prison, taking away the satisfaction of seeing justice served and having him exposed before the court. At least, I told myself, he saved taxpayers the time and money of housing him while he pled his way through the court system.

In the Jackson case I relied on modern-day methods, but in spite of advancement in scientific procedures in forensic work, good, old-fashioned interview techniques are still critical in police work. They require investigators to search for a common bond with the killer or perpetrator in order to establish trust and get to the truth. Sometimes this bond is real and sometimes it is fake. The main goal is to get a confession. Only God can put the jigsaw puzzle of a killer's mind back together again. An investigator's job is to keep them off the streets.

Robert Silveria felt that he was ready to "wipe his slate clean" and "to make peace with God." He said that he was shedding the old, "sick" Robert Silveria and putting on new garments. He was adamant when he said that he did not want to solve crimes for various police departments that implicated others and he told me he wasn't going to confess to any murders he did not commit

either, just to clean up paperwork for some cop. He was looking
after himself. It was his own being he wanted to face and bring to
peace. Hearing this, any earlier fears I had soon dissipated.

This is going to be a piece of cake, I thought, blissfully
unaware that the cliché would prove not to apply in this case.
Little did I realize at the time, but the challenges Silveria threw
out and the problems that developed out of them were going
to come back and haunt me over the years and I would not be
able to let this case go until the real truth came out — a truth
that has yet to be addressed in court.

Many times during our talks Silveria asked to turn the
tape recorder off so he could talk off the record about the
FTRA and murders in other jurisdictions, which he always
referred to as incidents. Of course, nothing in police work is
ever off the record when it involves a crime. We're not priests
or psychiatrists, we're cops. That evening, I probed Silveria
about his alleged crimes. I wanted to extract from him additional information on his crimes and to add in any way I could
to what I thought at the time was a great contribution made by
those detectives who questioned him before me. But most
important of all, I wanted to close the files on James McLean's
murder. As we spoke, Silveria not only confessed to committing
thirty-eight murders single-handedly and to participating in
homicides that implicated others, he stunned me when he said
he killed at least once in each of the thirty-eight states he passed
through and that the number of killings could be as high as one
hundred, and probably more.

Nodding his head, his cold, electrifyingly blue eyes
looked past me. "There's a graveyard out there," he said.

Another big shock wave struck when he told me about the
FTRA. Discovering the existence of a gang on rails, dominated by
death squads, stunned and flabbergasted me as it did the other
police officers who interviewed Silveria. That such a group existed

right under our noses and we had been blind to it was astonishing.

The system we were working under wasn't conducive to going beyond the crimes committed within our own little jurisdictions. As a result, we all came in and left with no follow-up questions. Everyone was first and foremost interested in solving the crimes in their own jurisdictions. We were also concerned that he might change his mind and stop talking. It was a race against time.

Silveria refused to discuss the murders committed by other FTRA members and remained extraordinarily loyal to the so-called death squad. He was definitely not a name dropper. Now that he was caught and locked up, his personal mission was, he said, to face his deeds and to cleanse himself of the past.

Before our meeting, all transient rail riders looked alike to me. Yet these guys could dress one way when they rode the trains and when they jumped off, they took off their grubby clothes which were typically military style camouflage or dark clothing. Underneath was a cleaner outfit, enabling them to mingle and mix with the public.

My talks with Silveria began with the speed of a garden snail moving across a yard. We both had had a long day and in my case, I'd also had a long, sleepless night. If I had to interrogate Silveria in his weary state, then he might lower his defenses. But then I realized I needed to be in prime condition myself to have an advantage over him. Still, I wanted to get to him as soon as possible. I began by reading him his Miranda rights after we'd established that he was familiar with the area of the crime. As we talked more, he convinced me he knew Emeryville well when he talked about the Emeryville indoor market and the aroma generated from rows of kiosks selling different ethnic cuisines. Detectives from Albany frequently ate lunch at the site. It's eerie imagining the probability that Silveria may have crossed paths with us there. Because the food was so good and cheap, a group of us used to eat at the market at least once a week. He talked on and on about McLean, admitting he killed him. He described the crime scene, including the unique green, cone-shaped stove and the bicycles strewn around. He recalled the victim's graying hair and "wolf-like" physical appearance and that the man had a bad leg. Silveria said he walked with a limp. He even brought up the fact that McLean had nine or nine-and-a-half size military style boots. Since no shoes or boots were found on McLean, I had no way to confirm this at the time. But I still needed a lot more proof that Silveria really did it. I needed all the bases covered for trial.

As I sat there growing more tired, I reflected that I didn't know how the guards did it — the colorless walls, the metal table, the hard chairs made me want to get out of the claustrophobic room. Though Barry and I badly wanted to solve our case, the atmosphere made me antsy. I turned to the prisoner. "Look, Robert, you are tired and so are we. We'd like to meet again with you tomorrow morning." Silveria agreed. "I didn't check, but are we allowed to bring you anything? Will they allow that?"

A faint grin appeared on Silveria's face. He shook his head, "No way. I've got pretty much everything." He told me he was looking forward to studying the Bible, which was the most important thing for him at that moment. I found this piece of information interesting and, as a Roman Catholic, suddenly felt a tinge of guilt for not reading the Bible myself as often as I should. I sputtered, "It's good reading, a very good book," and moved on feeling guilty.

Barry was about to request through the radio transmitter to the guards on the other side of the cell, our only link with the outside world, to let us out when Silveria popped one on me. "Hey, let *me* ask *you* a question now." He grinned, looking suddenly animated. "How come your hair is longer than a normal cop's? How come you've got those sideburns?" He arched his brows, studying me with a quizzical expression.

Barry and I exchanged glances. I had to grin and shake my head. "Go ahead. Tell him what you do," Galloway nudged, rolling his eyes.

I paused, looking back and forth from Galloway to Silveria. Taking a deep breath, I was about to begin my standard spiel when Silveria broke in. "Are you that Elvis cop?" I was taken back by his last question even more than by his first one. Even with feedback, it's hard to realize the impact one has when doing things outside the box.

"Yeah," I admitted. "I work on a grant as part of this singing Elvis and the Lawmen presentation at schools and community events."

"Well, are you going to sing a song for me?" Silveria said.

"You sing," I said. Silveria rose from his chair. He spread his legs and moved his hands like he was holding a guitar. Then to my and Barry Galloway's disbelief, he broke into a rendition of Elvis Presley's "Heartbreak Hotel," gyrating and mimicking the moves Elvis made famous.

"It would make a better story if he sang "Jailhouse Rock," but you take what you can get," I said later to Galloway. At that moment, Galloway and I stood there shaking our heads and laughing.

What amazed me was that he wasn't bad. In 1959, the year Silveria was born, there was probably at least one male kid on every big city block who at one time or another mimicked Elvis Presley. It was that year that I decided to go public for the first time with my impersonation of Elvis, creating a big stir in my junior high school with the students shouting for more and the Director of Activities wishing he could hide me in the janitor's broom closet. I knew then and there that Silveria's and my mutual affinity for Elvis Presley could very well turn out to be the common bond I was seeking to make Silveria open up about his past.

The following morning, Silveria showed a renewed willingness to cooperate. He joked briefly that Barry Galloway would make a good rail rider "because he's got that look," pointing out Barry's long mustache and long hair in the back. Barry was dressed in jeans, a black t-shirt imprinted with an image of the rock band Guns N' Roses and an open, flannel shirt. Leather shoes encased his sockless feet. I made an effort to look presentable by wearing a sports coat over my black t-shirt and jeans. Still, I couldn't hide my rock 'n' roll cop image, just as Barry couldn't hide his casual attitude and demeanor.

I reminded Silveria that he was still covered under the Miranda rights I'd recited at our previous meeting. I repeated that he was free to consult with a lawyer before speaking to me. Silveria said he knew his rights. I had already established from the previous day that Silveria was familiar with the area of the Albany, El Cerrito and Berkeley railroad tracks.

Silveria proved to be exceedingly open. He talked about how he liked facing his victims when he stabbed them in the rib area. He demonstrated a thrusting upward motion, as he described how he killed them. "Most of them I stabbed near the rib cage area, like God. God is pierced in the Bible in that same general area," he said. "I've used clubs, metal pipes, solid iron pipes…"

He added, "I've got a machete that I've used on a few people and it was used on a few people by the person I got it from, but his favorite way to kill was with a large buck knife with a brown wood-grain handle." He also used his foot to kill victims, referring to the steel toe boots he wore. He said he'd get pretty dosed on heroin and then he'd pick a fight with a victim. It could be anybody, even just somebody walking up the street asking for a quarter.

I was surprised to learn that guys like Silveria used the public library to get the railroad map and learn the routes. Although Silveria had already admitted killing McLean, I had him go over what he told us the night before, so we could flesh it out and learn more of the details.

Now Silveria recalled the incident happening in the middle of the summer. "What caused the incident?" I asked him.

He said, "What caused the incident was I was walking back with him to the camp. He was a belligerent kind of person. You know, if you were not doing things exactly how he wanted you to do 'em, he told you, 'Get the fuck out of here.'" I must have looked skeptical because Silveria added, "Excuse me, but I'm just telling you. He was a little bit scattered-brained and an older guy. He'd been doing speed most of his life."

As he talked, Silveria gave the details I'd hoped to learn, the needles he used as a ploy to get McLean angry and his own need to bring out the rage brewing deep inside of him to the surface so that he could kill. He described in detail how he killed McLean, first bludgeoning him with his goon stick and then stabbing him. He described removing McLean's boots and said that one of them had an extra heel added on to compensate for the man's bad leg. Surprised, I sat up when he said that and turned to look at Galloway. Barry returned my gaze. That was hold-out information that we, the cops, didn't know. I was anxious to corroborate this information.

I felt I had established an important link and analysis that the Department of Justice uses to bring together all known facts from a crime scene and what the criminal admitted. The Albany victim was a white male, fifty years old. Silveria's recollection was the murder victim was a white guy about fifty years old. McLean had a receding hairline and Silveria remembered his hair combed back "wolf-like." McLean had a gray beard and

Silveria described the Albany victim as having a gray beard. McLean was found shoeless and Silveria stated that he took from McLean black military boots, size nine with an extra heel on one of the boots. McLean had a deformed right leg and Silveria recalled that he limped and was unable to run. McLean was found with abrasion to his head and neck and Silveria admitted to striking his head with an oak axe handle. There were stab wounds found in McLean's chest and Silveria spoke of using a knife on the Albany victim. Family members and those that knew McLean described him as being cantankerous and belligerent. Silveria also described McLean as belligerent. Albany investigators learned that McLean was a meth user and Silveria said his victim in Albany was a "crankster." McLean was believed to have had two hundred dollars before his murder and Silveria admitted to taking two hundred dollars from the Albany victim. Silveria identified McLean from the photo I showed him. A link and analysis was also established in the crime scene: the den or the inside hooch of McLean's camp, items on branches of trees, the silver ten-speed bike, military-style jacket with patches and a Vietnam veteran's blue I.D. card. While Silveria had a hard time recalling McLean's dog when I spoke to him, he had told Wade Harper about killing an old transient who limped and had a dog.

The knife that he used to kill McLean, Silveria said, fell into the river when he was washing his pants in a creek near his Roseville camp. We tried to recover it. Detective Kevin Horn and Barry Galloway eventually made a thorough search of the area using a metal detector, but they couldn't locate the knife.

That morning I got a complete confession and Silveria gave me "something to remember him." I was well aware that I might have to turn it over to the D.A. if the case went to trial. As I questioned Silveria about his moniker, he told me that

when he signed his rail name on bridges and walls to indicate
he'd been there, he drew next to his rail name, "Sidetrack," a
crushed skull, railroad tracks and a spider web. He included in
this insignia "51-50," which is police code for crazy, and the
initials "F.T.W." and "S.T.P."

I pulled out a white cocktail napkin from my jean pockets, which I had picked up the night before in one of the local
bars in Auburn where Barry and I had a drink, and asked Silveria to draw me a sample, which he did. Then Silveria explained
the symbolism of his drawings. The rails stood for his home
address – indicating he was a rail rider and that was his only permanent address. The spider web was a warning not to come
near him for it meant that one was in danger of being "caught
up" and wrapped just like a cocoon when the spider crawls out
to kill its victim. "It spins a web around and you're going to
hang. He isn't going to try to handle society no more." Silveria's tone was matter of fact.

"What does the crushed skull mean?" I watched Silveria
for any emotional reaction, but he continued speaking in the
consistent monotone that he had throughout, although on
occasion he did display glimpses of an out-going personality
when he spoke about God or Elvis.

"That's how I kill my victims. I crush the skull." Again,
his eyes reflected no emotion. They simply looked right past me
with a cold, pitiless, steel-blue gaze that brought terror to so
many. Some say the "F.T.W." stood for the attitude of rail riders, meaning "Fuck The World," and "S.T.P.," which originally
referred to "Steam Tramp People," the original train hoppers
who rode on steam engines, now also stood for "Start the
Party."

When Silveria was explaining the symbolism to me, I got
more information out of him and another souvenir, a trophy of

my own. Taking it also made me realize how much investigators had in common with those they hunted down. It's only the spoils of war that reassure you that you're on the winning side.

I left Auburn feeling elated. I had my confession and Barry appeared impressed with my interview techniques, which meant that when he hung out with the others in the department, I wouldn't have to worry about gossip behind my back, at least this time. When you're an "Elvis" type of cop, it goes with the territory to have others always watching and talking about every move you make.

Getting into the car to drive back, I was excited and fascinated by the new information we learned, not only about Silveria but about the FTRA. Most of our conversation during the ride was animated, as Barry and I went over everything we learned in the last twenty-four hours.

Two days later I received another telephone call. This one was from Woodland Police Sergeant Doug Bera, who interviewed Silveria three days later, before the alleged killer was extradited to Oregon. Mike Quakenbush, I noted, sure worked fast. Mike was receiving credit for capturing Robert Silveria and all the cops were looking up to him. It was Mike's teletype and his constant telephone calls that led to Silveria's capture. Mike did an excellent piece of detective work and he shared the credit with other officers from Kansas and Utah.

Doug Bera also made a good impression on me when I spoke to him. He told me that he couldn't close the paper work on his own case in Woodland, because the murder in the boxcar happened in 1977, before Silveria began riding the rails. However, Bera was able to explore a lot of territory covering Silveria's long career in crime, which included a murder in Albany of "an old transient." This meant that in addition to confessing that he killed McLean and providing hold-out information that we cops didn't even know about and that I had to confirm afterwards, Silveria had also admitted to a second police department that he killed a man in Albany. Bera sent me a copy of the transcripts of his interview with Silveria. I was extremely impressed by Bera's interview techniques and very pleased to have another confirmation from Silveria that he killed McLean. I finished up my paperwork on the McLean murder and sent it off to the district attorney.

I felt my involvement with the case was over until the D.A. announced he was filing the case. I would next see Silveria in the Berkeley Courthouse when I would, for sure, be called to testify. However, events began to take a different twist. As I gathered up the cases and evidence and developed a timeline, I saw a conflict with a case in Kansas City. Silveria admitted to killing McLean on July 22 in Albany, but he also admitted to killing a Charles Boyd on July 26 in Kansas. According to the timeline the Kansas Bureau of Investigations developed, Silveria left El Paso, Texas with Boyd on July 23 and traveled through Colorado to Kansas. I called Kevin Horn into my office to discuss the matter.

"How the hell can he be in two places at the same time?" I scratched my head.

"Beats me." Horn shrugged. I asked Kevin to check with the rail companies and get back to me pronto. Kevin checked with the Oakland Rail yards and came back satisfied that our case against Silveria was still strong. He was told by the Southern Pacific Rail Company that Silveria could have jumped a priority train, or "hotshot," as they were referred to, and been in El Paso within ten hours.

The conflict, although momentarily solved, did not go away. In fact it would take almost eight years before I would learn how Silveria really did it and discover that the real story about him is different from the one presented to the world by the cops, the courts and the media. In spite of tightened security after 9/11, seasoned rail riders like Robert Silveria still have the know-how to circumvent the authorities and move around freely. They also know how to derail trains. To learn the whole truth, I decided I had to go back to discovering who Silveria, the so-called Boxcar Serial Killer, and his group of death squad members really were.

5

One of a Kind

"My friends always said I'd be famous someday.
They said I was one of a kind."
Robert Joseph Silveria, Jr.

I learned from Robert Silveria that he was born in Redwood City, a town on the San Francisco peninsula. When I think of Redwood City, I think of El Camino Real Road, meaning King's Highway in Spanish, which my high school friends and I used to cruise when I lived in San Francisco. The road is part of a trail, formed by a small group of Spaniards and Native Mexicans, which ran from San Diego past San Francisco to Sonoma, during the time the American Revolution was taking place. Today, Redwood City is lined with middle- and upper-middle class homes. It's ironic that while the community prides itself as a center of high-tech industry, the town got its early push in 1863 when the railroad line pierced through its jurisdiction, prompting an explosion in land values and population that can still be seen today. Ninety-six years later, Silveria popped up, making his own headlines in railroad history.

Silveria's life proved to be more complex then I figured it to be when he first began telling me about himself. But then again, anything having to do with Robert Silveria touches on conflict and becomes an enigma.

Silveria's parents worked at an airport for a major airline; his father was a supervisor, part of the management force, and his mother worked in the catering service department. He had an older sister and two younger brothers. He also had an older half brother from his father's previous marriage. The family appeared conventional, at least on the surface. However, behind closed doors and drawn window drapes there was serious trouble brewing. Its ugly head manifested at about the time Robert turned eleven. Problems with him started gradually: skipping school, forging notes, experimenting with drugs and then getting expelled from school. Silveria's father was a strong, authoritarian figure who reportedly often beat Robert for his rebelliousness, in the hope that he would knock some sense into him. Instead, the elder Silveria got trapped in a vicious cycle. The more trouble Robert got into, the more his father punished him with beatings. And the more the father punished him, the angrier the son got and the more recalcitrant he became. One thing for sure though, Robert Silveria, Jr. got into more and more mischief until he crossed the line into crime. The family moved at one point, but again, it's a matter of who you listen to as to why they moved. Was it because at the age of twelve Robert was caught burglarizing neighbors' homes or because his parents needed to be closer to work?

While he was still a pre-teen, three boys, two black and one white, beat Robert up in a park. Afterward, his father forced Robert to confront the three youths, insisting that he fight them one on one with a baseball bat in his hand. According to Robert, his maternal uncle, Lloyd Chapin was there too, egging the father on. That day, the twelve-year-old Robert Silveria refused to fight and ran back home. Years later, the baseball bat his father wanted Robert Silveria to use one-on-one had been replaced with a goon stick.

According to the Oregon psychiatric evaluation, Silveria showed early signs of destructive and deadly behavior. According to the psychiatrist's report, Robert killed a kitten his parents gave him as a present by throwing it across a cactus in their garden and then telling them it fell off the fence. They believed him. Robert's mother denies this. "Where did this thing about the kitten come from? It's true we had a kitten that someone poisoned, but it wasn't Robert. Robert loved animals. He kept a guinea pig and a snake as pets and looked after them. He promoted life and growth. He kept these creatures alive."

Another psychiatrist who evaluated Silveria characterized Silveria's relationship with his father as a war between the son and the father that started while Robert was in grade school and continued throughout his teenage years. It involved deadly games of sabotage, like the time the younger Silveria took the lug nuts off the wheels of his father's pickup. He removed all but one lug nut on each wheel. The report conjures up hateful images, which must have rushed through Silveria's mind as he pictured his father driving the vehicle back and forth to work with the wheels barely attached. The conclusion that I came to was that Robert Silveria was consumed by hate.

Silveria denied this when we met again later. "I don't know where this came from about me and my dad. He was a regular dad who used to take us camping. He gave us what he could," Silveria said and shrugged. Silveria's mother confirms this. "We weren't wealthy people. My husband was a supervisor working for Delta, so we had discounts in travel and we took the kids to Mexico City and to Hawaii. We did what we could with them." But there is one problem Silveria's mother doesn't deny. Silveria's older sister, with whom Robert was very close, became addicted to drugs at an early age and introduced drugs to her brother when he was fourteen years old. Both he and his sister became allies in cutting school, forging notes and the drug use that escalated into a serious problem for both of them. "Debbie doesn't like to admit this, but she was the one that got me started on drugs," Silveria told me.

His mother agrees. "Robert was very close to his sister and looked up to her." Yet Silveria also accepts much of the blame.

"I made it hard on my parents, very hard," he told me in a barely audible voice in the Placer County Jail in Auburn.

There were additional problems between Silveria and his father. When Robert Silveria was in his twenties, he took his father's truck without his permission and was caught by the police, who put the younger Silveria in jail and charged him with felony auto theft. Once out of jail, Silveria Junior soon started stealing cars regularly. Silveria didn't tell me this, but he told former Woodland Police Sergeant Doug Bera, now retired, that he traveled as far north from Redwood City as the Davis, Sacramento and Woodland areas to steal vehicles. He said he used a screw driver to start the stolen cars and then drove them to junk yards where he sold them for around five hundred dollars. This doesn't surprise me, because there are thousands of shipments of stolen vehicles that come into the docks in California. It's a multi-billion dollar racket.

Silveria did tell me that when he was in high school, his father allowed him to use his truck to go to school and back. He used the truck to help rob a drug dealer who was coming around to his high school. Silveria and another friend followed the dealer home one time to learn where he lived. Next, they took the friend's father's twelve-gauge shotgun and covered their faces with ski masks and robbed the drug dealer, confiscating the drugs he had on him. Later, the friend died from a drug overdose.

The older Silveria made attempts to help his son. He got Robert his first job as a luggage handler in the same airport where he worked. But Robert Silveria's problems continued to multiply and he continued to challenge his father's authority. Eventually, he was laid off from the job. Silveria told me that he believes he actually was fired because of his abuse of beer and drugs, but they gave him a layoff so as not to embarrass his father. Some time shortly afterwards, he was placed in a seven-month drug rehabilitation program through the county probation program. Unfortunately, the drug rehabilitation program didn't work. After leaving it, Silveria graduated to crack and later moved to amphetamines, but he lucked out and managed to get a construction job. While hanging drywall in a hotel building, he received a Christmas bonus of $1,000, which he spent entirely on drugs. By the time he was twenty years old, Silveria had been jailed on burglary charges, auto theft and motorcycle theft. His troubles were only beginning.

When he turned twenty-one, Silveria decided to leave California, hitchhiking to Arizona. That was the year he returned to robbery and committed his first murder. The victim was a white male, in his mid-forties driving a black, four-door sedan. The man spotted Robert Silveria walking with a backpack, pulled up and stopped his car and asked him where he was going. "I'm trying to get to Tucson," Silveria told him. The man told Silveria that if he could help out with the gas, he would be more than happy to drive Silveria there. Silveria gave him food stamps worth about twenty dollars. The man cashed them in to purchase ten dollars worth of gas and buy a twelve pack of beer. Climbing into the man's black sedan, Silveria

noticed a gun partially covered by newspapers with advertise-
ments that included images of a green clover, signifying St.
Patrick's Day. After they crossed an area with a fruit check
point, the driver pulled off the highway onto a narrow dirt road
and drove three miles inland before pulling up by a wooden
post with a broken-down gate. "I want to stop and drink a
beer," he explained. Turning to Silveria, he asked if Silveria ever
fooled around. Silveria was trapped in an isolated place with a
stranger with a gun and in danger of rape.

Silveria asked the man if he would teach him how to
shoot the gun. The man asked, "What gun? What gun are you
talking about?" Silveria pointed to the one under the newspaper. He told the stranger he never shot a gun before and
wanted to learn. "All right, well, let's make it fast," the guy
said, according to Silveria.

They got out of the car and the man began showing off
his skills with the gun, boasting, "Drink that beer real quick and
let me have the can. You can throw it up in the sky and I'll fill
it full of holes." Silveria threw the can high up in the air and the
man shot a series of rounds, peppering the can with holes. Then
the stranger reloaded the magazine with nine shells. The gun
was a German Luger — a nine millimeter handgun. He held it
away from Silveria and said he was going to stand behind him
and show him how to hold it. Then he put the gun in Silveria's
hand. Silveria wasn't sure what was going to happen next, if the
gun had a safety on it or what. But the man put his arms around
Silveria, squeezing him, and without hesitating, Silveria whirled
around and shot the man in the face. He fell instantly.

As he told this story, there was a sudden dead silence in
the room. I could tell that though the past no longer existed,
its memory still haunted Silveria. His glazed eyes appeared to
be staring into some faraway space. I found no reason not to
believe him.

I leaned forward empathetically, but asked no questions, giving him room so he would continue the story. He did, telling how he'd regained his composure that day. He grabbed the stranger's body and dragged it next to the car. He thumbed through the man's wallet. Inside he found a Kentucky ID, which Silveria wound up keeping along with the man's social security card and military veteran's card. He also pulled out car keys from the man's side pocket and opened the trunk, wondering how he was going to get rid of the car and the body. The thing that stuck in his mind was he had to make it quick to run from the law.

Managing to lift the body, he shoved it in the trunk. Next, Silveria put the gun in his backpack. Then he drove through the desert until he came upon a ravine surrounded by a pile of old railroad ties. Silveria pulled the car up facing the ravine and stopped. Getting out, he pulled his gear from the black sedan and put it on the ground a few feet away. There were some flares in the car, which he took, too. He managed to break off a piece of a manzanita bush growing nearby and wedge it in between the gas pedal and the seat. The car gearshift was in park and the motor started revving up full blast. Silveria shifted it into drive and drove the car down into the ravine, clinging to the wheel, as his whole body vibrated with the movement of the sedan. He rolled into the hole in the ground with the sedan's nose in the ditch and the back wheels still rolling. Suddenly, the car started blowing pure white smoke from the exhaust pipe. Silveria climbed out of the ditch and ran, stopping only when he felt he was at a safe distance from the burning vehicle still blowing smoke. Then the smoke suddenly stopped. Silveria stood watching and wondering why. "What's going on?" he murmured. He thought maybe all the oil moved to the front of the engine and no more was left to burn. He decided there was nothing more to do but to crawl back into the ditch and find a way to blow the whole thing up. Taking the gas cap off, he stuffed a bunch of manzanita branches in the tank spout with other little pieces of twigs and splinters of wood from railroad ties. Then he lit the flare. It took a while for the flare to light the wood, but finally it caught fire. Silveria rushed out of the ditch, running back to a safe distance before the car blew up. Sitting on a log, he watched from afar as the smoke and flames rose into the air. The trunk never opened.

Afterward, Silveria walked back to the burning car, throwing railroad ties on top of it to create more heat. Then he moved back and sat watching it burn completely, before walking back to the freeway and catching another ride all the way to Tucson.

Silveria kept the gun. Later that same year, Silveria started riding rails, but only recreationally.

Sometime later (Silveria didn't remember exactly when), he traveled to Kentucky to apply for welfare under the dead driver's name. Pinning Silveria down to the exact times was hard. He remembered details of incidents well, but when it came to dates and times, he said it all blurred together.

Securing welfare was relatively easy since Silveria had the stranger's veteran's I.D. card, but more importantly, Silveria had his social security card. The Kentucky welfare clerks told Silveria he was eligible if he wanted to apply, because "he" had no open case there. Silveria claimed he never collected and never used the welfare card. He also said he went back later to the same spot in the Arizona desert where he had set the black sedan with the body of his first victim on fire. He was surprised to see there was no evidence of any incident there. It was like it never happened. There was only sand.

Silveria had relationships with girls before he married his first wife, whom he met when she was just fourteen and he was doing tattoos on her father. They got married on May 19, 1984 at the Methodist Church in a small town on the Western slopes of the Sierra Nevada mountain range, Quincy, California. This was the same year the FTRA was being christened in a bar in Whitefish, Montana.

Silveria was hired as the airport manager for the Chester Airport near Quincy. No doubt it was because of his father and his airline industry connections. But soon the younger Silveria lost his job; he was caught embezzling money to feed his drug habit. The couple separated about eighteen months later and Silveria took up with another woman. The separation, however, turned out to be brief and the couple was back together again in the summer of 1986, had a daughter and moved to Kentucky. Before they had time to settle down, Silveria was arrested and extradited to California on embezzlement charges. He spent a year in jail waiting to go on trial. His first wife later told Detective Quakenbush that in October 1987, she and Silveria began frequent trips to visit his uncle in Stockton, California. It was during this period that her husband kept telling her that he was going to the store and would be right back, but he didn't return for several days. It was around this time that the young wife learned her husband was a druggie. According to her, one time Silveria left and she never saw him again. Periodically he contacted her mother and talked briefly with her. It was through her mother that Silveria learned his wife had divorced him.

I don't know if his first wife realizes how lucky she was that he walked out on her. Silveria told me he took up rail hopping, because he woke up one night in a sweat, having dreamed that he killed his wife and their infant daughter. He woke up very early the next morning with urges to kill his wife and baby girl. That morning he packed a few things while his wife still slept and left for good. "I didn't want to follow through with what I was feeling; I didn't want harm to come to them," he said. I suppose it's one thing to fight an enemy outside of you, but when it's the enemy within you, the struggle becomes tougher. Silveria confirmed what his first wife told Mike Quakenbush, that sometimes he'd phone his mother-in-law to ask about his wife and daughter, who by then had moved back home. He told me, "Many times I'd phone and hold the receiver to my ear and say nothing." Silveria eventually remarried and tried to make a fresh start with a second family.

Silveria's second wife was still wearing his wedding ring when I talked to her. She met Silveria when cousins of a man she was dating came from California to visit him and Silveria was with them. She and Silveria struck up a conversation and soon realized that they really wanted to be together. She said she found Robert easy to talk to about everything and anything. The gabbed for hours on end. Silveria told her that his father rode with the Hell's Angels and beat his mom. Years later she heard from Silveria's mother that the story was untrue.

The couple moved in together shortly after meeting and became almost inseparable. In November of 1990 they moved to Mississippi and got married. Silveria and his wife and her children settled in a trailer. He got a job working for his wife's brother-in-law and another friend of the family doing roofing. At this point, Silveria phoned his first wife to tell her the news.

When I talked to Silveria's second wife, she said she has a hard time reconciling herself to the fact that the Robert Silveria she knew is the same man dubbed the Boxcar Serial Killer. She told me that Silveria was probably the nicest guy she ever knew. At least that's what she thought when she first met him. Her family, friends and acquaintances thought the same about him. He was "just too nice," she repeated numerous times. She still loves the man she remembers with all her heart. The horrible man she ended up reading about in the press or watching on television was entirely different. The Robert she knew was always there for her, even when her mother needed to be driven to places to run errands. He did her mother's yard work and took her to garage sales. Even her kids liked him. She had no objections when Silveria convinced her to allow him to do tattoos on the kids. He was charming, polite and a very hard worker. She never saw him drink hard liquor or beer. The only thing they drank at home, in their house trailer, was sparkling wine, which they called "Champagne." She never saw him do any drugs either. She herself was strongly opposed to even smoking pot. Her own family viewed drugs as taboo.

However, there were some discordant things she noticed about Silveria, which she just couldn't pinpoint. He would be gone for many hours at a time and she didn't know where he went and what he did. She was never concerned there was another woman, but felt there was something lingering from his past that was intruding into their present. One day Silveria phoned his wife to pick him up at a bar. She drove over to get him, but when she saw him she was astonished. Silveria was badly beaten; blood, bruises and open wounds covered his face. He told her some men jumped him. She wanted to telephone the police, but he said, "I'll handle it in my own way." His wife drove him home where she washed him and bandaged his wounds. The next morning he was up at dawn, back at work as a roofer, doing his job as if nothing had happened.

About four months into the marriage, things began to sour. His wife's son came to her, told her to sit down and pay attention to what he had to say to her. He told her that Robert Silveria was a drug addict, using crack cocaine and heroin. She didn't believe him and went into a state of denial. Maybe, she thought, her son was being overly protective of her. Maybe she imagined he and Robert had an argument and exchanged a few words. Or maybe, she considered, this was his way of breaking them up, because the boy was jealous of the relationship. She decided to do nothing, just sit back and watch for any clues that would help her size up the situation.

Then a drug agent from Cleveland, Mississippi made an appointment to see her. He came to her home to speak to her privately. He told her straight out that she married a very bad guy. She disagreed with him and told him so. But the agent was persistent. He told her Silveria had been in trouble for a long time with the law and that he was on probation, but the agent couldn't or wouldn't tell her more than that. She still had trouble believing that Robert Silveria was anything but a wonderful and caring man. The agent told her that Silveria was under investigation. He said, "I don't care what you do, but you need to get him out of your life — now."

She told the agent that she would think about what he told her. After he left she sat down, still unable to understand the circumstances in which she suddenly found herself. She knew some people who worked in different police departments and phoned them to ask that they check out what the Cleveland agent said was true. They confirmed everything the agent told her. Soon, she began to notice money missing from her wallet and then she realized that a lot of cash was disappearing from the house. It was a sure sign that all was not right in her household.

By mid-April in 1991, his second wife finally got enough nerve to approach Silveria about his drug use. When he came home one day from work, she asked him point blank if he was doing drugs and he said, "No." She told him that if he was doing drugs that was a big problem. He said, "The only problem I have is you." It was then that she told him to leave. They maintained sporadic contact after that. Silveria moved in with another woman, but he phoned his second wife wanting to get back with her. She met him in a motel. They talked for a while and she almost agreed to take him back. But she told him that if he wanted to get back with her, he would have to give up all drugs. He told her that he used only marijuana. By then she knew better and adamantly told Silveria, "You can come back, but no drugs and that's that." That year, Silveria adopted the rails as his permanent home address and became a member of the FTRA.

6

The FTRA

"We carry our homes on our backs."
Robert Joseph Silveria, Jr.

Everything Robert Silveria told me about the FTRA matches what I learned gradually over the following years in my own inquiries. Nevertheless, how the group got started remains cloudy. One version is that the name grew out of the freight trains with the logo XTRA that changed over time to FTRA. Silveria said the group was started by Vietnam veterans who, after they did their stint in the service, dropped out of society, feeling used and neglected by the government. When they dropped out, they formed a brotherhood along the rails to help look out for one another. The first group went by the name of the "Hole in the Wall Gang."

There is no dispute that the brotherhood got started with the Vietnam veterans, as Silveria said, but other riders with whom I spoke in several different cities insisted that the name FTRA originated as a joke made in a bar in Whitefish, Montana by a man with the frontier-sounding name of Daniel Boone. According to them, Boone, who later became a Pentecostal preacher in Montana, first suggested naming the group "Fuck the Reagan Administration," or FTRA for short, in the summer of 1984, the same year Ronald Reagan was reelected the forti-eth President of the United States. According to these veterans, their attitude was a reaction to Reagan's cuts in social programs and benefits that severely impacted down-and-out veterans.

Time kept the initials but changed the meaning to the Freight Train Riders of America. A strong anti-government sentiment exists among rail riders even today. Except for Silve-ria, most train riders remain mum on the food stamps they get and trade, but justify buying other men's identities on the black market as a form of survival. It's a technique they teach to new-comers to get a bigger piece of a very meager pie. As Silveria expressed it, "If the government took time to help us, most of us would be out of there."

Drinking plenty of booze and smoking reefer helps FTRA riders ignore the filth and unwelcome odors in the camp-sites they call *jungles,* where they chill out and wait to catch the next freight train. Typically, there are plentiful supplies of drugs and liquor in the secluded spots where seasoned, hard-core rid-ers hang out. These die-hard FTRA members, the more violent breed, rob and steal drugs that they share willingly with others in their group. Sharing is a big thing among the FTRA mem-bers. It provides a sense of brotherhood, a replacement for the families they once had. I can't think of a single FTRA member to whom I spoke who didn't tell me that he took up rail riding after a separation, a divorce or the death of a spouse.

They survive on social security checks, veteran disability

checks and food stamps. At one time Robert Silveria had as many as fifteen aliases on him, most of them belonging to his dead victims. He knew the rails like most people know the roads leading to their local market or as some folks know which back roads to take from their favorite bars to avoid tailgating cops, all of which made it difficult for law enforcement to track him down, let alone identify and catch him. By the time police discovered the bodies of his brutally murdered victims, Silveria was thousands of miles away, looking for new prey. Usually, he took his victim's personal documents with him, making it difficult to identify the deceased and buying time for himself.

To become a member of the FTRA, Robert Silveria had to go on a "quick" ride around the United States with a seasoned FTRA rail rider. At that point, he was studied and observed to ascertain whether he had the toughness and the personality to make it in the Brotherhood. It's during this initial trip that a name is designated for each prospective member. An individual's tag is based on faults and weaknesses that the members spot during the trip around the country. For example, Silveria said, "If you like to stop and do laundry frequently, you might get the moniker of 'Mr. Clean.'" In Silveria's case, he got tagged "Sidetrack," because the first train he was on as a fledgling FTRA member got sidetracked. They sent him out to buy beer and he got distracted and didn't come back for days. The name stuck and seemed apropos later. He got sidetracked diving into dumpsters or doing "other things." One time he disappeared from the group for a couple of days, only to show up in a stolen truck at the camp where his group was waiting for him.

The tagged name you get is very important in the FTRA. That is how you're identified along the rails. There are no first names or last names used among members, only the assigned monikers. If a man uses another's assigned name and commits a crime against the brotherhood, such as snitching to the cops or stealing from another FTRA member, the wrong person can get beaten up or even killed by one of the enforcers.

Silveria impressed the FTRA and was judged to be the right kind of prospect for the toughest element of the group. He was recruited by the executioners in an enforcement group. Each time they met up they asked each other "How many did you kill?" Silveria claimed he killed about thirty men with just the death squad alone. But when he was caught he wouldn't divulge any of the death squad members' names or monikers to any of the cops interviewing him.

When a new FTRA member is initiated, there is a big party at the camp. Each group has its own concho and each member of that group will wear an identical concho. Silveria's group was made of five members. In addition to their conchos, each had the same "Flashback" button. They carried them in their Indian medicine pouches. Had the police ever stopped all five of them together, they would have had the entire death squad. Of course, that never happened.

Most of the original FTRA, such as Catfish, are qualified to wear a gold concho. They have covered the million miles required to earn them. The rest of the FTRA wear silver. An initiate receives his silver concho from the head guy, in whose camp the initiation takes place. During the initiation, which begins with Thunderbird wine and Jack Daniels, the concho is placed over the fire. Members cut their fingers and drip their blood over the concho. The members all wear rags or bandannas, which denote their geographical locations — the routes with which their camps are associated. For example the southern rail route's starting point is in Yuma, Arizona, but members of their goon squad hang out at an old, abandoned ice warehouse in Mobile, Alabama.

Silveria's group's starting point was in Vancouver. The black rags they wore signified the northern routes that moved along the Hi-Line through the northern states. Before the initiate earns his rag, the other members piss and stomp on it so that when they finally give the rag to him to tie around his neck, it's dirty and smelly, but he has to wear it for a week before washing it.

The initiation is rough. During it each initiate gets challenged. Then they pour beer over his head. The beer is never finished to the last drop. About a half inch of brew remains in the bottle to be poured on the ground in a circular motion in remembrance of brothers and sisters in the spirit world. I've also seen them pour some beer out first and then drink it. Each time I had an encounter with any of the FTRA, the beer ritual was one point they stressed as very important. Rituals for the dead were part of the FTRA practices. They were even known to create shallow graves for victims and plant makeshift headstones. Silveria took trinkets from his victims as souvenirs for his medicine pouch, in order to keep their spirits with him. He was not alone in these rituals. Many of the FTRA enforcers had leather Indian medicine pouches hanging from their necks, in addition to the conchos and the bandannas.

The person in whose camp any party is held is considered in charge and may order anyone to leave if the person disobeys his rules. However, the holder had to be strong enough to defend the rule. Females are treated with utmost respect, primarily because they are rare in the FTRA's world. Silveria told me that if he saw a woman disrespected at a party and a brother sitting nearby witnessed it and didn't come to her aid, then it would be Silveria's job to beat up the one who failed to act in defense of the woman.

FTRA members also have their own slang. *Good guys* stands for the modern day FTRA, which I see as the next generation of traditionalists. They are usually in their late twenties and early thirties. *Flintstones*, who seem to be more acceptable today than they were a number of years ago, are the new rail riders. They pierce themselves and like heavy metal music. *Sil-*

ver mining is hitting the casinos and going around seeing if a player forgot small change in one of the machines or didn't finish playing a hand, as well as getting free booze from the cocktail waitresses. *FTW* means Fuck the World, and *butchered up* means fell under a train. *STP* once stood for Steam Train People, what the rail riders were called when there were steam locomotives. It's meaning has changed to Start the Party, when members form a *San Francisco Circle* and whatever money anyone has on him is thrown into a hat — they all pony up to buy "grub, beer, whatever." *SWP* stands for Supreme White Power. Most of the racial slogans seem to derive their origin from lingo in the prisons, where prison gangs are divided along racial lines, intensifying prejudices and anger.

Members of the group claim to have dropped out of society voluntarily. They like to sound like the last of the free men, with no obligations or responsibilities, but the idea that it's an act of volition seems to be inaccurate. Most of those with whom I spoke had dropped out and started riding rails after divorces or the death of spouses or major problems finding jobs. Many have not been trained to hold jobs or "programmed" to survive in the mainstream. Many are ex-convicts, and this strikes against their job possibilities. The rails have become a refuge for thousands of such men; only a handful of women ride the rails.

Most of the men to whom I spoke don't see themselves as homeless. Drawings depicting rails next to monikers signify that these individuals, including Silveria, are FTRA rail riders and the rails are their address. "Don't call me homeless, because I'm not. I have a country. The United States is my home," said a former Navy enlistee who traveled the world on a ship during the Vietnam War.

The personalities of the men I met in the FTRA vary. Some were sharp and articulate. One, whom I spotted dumpster diving with another FTRA rider, said he had been a law student. However, some men appear to be possessed, their mental illness so severe it is instantly visible even to an untrained eye. Yet they all rode together and looked after one another, the exception being factions like the Wrecking Crew or the Goon Squad, which I was told were hiding out in Mobile, Alabama, in an abandoned ice house.

Older FTRA men frequently team up with young men whom they know they can trust. I asked, "How can you know when to trust the person you're riding with?"

Silveria dryly responded, "When you wake up in the morning," but other riders told me, "It's in the eyes." They watch the person's eyes and movements and if they don't feel safe, they throw that person off the boxcar.

One rail rider I met claimed to be a grandson of one of the Dalton Brothers, who robbed trains at the turn of the century. He said that hobos got that name because they would jump off of trains, fix rails and clean debris with the hoes they carried. Many were seasonal farm laborers. Somehow the romantic image of being hobos started with these guys and became perpetuated in folklore throughout the years as the number of freight train riders swelled with each war and with severe downturns in America's economy.

However, I observed that the more violent character of the FTRA developed with the second generation of post-Vietnam riders, guys like Silveria, Dogman, Catfish and Daniel Boone, all of whom were too young to fight in the Southeast Asian war.Outsiders typically are not trusted and many deadly fights have broken out between FTRA and the wannabes who can't prove they've been "tagged." The so-called Home Guards, men who live in missions, also can be dangerous to a visiting rail rider, because they tend to be very territorial and are not part of the Brotherhood. I learned that the FTRA doesn't like or trust Home Guards, referring to them as yellow-bellied pussies.

This is the violent world into which Silveria settled. Trained by former Vietnam veterans whom he looked up to, he became a proficient rail rider leading a nomadic life. His weaknesses were his rage and his drug addiction pulling at him. In the beginning he survived through food stamps, but he needed more and more money to feed his habit. To get cash, he took a route through twelve states where he had set up welfare benefits under different aliases. In fact, Silveria might have continued doing his juggling act were it not for the crime that proved to be the first step in bringing him to the attention of law enforcement. It happened in Salt Lake City, Utah.

7

A Killing Rampage

"The only thing my victims asked me was 'Why me?'"

Robert Joseph Silveria, Jr.

Silveria's life might have been completely different had he not met a twenty-nine-year-old rail rider named Hooter and his twenty-three-year-old girlfriend, Blondie. Hooter would be alive today if he hadn't invited Silveria to keep him company. Hooter's real name was James Lee Bowman. He was originally from Tennessee, but his image and behavior were a far cry from the southern gentleman. Instead, everything about him shouted punk rock: spiked hair, pierced ears, nose and tongue. He also attracted notice because of his very tall and narrow frame. Hooter belonged to a new breed of train hoppers who listened to heavy metal rock and tried to project tough images.

Some tramps refer to them as nothing more than Aryan drug heads, "out to take control of the rails."

Like many of the Flintstones, the nickname of the new breed of FTRA riders, Blondie sported many piercings. Aside from their dual piercings, they looked like a strange couple, despite their similarities in outlook. Hooter was tall and slim; Blondie was short, built like a pixie, with a heart-shaped face beneath mounds of golden hair. She and Hooter met in California, where they quickly bonded. Together they traveled the rails for three months before settling in Salt Lake City in early April 1995.

That April was a busy month for me. My photograph appeared on a Pepsi soda can in the San Francisco Bay area when Elvis & the Lawmen were featured with two crash dummies and a forty-thousand dollar Mitsubishi Montero donated to the program, announcing a local teen driver song and music video contest. I was also busy doing my Elvis presentations at schools, while conducting surveillance of a motel in Albany. We were about to clamp down on the motel because of the prostitution that was going on there. That same month, my first-born son, Will, graduated from the Police Academy.

In many parts of Utah, spring was showing signs of settling in that April. However, not in Salt Lake City, which is crowned by high mountains on the south and east. There the temperature was still in the thirties. The city sits in an area once covered by 900-foot-deep Lake Bonneville, which extended 20,000 square miles over parts of Idaho and Nevada. Today there are only remnants left of the prehistoric body of water. The largest is the Great Salt Lake, which lies fifteen miles east of Salt Lake City and is a popular tourist attraction, being six times saltier than the ocean and second only to the Dead Sea for high salinity. The population of Utah is predominantly Mormon and Salt Lake City is world-renowned for its Tabernacle Choir.

When you live outdoors, as Hooter and Blondie did, the chill in the air is penetrating. The couple were hiding from the cold and sleeping under a culvert in corrugated pipes near a temporarily abandoned construction site. The location was not far from the downtown area and close to the Southern Pacific rail yard, where rats, their nearest neighbors, burrowed under the pipelines. The couple told the local homeless agency that they had come from Sacramento. An old timer in the area, Pinky, met and befriended them. He gave Hooter another moniker, "Youngster." Pinky helped Hooter and Blondie to settle in, showing them where to register for food stamps, where to cash them in and where all the critical departments were located that served the needy. On Friday, April 21, Hooter picked up his food stamps. He exchanged them through Pinky, getting sixty cents on the dollar, and set out to fill his thirst.

There are three types of places in Utah where a visitor can get a drink. The first is in private clubs that sell almost every type of liquor available for a moderate, annual membership fee. These fluctuate within a twenty dollar range among the different clubs. Tourists can also purchase a temporary membership for a small sum. Most fine restaurants also have liquor available with lunch and dinner. Finally, brew pubs, which included beer bars and taverns, sell wine and beer on their premises. Pinky helped Hooter buy liquor from one of the clubs. Hooter purchased several fifths of vodka and cigarettes. Giving Pinky one of the bottles of vodka, Hooter headed back to camp, keeping the other two bottles of liquor for himself and Blondie.

That day, Robert Silveria was also in Salt Lake City, traveling under the name of Brad Foster, an identification he purchased for ten dollars at a flea market. He was in town to establish welfare assistance so he could get food stamps. But at the welfare office he discovered that someone else was using the same identification, not only in Salt Lake City, but in California, Washington state, Oregon, Texas and Idaho. According to the welfare worker, the downtown welfare office had all the information in their computer files. Hearing that, Silveria grabbed his gear and got out of the building fast, running most of the way until he reached the Southern Pacific railroad tracks.

Hooter and Blondie were hanging out by their culvert when Silveria got there. Normally, FTRA know each other by their rail names, but Silveria used Brad Foster, the same name he used in the Salt Lake City welfare office, when he introduced himself to the couple. He didn't trust them enough to give his rail name. They were a different breed of rail riders from the group he hung out with, but they were friendly and no one he knew was around.

Hooter should have known immediately that Silveria was a member of the FTRA by the black bandanna around his neck. But in spite of the hostilities between the FTRA and the so-called Flintstones, Hooter nevertheless asked Silveria to have a drink with him before Silveria left to *catch out,* that is, jump a freight train. Blondie left temporarily to see if she could score some dope.

That week had been rainy with over eighteen mile-per-hour winds, but that Friday, the rain started to ease up and at times to stop completely. Hooter and his visitor decided to make cocktails to warm themselves. While Blondie was gone, they walked to a nearby market and returned to the culvert with a carton of chocolate milk and a container of orange juice. They made concoctions: first mixing chocolate milk with the vodka and later mixing the vodka with orange juice. When Blondie returned to the campsite, Hooter and the man she knew as Brad Foster had been drinking and she noticed that Hooter was getting drunk.

The trio wandered off towards the central district, passing wide boulevards, parks and shops. They settled down on the front steps of one of the public buildings, joking and passing the cartons of cocktails covered in paper bags among them.

Hooter suddenly turned and looked hard at Blondie. He eyed her up and down, before pulling out a ten dollar bill from his bill-fold. "Here, go buy something to pretty up."

Blondie grabbed the money from Hooter's hand to show her annoyance. She stormed down the stairs and soon vanished from the men's view. She returned shortly afterwards, carrying a small bag with a razor and hairbrush inside. Hooter's face twisted into an angry scowl when Blondie displayed her purchases. "You wasted the money," he said, scolding her loudly. A small argument ensued. Robert Silveria sat on the steps and watched the domestic rift from the sidelines. Not wanting to create a bigger scene, Blondie turned around and stormed away. She wanted to give Hooter time to cool down.

It had started to drizzle when Blondie caught a bus on south Main Street and rode it uptown, where she transferred to another bus, Number 16. The bus let her off across the street from the mission shelter. Whatever thoughts ran through the young woman's head as she stared out the bus window brushed with delicate trails of raindrops, the warmth and comfort of the bus had to be a break from the hard ground she had been sitting and sleeping on by the Southern Pacific Rail yard. At the mission, Blondie ran into Pinky and his old lady and had lunch with them.

After she finished her meal, Blondie purchased seven dollars worth of marijuana outside the mission. She smoked it near the vicinity of the shelter, talking with some of the mission regulars. By then the rain had stopped, so she strolled over to a nearby park and hung around there for a few hours with other homeless people. Finally, she figured she had given Hooter enough time to cool down. Perhaps he might even be missing her. She headed back to the campsite before it grew too dark.

Shortly after Blondie stormed away, Hooter and Silveria also left the steps of the building to meander back to the couple's campground. By the time they reached the culvert, the light rain stopped. Silveria and Hooter had finished two bottles of 80 proof vodka in a period of about an hour and a half. It was then that the differences between the two men began to emerge. Hooter started badmouthing the FTRA, telling Silveria, "They're all screwed up," unaware that he was talking to one of its most deadly members and that he was igniting a rage that, once lit, wouldn't die down until it had exploded.

Though his face was reddening, Silveria tried to act cool, letting Hooter egg him on. Inside he was fuming. His only satisfaction was that he knew his fury was about to be revenged. Finally, he asked Hooter, "Do you know who you're talking to?"

Hooter grinned, "No, but by the way you're acting, I think you're an FTRA member."

"Well, maybe I am and maybe I'm not, but either way you shouldn't be talking about people like that." Silveria stared at Hooter, "Do you want to challenge me to a fight?" Hooter shook his head and said he didn't. But by then it was too late. Silveria's wrath had reached a boiling point. He threw such a hard punch that he broke his knuckle when it landed on Hooter's right brow. Hooter fell back, hitting his head against a boulder. Then he stumbled, falling on the cold, wet ground. Crawling under the culvert, he tried to escape Silveria, but he didn't get far. Silveria crawled in after him and dragged Hooter out, then pulled him up on his feet. Blood poured over Hooter's right eye where Silveria punched him. In the struggle, Hooter got smeared with wet dirt over his face and clothes. Silveria's own clothes and hands were covered in mud and blood. He leaned his face close to Hooter's. With steam rising from his breath, he asked Hooter, "Have you had enough?"

"As soon as I get sober, I'm going to kick your ass." Hooter stared defiantly at his guest.

"Well, you look sober enough to me right now," Silveria glared back, pulling Hooter by the collar of his jacket closer to him.

"Well, I'm not." Hooter tried feebly to push him back.

"I'll tell you what," Silveria released the hold on the younger man and stood back. "This is going to be like in the army. To me you're nothing but a gook and if you don't do something to me, then I'm going to do something to you. I'm going to kill you," Silveria said, recreating in his imagination a Vietnam War scene that both men were too young to have ever experienced. Seconds later, pulling out a small, folding buck knife, he stabbed Hooter in the right rib cage. Hooter grimaced, moving his hands to his side.

"Had enough?" Silveria paused, but the younger man just would not give up.

"That didn't hurt. I feel nothing." Hooter's continued defiance pushed Silveria deeper into violence.

"Come on, punch back," Silveria hollered, his face crimson red. Hooter refused to fight, pressing his hands over the wound where Silveria had stabbed him.

Hooter told Silveria, "Fuck off. I'm going to kick your ass when I sober up."

Enraged, Silveria threw the wounded man towards a cardboard box spread between large boulders over an incline by the culvert. Hunched over towards his right side and holding his hands over the stab wound, Hooter fell with a great thump. Silveria ran up to a wooden crate filled with discarded building material that he had noticed earlier. He grabbed a two-by-four and returned to the spot where Hooter lay cold, drunk and wounded. Silveria raised his arms high up in the air, gripping the board in his hands, and then smashed it down against Hooter's head like it was an axe. Blood splattered in all directions. Silveria kept wildly wielding the weapon on Hooter's head until the blood-stained board broke in half, forcing him to stop. At this point Silveria was sweating, breathing hard, his hands hurting. Looking down at his former host, he saw there was no more warm breath coming out of Hooter's mouth and nose. His face and head were swollen and butchered up, with deep lacerations revealing muscle tissue and a bloody skull.

Silveria let the broken piece of board slip from his hand and drop to the ground. He stood there, momentarily mesmerized, looking at Hooter's body. Holding onto his swollen right hand with his left to ease the pain, Silveria realized he had to get out of there as soon as he cleared any evidence of the fight. After picking up the pieces of board and discarding them some distance away, he picked up his gear and left the campsite with Hooter's blood still splattered on his clothes and face. Unlike the others he had killed, this time Silveria walked out without taking a single trophy or memento from his victim. In his madness and drunken stupor, it did not feel like a victory to him.

According to Silveria, shortly after this incident he sought help at a mental clinic in Vancouver, Washington, only to be told to take a number and sit down and wait. He stormed out, wanting to go on a rampage and kill the next man he saw.

Later, he told Woodland California Police Sergeant Doug Bena and others, "When they turned me down a year ago in Vancouver, that's when I started getting real brutal in the incidents, because the whole time I was taking the victim's life, I kept thinking, give me a number and maybe go sit in a mission."

From the distance, as Blondie headed back to the culvert, it looked like Hooter was lying on a piece of cardboard on the raised incline by the culvert sleeping off his drunkenness. It wasn't until she got closer that she began to suspect something was wrong. In the fading light she saw the blood and the trauma etched across his face. She called out his name several times, each time louder and louder until she screamed it out. But there was no answer, only the sound of a moving freight train in the distance. Frightened and near panic, she ran out of their campground area. Shaking, she headed towards the eastern part of the tracks where another couple lived in a car under a viaduct. She convinced the homeless man to go back with her to the camp. Half-running, she led the man to the spot where the bloodied body of Hooter was sprawled. Neither one touched the victim, but they both noticed that Hooter didn't seem to be breathing, although they were not quite sure if he was dead. Blondie and the man rushed back to his car. They told his wife and he drove Blondie to a 7-11 store on 1300 South and Main Street, where Blondie used the public telephone to call the Salt Lake City Police Department. When she came back outside, the driver and his wife had left, leaving Blondie alone in front of the market to wait for the police to arrive so that she could lead them to the spot where Hooter's body lay.

Around dusk Pinky had headed out to the culvert where Hooter and Blondie were camping. He wanted to invite the young couple, to whom he had taken a liking, to come back with him to his camp, which he shared with his old lady. He figured it would be nice to have some drinks together. When he got there he was surprised to find police cars with flashing lights parked around the culvert. He was further shocked to find himself being questioned by the police as to whether he knew anything about the death of James Lee Bowman, or Hooter, whom Pinky had renamed Youngster.

A short while later Detective Guy Yoshukawa arrived on the scene. By then, darkness had settled in and it looked like Hooter had slipped and fallen, hitting his head against one of the boulders. Yoshukawa agreed with the other officers that

Hooter's death appeared to be an accident. According to his girlfriend, the young transient had been quite drunk. It made sense that he could have fallen.

It wasn't until the medical examiner performed an autopsy that they learned that James Lee Bowman did not die an accidental death as the police had at first thought. Their report was changed to read homicide. Blondie told investigators that she last saw Hooter in the company of Brad Foster and described him being sandy haired with a thin mustache and a light beard and in about his early thirties. She also recalled a tattoo of the word "freedom" written on Foster's neck and that his eyes were a striking blue.

Detective Yoshukawa, who headed up the investigation into James Lee Bowman's death, was born and raised in Salt Lake City, but his parents were originally from Hawaii. He decided to become a police officer when he wondered in high school what he could do to give meaning to the rest of his life. Years later, called to the culvert, he didn't realize the part he would play in the chase after Silveria. For the most part, the modest Yoshukawa took his excellent record of solving crimes in stride. He was successful because he was sharp and meticulous in his details and also because he knew the town so well. He also worked in an excellent law enforcement unit. Even so, the job was not easy and the crimes he investigated, though they may have been solved, continued to haunt him. He wondered what it was in human nature that caused one to harm another individual.

That year, Salt Lake City had an unusually high number of murders, most of them the result of a drug turf war. With all of that going on, the death of a transient that easily could have been the result of a drunken brawl, would have been simple to put on a back burner. Yet Yoshukawa diligently persisted investigating the case. He was aware of the existence of the FTRA and the department had done a roundup of some members of the group back in 1991. Several weeks before Hooter's murder, one of the detectives in the weekly staff meeting commented that he noticed a number of new FTRA graffiti around town. But the connection to Hooter's murder with a member of the group would not become evident until almost a year later. Hooter was not affiliated with the FTRA and the one key witness to last see Hooter alive, Blondie, was unaware of any connection. However, Salt Lake City Police were miles ahead of those of us in California and in other states, who were not yet tuned in to the fact there was a group like the FTRA.

Blondie's description of "Brad Foster" eventually helped Yoshikawa to single him out as someone wanted for questioning. This was the first time local police ever had an eyewitness to the last person seen with one of Silveria's victims. The eyewitness description was the kick-off for the domino effect. All the blocks around Silveria began tumbling one by one. Continuing his investigation of the murder of James Lee Bowman, a.k.a. Hooter, Detective Yoshikawa sent out a teletype to all western law enforcement departments describing the crime against Hooter and asking if anyone had a similar case.

Next, he checked with the agency providing food stamps and found out from one of the personnel that indeed a Brad Foster did try to pick up food stamps in Salt Lake City at around the time of the murder. The county jail had a tracking system of people they booked. Yoshikawa gave them the description of Brad Foster based on Blondie's description and placed a request for a search for any individual booked with a tattoo on the neck with the word "Freedom."

It was this search that revealed the name of Robert Joseph Silveria, Jr. A new teletype went out stating that Brad Foster and Robert Silveria were wanted for questioning in the murder of a James Lee Bowman with a description based on the one given the Salt Lake City police by their witness. But finding Silveria was more complex, like looking for a worm-infested apple in a large orchard.

Later, Angel, a thirty-six year old FTRA rail rider who rode with Silveria numerous times, recalled Silveria telling him back then about killing someone by the rail yards in Salt Lake, but he didn't take it seriously. At the time, twenty-seven years old and riding the rails since his early teens, Angel heard all kinds of talk. "Here," Silveria said, handing him identifications belonging to Brad Foster, "if you want it you can have it, I've burned it up." Today, Angel laughs when he recalls taking the I.D., trying to use it and then being arrested for possession of a false identification.

Spring merged into summer in early June and Silveria continued his travels. About one-and-a-half months after killing Hooter, Silveria was outside Tucson, Arizona looking for drugs. He entered Loco, a roadside saloon decorated with large green cacti on the outside walls. Once inside, he was greeted by melodic Mexican music wafting out of a jukebox. Planting his pack down on the worn-out linoleum floor next to his bar stool, Silveria sat and ordered a beer. He looked around the room and spotted a couple of Mexican men who looked like they could have in their possession the merchandise he wanted. He walked up to them and asked, "Do you know where I can get some meth?" They pointed out a man at the other end of the bar and told Silveria to check with him. Silveria waited a while before approaching the dealer. Finally, he walked over to the man and told him he was looking to buy some methamphetamine. The short, dark-haired dealer spoke good English in spite of a heavy Spanish accent. He told Silveria that he had some he was trying to sell.

"How much?" Silveria said.

The Mexican dealer turned the question around. "Well, how much do you want?"

Silveria told him he wanted to see it first. "I'm not going to buy any until I try some." The dealer shrugged and told him that wasn't a problem.

The two men walked outside through the front door of the bar. On the left side of the one-story building housing the saloon was a trailer park; on the other side was an open field where the dealer's car, an old, dark Cadillac sitting low to the ground, was backed up close to a barbed wire fence. Silveria followed the dealer to the vehicle. The man opened the large trunk and pulled out a beat-up brief case. He opened the case to reveal its contents and let Silveria examine it. Silveria told the dealer that the merchandise looked good, but that he had to call his friend who was the real buyer. The Mexican dealer's face was troubled as he watched Silveria walk over to a public telephone booth near the entrance to the saloon.

Silveria picked up the phone and pretended to make a call. After a minute or two, he hung up the receiver and walked back to the dealer whom he had left standing by the car. Silveria told the dealer that his "friend" was going to meet them just up the road. The Mexican dealer, somewhat hesitantly, agreed to drive with Silveria to the designated spot. Silveria dumped his roll and pack beside the beat-up briefcase loaded with drugs inside the dealer's open trunk and climbed in on the passenger side of the Cadillac.

The Mexican dealer and Silveria hadn't traveled far before Silveria pointed out where the dealer should pull over and park the vehicle off to the side of the road. The dealer followed Silveria's instructions. He kept the key in the ignition and the car running, in order to allow the air conditioner to flow cool air while they waited for Silveria's "buyer/friend." There was a newspaper lying in the back seat of the vehicle, which Silveria noticed when he climbed into the car. He turned and tilted his head to exam it briefly and saw that it contained headlines about a rail derailment in Arizona, with a photo underneath showing an Amtrak train with three of its cars lying on their side. Several months later another FTRA member, Dogman Tony, would be accused of the derailment because of some incriminating papers found near the scene of the crime with reference to the "Sons of Gestapo."

Silveria turned to the dealer. "Let me check the contents in your briefcase again," he said. The dealer told Silveria he wanted to wait for the other guy that Silveria had said was coming soon. It is the nature of the drug business to be suspicious, but the dealer still believed that Silveria's friend would show up, unaware that the man next to him had a loaded pistol.

"Let's just look at it one more time to make sure it's what this guy wants." Silveria pushed harder.

"No. Just be patient and wait until he gets here." The dealer paused, turning his head. "This isn't a rip-off, is it?" The dealer looked questioningly at Silveria.

"Oh no, it's not a rip off." Silveria tried to sound innocent.

"Okay, man," the dealer nodded, "because I'm just trying to get somewhere."

Silveria leaned back in his seat and stretched his legs to give the impression of nonchalance; a denim vest hid the gun lodged in the waistband of his jeans. He lowered his arm to get ready to pull out the pistol, but then hesitated. A car appeared in the distance moving fast from the opposite direction towards them. "That might be him," Silveria said and motioned with his chin towards the road.

"Oh...really?" The dealer sat up in his seat. He watched silently as the car moved closer. Silveria's eyes shifted between the dealer and the approaching vehicle. Neither he nor the other man spoke. The only sound inside the Cadillac was the humming of the air conditioner. Silveria knew he was stuck.

Silveria didn't want to pull out his gun and shoot the dealer until the automobile heading towards them was far enough away from them that the driver and any passengers who might be inside the car couldn't hear or see anything. He also had to time it just right, before the dealer got wise. Silveria had no idea what thoughts were racing through the dealer's mind, although the man's expression was puzzled watching the car speed towards them and not slow down as it got near them. Suddenly, the vehicle zoomed past them. Questions raced through Silveria's mind. He wondered if the drug dealer had gnawing suspicions or if he had learned to accept such problems as part of the drug business. Did he have a weapon hidden on him to protect his merchandise? Silveria knew no seasoned drug dealer went out on a sale without carrying a weapon.

A few seconds after the car passed them, Silveria pulled out his gun. At that moment the dealer turned to Silveria, but he froze when he saw the muzzle of Silveria's gun pointed at him. Before the dealer could make a move or say anything, Silveria pulled the trigger. The bullet ripped through the dealer's body and blasted out the car window, shattering the glass outward from the car door with a loud bang and an echo. The glass rained down onto the hot asphalt. The dealer fell forward on the steering wheel; a heavy flow of blood streaming down from his mouth and nose, soaking everything below.

Inside, Silveria felt "major panic." He sat there thinking about how he was going to have to move the dealer with all that blood spilling out from his face and body. But Silveria realized he couldn't wait; another car might drive by. Quickly, Silveria pulled back the man's head and reached to get the car keys from the ignition. Then, feeling a burst of energy pumped by adrenaline, he climbed out of the car and ran to the back of it. Opening the trunk, he pulled out both the beat-up brief case containing the meth and his sleeping bag. Untying the two strings over his sleeping bag, he dumped the contents from the brief case into it. Then Silveria rolled the bedding back up again, tied it and put the bedding back in the trunk with the empty briefcase. Next, he walked back to the front of the car, opened the door and got in the driver side. He shoved the body of the dead victim over to the passenger side. Then Silveria took the newspaper from the back seat and covered the victim with part of the paper. In a matter of seconds blood soaked through the headlines Silveria read earlier, but he tried to ignore it. He started the engine and drove down the road until he came to a shallow ravine containing a number of discarded vehicles. Removing all his belongings from the Cadillac, Silveria rammed the car into the shallow ditch.

Afterward, Silveria got out and walked to the back of the car again. He pulled out some rags that were in the trunk and took a clean section of unused newspaper that he saved for this purpose, rolling it around the piece of cloth into a cone shape. There were some dry twigs lying around on the ground from tumble weeds. Silveria gathered a few up and stuck them inside the cone; then he unscrewed the top of the gas tank and shoved the roll into it. Lighting the rags and the newspaper with matches he pulled out of his side pocket, he tried to set the cone on fire. It didn't catch right away and he had to relight the cone a number of times before the fire caught. Then Silveria stepped back, all the while watching, making sure that this time the fuse, made up of scrounged up material he found inside the Cadillac and laying on the ground around it, would do the job. It seemed to take longer this time than the countless other times he was in similar situations, setting fires to vehicles with dead bodies inside them. He wished the dealer had flares in his trunk so the whole process would be easier.

Once Silveria was satisfied the burning cone would not go out, he climbed out of the ditch, grabbed his gear and moved quickly to distance himself from the ravine. Satisfied that he was safely far away, Silveria stood in the vast Arizona desert, where in a short while the setting sun would be casting brilliant hues across the sky, waiting anxiously for the evidence of his crime to go up in smoke. He watched tensely as the dark blue Cadillac with the dealer's body inside burst into flames.

Most of the loot Silveria got from the dealer outside of Tucson he gave away to his FTRA buddies; what was left he saved for himself. Later, Silveria placed himself in Arizona about the time of the Amtrak train derailment that Dogman was suspected of doing. I wasn't involved in the investigations of the derailment, but I uncovered that Silveria's train rider friends included Crazy Angel, Cowboy, Desert Rat, Dogman and several others who were part of a close inner circle of people in the FTRA. I suspect Silveria was there when the train derailment happened. He knew too much about it.

The last time I saw him, Silveria revealed to me that Dogman Tony did know how to derail trains. Then Silveria proceeded to describe the technical aspects of it, indicating he also knew a lot about train derailments. "Where it happened, you could drive down with your car and see it." Silveria suddenly paused, as if for a few seconds he had moved to a different time and place. Then he continued, "There was this old engine just standing there and Dogman got in and started it up." Silveria grinned and added, "He derailed it."

That's whitewashing it, I thought. *First he steps forward and admits it, then he moves from an Amtrak passenger train derailment to an old freight "engine just standing there."*

8

Death in Kansas

"I'm running with the devil and it's touch and go."

Robert Joseph Silveria, Jr.

It's uncertain what Silveria's next move was or who he shot, bludgeoned, executed or pushed off a train in the days after he finished off the Tucson drug dealer. I've asked him myself and tried through other means to discover his path, but it's nearly impossible to tell where he was. What is clear, though, is that eventually, Silveria, Dogman Tony and others moved their partying to Vancouver, Washington to join Catfish. Then Silveria started moving southwest again.

Scorching rays from a mid-day Texas sun showered Silveria as he stepped from the El Paso welfare building on July 17, 1995. Adjusting the heavy roll on his back, he didn't notice a white truck pull up along the sidewalk until a man with a mustache and a cowboy hat, well over six feet tall and built like a football player, climbed out of the passenger side and headed straight towards him. He introduced himself as Charles Randall Boyd. Then he came right out and told Silveria he was looking for a strong "buck" like him to help out at a Christian mission. He said he was from Double D Ranch, about one hundred miles outside El Paso in a rural area in Van Horn. The ranch was just starting out as a future mission for the homeless. Boyd told Silveria that they were in town to buy some supplies, which Boyd paid for with his own money. He explained he was working in the mission for free and on top of that donating his personal funds to it. He told Silveria that if he came to work at the Double D Ranch, there would be no money for him, just room and food and all the work he did would be for Christ. Then he paused and asked if Silveria would be interested in helping out.

The idea sounded good to Silveria. It was even inspiring and he agreed to give it a try. He knew Van Horn had a railroad that passed through on the southern side of the town, which would enable him to move easily between the Pacific and the southern routes. Silveria gave his name as Lester Paul Dykeman, the same name he just used at the welfare office to get food stamps. It belonged to one of the few victims Silveria told me he "let live." Boyd walked him over to the truck and introduced him to the driver, who he said was his boss and the evangelist in the mission. Boyd said he and the preacher hadn't eaten lunch yet and were about to get some hamburgers. He invited Silveria to join them before the three of them headed out to the ranch.

Over lunch, Silveria told Boyd and the preacher that he had been staying at the Christian Home in El Paso and that he was from Southern California originally, where he had once been involved in gangs and arrested for joy riding when he was a teen. He concocted the story to provide an excuse for his lifestyle without revealing he was one of the enforcers for the FTRA and a killer. Both Boyd and the preacher were very sympathetic and forgiving. They told him many people had problems in the past and they would be happy to have his help on the ranch. Boyd laughed half-heartedly, saying that he was divorced several times. He spoke about having family in Kansas, among them a daughter and grandson. He told Silveria that he was from Virginia, where he used to work as an accountant. He grinned and said that it was his mother who pushed him to come down to Texas when she heard through her church that a preacher was looking for someone to help him build a church with a mission. She even wrote to the preacher herself.

While Boyd and Silveria were biting into their hamburgers, it became the preacher's turn to talk. He told how he had first gotten a letter from Boyd's mother, then Boyd phoned him several times from Richmond asking all sorts of questions. "One day, several months later," the preacher shook his head chuckling, "he just shows up at the ranch in a blue 1989 Plymouth minivan with a trailer hitched to it filled with all kinds of power tools, equipment, two mountain bikes and even a computer. The man was sent from God."

Boyd grinned proudly and, in between bites of his burger, took the opportunity to brag, telling both men how he built the flat trailer himself. Boyd said that he was thinking of some day going into the construction business, but first he had to learn the trade. He figured he could do that by working at the Double D Ranch and help Christ out at the same time.

"Amen," the preacher nodded. Silveria mentioned casually that he had experience in roofing. Boyd sat up. This was new and very interesting information about Silveria. It was a lucrative enterprise, Boyd said, because there would always be a demand for roofing in construction and there will always be a need for construction. Boyd didn't say anything then, but a seed was planted in his mind to go into the construction business with Silveria.

After lunch, the three men headed out on a long drive in the direction of Van Horn, which prides itself with the motto, "The town so healthy, we had to shoot a man to start a cemetery." The town was originally named Van Horn Wells after the discover of water wells in the area by Jefferson Van Horn, an army major who later commanded Fort Bliss. Van Horn Wells then became a stage stop on the San Diego–San Antonio mail route. During the Civil War the Confederates captured the wells. Ironically, the Union officer in charge was James Judson Van Horn, who was no relation to the other Van Horn. It's uncertain which Van Horn the current town is named after, the discoverer of the wells or the Union Officer who lost them, but the county, Culberson, is named after a Confederate. Town history was made again in 1881, when the Texas and Pacific Railway passed through Van Horn. The original Texas and Pacific Railway Company was the only railroad in Texas and one of the few in the country to operate under a federal charter. Less than a hundred years later it would be taken over by the Missouri Pacific Railway, but in the town's early period it was responsible for a population boom, which in 1890 reached nearly five hundred people. Then the town shifted, leaving the old Van Horn Wells south of its present site, twelve miles from the old ghost town of Lobo. Although Van Horn's population remains low, under 3,000, it has numerous inexpensive hotels for tourists attracted to the region by the Guadalupe Mountain National Park and the Carlsbad Caverns or passing through on a highway route leading east to San Antonio, Houston, Baton Rouge, New Orleans, Mobile and all the way through Tallahassee to Jacksonville, Florida. The town itself is a typical rural desert community in the southwest, easily accessed from El Paso by I-10 and U.S. 80. It's also where

the central/coastal time line runs through Texas, dividing the
state into two different time zones.

When they finally reached the ranch, Silveria thought it
was pretty nice. He was placed in what was referred to as a guest
house, but in reality was only one room which he shared with
Charles Boyd and a Mexican named Jose, the head cook at the
ranch. Regardless, it was better than living outdoors in the blaz-
ing heat and sudden rainstorms.

The work on the ranch was hard and involved a variety
of projects ranging from planting watermelon seeds to putting
up concrete slabs. Silveria impressed Boyd and the other residents at the mission with his diligence, hard work and, in particular, his welding skills, which Silveria told them he acquired
in an Arizona prison. He also told residents at the ranch that he
spent time at the Manna Outreach in Hobbs, New Mexico. The
mission had strict security and required photo identification
and fingerprints before they would allow anyone to stay there.
Nevertheless, Silveria established himself quite well with his
made-up identity and background. No one pegged him for a
killer. He and Boyd soon formed a bond, working closely on
different jobs and just hanging out.

Silveria noticed, however, that Charles Boyd frequently
disappeared when there was strenuous work to be done, leaving the bulk of the work to Silveria. Boyd also started having
blow ups. Mostly he appeared to be angry with himself, but he
was also irritated with the preacher. Boyd told Silveria he came
down to Texas with $10,000, which had dwindled down to
$5,000 in a matter of weeks, and he couldn't go on like this.
He already had spent enough on supplies and materials for the
ranch. Boyd began talking to Silveria about leaving. He said he
had attended college in Kansas and had thought for a long time
about going back to Kansas to settle there, to be closer to his
daughter, infant grandson, ex-wives and in-laws. He invited Silveria to join him, telling him, "We could do roofing together."

One day, when the preacher was out on an errand for the mission, Boyd told Silveria that since the boss wasn't there it was a good time to pack up and go to church. The two men drove to a small church just outside El Paso with white stucco walls, painted icons and simple wooden pews. They sat at the end of one of the pews near the back. The entire service was in Spanish. Suddenly Boyd stood up and moved to the aisle of the pew. "Come on, let's get a burger. Do you understand anything that's been said?" Disgust was written all over his face. He didn't care who knew it or heard him.

"No, but we're in the House of the Lord and we should sit here till they're done with the sermon," Silveria said and looked up at Boyd's giant frame towering over him as he stood in the aisle.

"Let's go." Boyd's tone was commanding as he turned around and headed towards the back of the church. Putting on his cowboy hat, he walked out the front door. Silveria sat there smiling sheepishly at the small group of dark-haired worshippers in nearby pews who had turned to see what the commotion was about. Feeling uncomfortable, Silveria got up and followed Boyd's lead, walking out the front door as all eyes followed him.

He and Boyd headed to El Paso, where they had lunch. It was then that Boyd decided he wanted to move on. They returned to the Double D Ranch and loaded Boyd's trailer and the van with all of the equipment, tools, mountain bikes and clothing Boyd brought down with him from Virginia. By then, Boyd was eager to get out of there as soon as possible.

At about this time, my case involving J.C. McLean was to begin. In the interval between the time that Boyd and Silveria first met and then took off together for Kansas, Silveria left Boyd and the Double D Ranch long enough to head out to Berkeley, catch up on his drugs and kill McLean. Then he headed back to Texas and left with Boyd for Kansas. The mystery at that point takes on more twists and turns. Silveria claims that he and Boyd headed towards Kansas via Albuquerque, New Mexico, where they met up with Silveria's FTRA "brother," Arkansas Bobcat. Meanwhile, the detectives in my department and I were busy going over the details of McLean's murder and questioning any witnesses we could find. As we labored searching for clues, Boyd was having trouble driving up the Colorado mountains. Boyd, Silveria and, rumor had it, Arkansas Bobcat crossed the Colorado border to Kansas.

Around 3:30 P.M. on Wednesday, July 26, 1995, Boyd's blue van pulled in front of his daughter's home near Pierceville, Kansas. Boyd told Silveria to wait in the car while he went inside. Silveria watched as a young woman opened the door and let Boyd in. Silveria caught a glimpse of her looking at him before shutting the door. I asked Silveria where Arkansas Bobcat was during the time he and Boyd were visiting Boyd's daughter, because I knew there was no evidence of a third man being with them. Without hesitating, Silveria said, "He was dropped off. He was looking for drugs. We picked him up later."

Silveria said he remained in the car waiting for Boyd for a long while. Then he got out of the van and stretched, feeling cramped and tired of sitting there waiting. Silveria opened up the hood to check the oil. He was surprised to see that the engine in the van was brand new. Silveria was filling the water reservoir for the truck's automatic windshield washer with a hose he saw lying on the lawn when Boyd stepped out from inside the house and asked him if he wanted a soda. Silveria said "Sure." Boyd paused and studied him for a few seconds.

"Well, I'm fixing to go out and get myself a six pack of Coors. You ever drink Coors beer?"

"I thought we were all going to be good Christians." Silveria studied Boyd's face. There was a big emphasis at the Double D Ranch against any kind of liquor.

"Well, I'm getting run out of here, too," Boyd snapped. He paused again, as he studied Silveria.

"Come on in the house," he waved.

Boyd introduced Silveria as Lester Paul Dykeman to his daughter. Her responses were curt: "Yeah, hi," and "Great," and "Excuse me, I have to go and check on my baby." She soon left the room and went to the rear of the house. In the short time he was with her, Silveria got the impression that Boyd's daughter wasn't happy to see him or her father.

"Come on. Let's go," Boyd turned and strode towards the front door with Silveria following close behind.

"Where are we going?" Silveria looked over at Boyd, who seemed preoccupied as he opened the door and stepped outside.

"I'm not wanted here, I told you," Boyd said. As they walked toward the van, he said he knew a campground where they could stay until he figured what to do next. "Let's go and get a six pack of beer. It's hot and it will be just the right thing to quench our thirst and discuss where we're going." Some time after this, Silveria said, they picked up Arkansas Bobcat at a designated meeting place.

The campground Boyd had in mind was located at Kanopolis Lake, in rural Ellsworth County, Kansas. The lake is man-made, built by the United States Army Corps of Engineers in 1948. It's considered to be one of the best examples of mankind working cooperatively with nature. The lake and its surrounding 22,000 acres offer an abundance of fishing and wildlife, making it popular with campers.

It was late and dark when the men reached the campground. Because it was after hours, there were no rangers stationed at the entrance, but there were envelopes provided for late arriving campers to use when depositing their checks in a designated slot. Boyd filled out a check. Originally, Silveria told Officer Mike Quakenbush and Roseville Detective Mike Allison that it was his fingerprints on the envelope. He made a point of mentioning that his fingerprints were all over the camp. I don't know if he was hinting for them to follow up on the fingerprints, but it doesn't work that way. It wasn't their jurisdiction.

Later, he told me the fingerprints belonged to Arkansas Bobcat. According to Silveria, Bobcat sealed the envelope and climbed out of the car to deposit it. Then they drove on into the camp.

Boyd didn't like the first campground they entered even though Silveria pointed out it had showers and other amenities. Boyd complained, "There are too many cars." He turned the van around and drove up dark winding roads until they came upon the Cottonwood Campground, located on the opposite side of the lake from the first camping facility, near a cove and a boat marina. The place was isolated and private. The men unloaded their camping gear and set up Boyd's blue, dome-shaped tent with a mesh screen window, which was large enough to sleep five men. Boyd sharpened the axe; Silveria cut down some wood and built a small campfire over which he cooked some stove top stuffing. When they finished eating, they washed the dishes under an elongated water pipe and Boyd cleaned some of his equipment. Silveria started to roll out his own tent, but Boyd told him not to bother. "There's plenty of room for you in my tent. Arkansas Bobcat can sleep outside and use his own roll." Silveria threw his gear back in the van. Boyd went inside the tent and settled in his sleeping bag. Then he did something that appeared to Silveria to be out of character.

While Silveria was rolling out his sleeping bag inside Boyd's tent, Boyd told him that he had lots of money and that the two of them could be more than just friends. He repeated several times that he had lots of money, in case Silveria didn't understand what he meant by that. Silveria ignored him. Then Boyd held out his wallet and asked Silveria to put it in a special hiding spot he had built on the passenger side in plastic mold-ing underneath the seat. He explained to Silveria he didn't want to get up and do it himself, because he was undressed and already settled in his sleeping bag. He said he wanted to learn to trust Silveria with handling his money. Silveria took the wallet, wondering why Boyd didn't just sleep with it tucked under his sleeping bag and feeling annoyed by Boyd's innuendos. It didn't matter to him that he liked Boyd or that he felt sorry for him. He had had enough of the man. The new twist Boyd had introduced into their relationship made Silveria more irritated. Before he even reached the van, Silveria made up his mind to rob Boyd and get as far away from him as possible.

When Silveria reached the passenger side of the van, he opened the door and pretended to poke around. Then he called out to Boyd, "I can't find the hiding spot." He told Boyd to get up, come over and show him where it was so that the next time Silveria would know. Boyd grumbled, but he rose reluctantly and walked over with a flashlight to show Silveria where the hiding spot was. Boyd held the flashlight underneath the passenger seat; Silveria slid the wallet into the compartment. In a flash, as soon as Boyd turned and pointed the flashlight in another direction, Silveria pulled the wallet out from the hiding spot and closed the door to the van.

They were halfway back to the tent when Silveria switched directions, telling Boyd he was going to make sure the campfire was secure before he bedded down for the night. While Boyd went back inside the tent, Silveria knelt down and slipped the wallet into his sock. His plan was that in the morning, when Boyd went to look for his wallet, Silveria would tell him that he had no idea what happened to it and remind him that they both put the wallet away together. As I pieced together what Silveria told me in the past, what he told other cops before and what he is saying now — that he was not alone with Boyd — it is uncertain what Arkansas Bobcat was doing or even if he really was there.

Silveria slipped out of his clothes and got into the sleeping bag. He lay there planning how to leave Boyd. He even considered sneaking out during the night before daylight. Suddenly he felt Boyd beside him. At first Silveria thought Boyd had just rolled over in his sleep and he was about to nudge him to scoot over, but when Silveria turned, he saw the silhouette of Boyd's head, darker than the darkness in the tent, leaning close to him. He suddenly became aware of his breathing. "Did you ever fool around?" Boyd whispered.

Enraged, but holding his feelings in, Silveria sat up and leaned back on his elbows, thinking how he was going to overpower Boyd if he had to. However, Boyd was more than six feet tall and weighed 250 pounds. "No, and I don't." Silveria told Boyd he thought of him like a big brother.

"Well, I've got a lot of money, man," Boyd persisted in a gentle voice. Then he grabbed Silveria's forearm, pressing down on it. "Do you want to try?" He leaned closer.

"Fuck off," Silveria told him, but that made Boyd only more persistent. He squeezed Silveria's arm, reminding him that he'd been buying all this food for him and that he'd been paying Silveria's way all along and now he wanted his way. "I plan to pay you back when we get our first construction job," Silveria said. That was their agreement. Suddenly, Silveria said later, he saw an image of another man, in another time and another isolated place, making sexual advances toward him. Silveria was only twenty-two that first time and hitchhiking to Arizona. He recalled images of killing the man, shooting him with his own gun. It was that man, the driver, Silveria said, who became his first murder victim.

Silveria jumped up and pulled away from Boyd's grip. He grabbed his clothes and sprinted out of the tent.

"No, no, no. I'm just kidding around. I'll give you time to think about it. Come back here and go to sleep," Boyd pleaded. At that point, Silveria said, Arkansas Bobcat woke up and joined in the squabble. After some negotiation, Silveria finally went back inside the tent. He lay there for a long time wondering if he could kill Boyd. Killing strangers was one thing. FTRA rail riders do that if they perceive danger or they're stoned or drunk. However, killing someone you've lived with and liked was another matter for Silveria. At the same time, Boyd wanted to subject Silveria to a subservient sexual role and Silveria was not going to do it. He kept mulling over whether he had it in him to kill Boyd. Finally, dark thoughts revolving in his head, Silveria dozed off.

Silveria was awakened by dawn's light filtering through the dome tent. Boyd was still sound asleep. Silveria eased out of his sleeping bag and slowly unzipped the tent door so as not to wake him. Outside, the scent of dew brought freshness into the air. The light falling on the peaceful lake added serenity to the setting. But neither the dew nor the light on the lake could hold Silveria's attention and ease his turmoil. His mind was once again preoccupied with murder. One of the first things to attract his attention was the axe leaning against the ice chest.

According to Silveria (when he first told the story), he picked up the axe, running his fingers over its handle. He thought of the gun in his pack, but decided it would make too much noise, attracting campers and rangers. Then he saw a large piece of concrete block lying to the side that somebody had probably used as a tire wedge. He put down the axe, walked over and picked up the concrete block. It was big enough and heavy enough. It looked like a piece of sidewalk ripped off, one end longer and sharper. He guessed the block weighed at least thirty pounds. Silveria was thinking that Boyd was a huge guy and probably could rip Silveria to pieces if he put his mind to it. Silveria had to do it right the first time. He couldn't screw up and just run. There were no rails nearby. But then Silveria put down the block. He just didn't have it in him to kill Boyd. He needed more time. He started a fire and made a pot of coffee.

The sound of Silveria moving around the camp woke up Boyd. Peeking through the tent window, he asked Silveria what he was doing up so early. Silveria told him he was going to fix them breakfast. "Go back to sleep," he said. Boyd lay down again and dozed off.

One has to question Silveria's two different accounts of the events. Did Silveria stand there stirring his coffee and telling himself not to think about it, but just to go ahead and kill Boyd. Did, as he said later, Arkansas Bobcat nudge him on by saying, "Just think about the hurt, then just go and kill and get out of there fast."

Whatever the real truth, Silveria admits to next picking up the piece of concrete block and carrying it to the tent. The screen window in the fabric of the blue domed-tent allowed Silveria to see exactly where Boyd's head was. Closing his eyes, Silveria said that he lifted the concrete block high in the air and with all his strength threw it down on the tent in the spot he knew Boyd's head lay. The block ripped through the fabric and landed on Boyd's head. Silveria opened his eyes when he heard Boyd moan. There was a large rip in the tent. Silveria dove down halfway through the torn opening in the dome and picked up the concrete block to hurl it again. Boyd started to lift his arm over his bleeding head, but Silveria smashed the large concrete block against Boyd's head before he could stop it. This time Silveria had his eyes wide open.

Boyd didn't move. Silveria didn't wait to find out if he was still breathing. He raced to the van with Boyd's wallet already in his possession and his gear in the vehicle. Then he sped away with the trailer still attached in the back. Again, it depends which version of Silveria's story you believe whether he was with Arkansas Bobcat. When he got to the end of the road, Silveria realized that he had not checked to see if Boyd was dead or alive. He made a U-turn and drove back to the campground, passing a ranger along the way.

Returning to the campsite, Silveria peered through the large rip in the tent and saw Boyd sitting up dazed, blood dripping over his head. Silveria ordered him to lie down, because he didn't want to kill him. But Boyd just sat there in a state of shock, his head swollen and blood-soaked. Silveria said it was Arkansas Bobcat who picked up the axe Silveria handled earlier, returned to the tent's opening and swung the blunt end against Boyd's neck from the back. Boyd fell forward instantly. And it was Arkansas Bobcat, Silveria said, who pounded Boyd with the blunt end of the axe, ripping through a new section of the blood-soaked tent; forcing part of it to collapse over Boyd's body and reveal, through a new tear in the fabric, the crushed skull and mangled neck. Finally exhausted, he stopped, feeling the strain in his hands and arms from the wild hammering with the axe. I feel Silveria's version of events is fanciful. Maybe Arkansas Bobcat was there, too, but I believe the m.o. fits Silveria.

Next Silveria rolled Boyd's body over in the tent, covering him with fresh new sections of the fabric that had escaped the splatter of blood. Then he threw miscellaneous tools over the tent. He wanted it to appear that some camper unloaded the tent and left temporarily before finishing putting it up. It was all to look like a work in process. This was his short term plan. But his long term plan was different. When staging the scene was completed, in order to buy time to escape, Silveria then did something completely the opposite. He claims he walked around the camp touching different objects: coffee pot, Coleman green box, ice chest. He then left the axe with his finger prints on the handle leaning up against the ice cooler and the concrete boulder besides Boyd, knowing the FBI had a file on him. While he was telling me this I wanted to say, "Come on Robert, even a sixth grader can see through that," but I wanted to learn more so I remained silent.

Silveria took off in Boyd's van. The wallet Boyd used as a tool the night before in attempting to lure Silveria into an intimate relationship with him was in Silveria's pocket and Boyd was dead. Silveria sped out of the park, going at times as fast as one hundred miles per hour, causing the back wheel bearings of the trailer attached to the van to smoke. He stopped at a truck stop outside the park and unhitched the trailer, leaving it behind with all the equipment and tools still tied to it. He unloaded the two mountain bikes under a tree at another location, thinking he might come back for them at another date, but he says he never did. His next stop was Kansas City.

In the middle of downtown Kansas City, Silveria ran out of gas, but he managed to pull into a gas station. It hit him that he never went through Boyd's wallet to see what he had in it. He did that now. Inside there wasn't that much money, but there were all kinds of credit cards. Silveria examined each one closely. Silveria never owned a credit card and wasn't quite sure how to use one, but he did know they contained a lot of possibility for acquiring cash quickly. Silveria climbed out of the van and walked up to the female gas attendant behind the counter. He explained to the clerk that he needed to use his credit card, but he didn't have on his glasses. She told him to just go fill the tank up, come back and sign for it. Silveria went back to the van and copied Boyd's signature on the palm of his hand. After filling the tank, he went back to the attendant and she processed the credit card. Silveria signed Boyd's name to it. Then Silveria asked the clerk, "Is there any place I could get a cash withdrawal, because I'm having a hard time with the fuel tank and I need a mechanic to take a look at it." The clerk explained how to take out money on a credit card in the bank across the street. No password was necessary.

Silveria made a two-hundred dollar bank withdrawal using one of Boyd's credit cards again. Later he withdrew about

five times as much as he headed from Kansas City to Little
Rock, Arkansas. In Little Rock, Silveria used the card to purchase half a dozen VCRs from a store in a mall at two hundred
dollars each. He later sold them in a flea market in Texas for
one hundred and fifty dollars each. Since he paid nothing for
them, he thought it wasn't a bad profit.

During the day of Boyd's murder, rangers passed by the
campsite but didn't enter it to check. Silveria's ploy to fool
them worked. From the distance, it appeared to them as if
someone simply didn't finish putting up the tent and had to
leave. Then, on the second day, July 28, 1995, one of the
rangers passing through the Cottonwood campground became
suspicious and drove in to check. When he climbed out of his
vehicle, the stench of death greeted him. Its putrid odor
increased with every step he took towards the blue collapsed
dome. He held his breath and covered up his mouth as he
pulled up the tent, which revealed his worst fear—the decomposing body of a man. He was dressed in a white tee-shirt and
boxer shorts laying face down in a sleeping bag. As the ranger
got closer he saw the man's head was bloodied and there was a
bloody concrete block nearby. He summoned the sheriff's
office. A short while later the body was removed, with the area
closed off for careful inspection. There were no documents,
credit cards or a vehicle to identify the body inside the tent. The
check that Boyd deposited the night he got there was already
being processed, but there were too many people coming and
going to determine who wrote the check.

The autopsy report concluded that the victim had been
murdered two days earlier. He suffered multiple abrasions and
lacerations of the head with extensive injuries to the skull that
resulted in fatal damage to the brain. There was no damage to

other parts of the body, except the murdered man's neck was bloated and one of his front teeth was loosened from its socket. Maggots were found on the upper body along with clumps of insect eggs in different sizes. They were scraped and taken as forensic evidence to determine time of death. His death was listed as a homicide. The evidence found led to the conclusion that Boyd had been beaten to death with a heavy, blunt object.

Because the murder occurred on the premises of a state park, the responsibility to investigate the case fell on the Kansas Bureau of Investigation, KBI, which was established in 1939 by the state's legislature as part of the Office of Attorney General. Their mission was to fight crime in Kansas. When the KBI was first formed, its original intent was to focus on bank robberies, but over the years, as crime spread into other areas, the responsibilities of the agency increased. Today the agency has expanded to include running forensic labs, providing assistance in local officer training and to keeping and providing crime data to the legislatures and the public. It's headquartered in Topeka, with regional branches in Overland Park, Great Bend, and Wichita. The KBI employs about eighty-five special agents and 150 civilians.

Special Agent Bruce Mellor, a twenty-year veteran of KBI, was appointed to head up the investigation of the murder. His first task was to establish who the victim was and then who killed him. Boyd once had worked as a bank accountant and his position required him to be fingerprinted. Using the Henry fingerprint classification method, in which fingerprints are sorted by physical characteristics, the body in the collapsed tent was identified on September 16, 1995. The KBI learned that the victim was Charles Randall Boyd, a white male born on December 3, 1948, from Midlothian, Virginia. KBI special agents contacted Boyd's family members and found out that Boyd had a daughter living in Kansas whom Boyd had visited recently.

Shortly afterwards the agents contacted Boyd's daughter. Her recollection differed in some details from the story Silveria would later tell.

The young woman described her father's van as blue-grey with simulated wood panels on the sides. She described a white two-wheeled trailer pulled by the van with two mountain bikes inside the trailer. His daughter said that Boyd had told her that his van almost overheated a couple of nights ago as he and his fellow passenger, whom he introduced to her as Lester Paul Dykeman, made their way up the Colorado mountains. According to the daughter, her father revealed that he had met "Paul" approximately nine days earlier at a Christian ranch for the homeless in Van Horn, Texas, where Boyd had put up window screens that he purchased himself and did some masonry work. She told Mellor and his partner, Galen Marple, that her father had first visited another address, only to find that she had moved. He phoned her grandmother from his cell phone and she told him his daughter's new address. Boyd's daughter told investigators the man accompanying her father appeared to be thirty and had heavily tattooed arms. She described him as light-haired and deeply tanned with unique blue eyes. She also recalled the word "freedom" tattooed on his neck. She said that Boyd took a short nap at her house and spent time playing with her son. Afterwards, he thumbed through a phone book, explaining to his daughter that he and Paul Dykeman had roofing experience and wanted to do some roofing in the area. The daughter's impression was that her father had planned to stay with her overnight, but then decided suddenly to push on. He left with Dykeman between 5 and 5:30 P.M. without telling her where they were headed. Two hours later, after dinner, she phoned her mother to tell her of the visit. Neither of the women realized at the time that they would never see nor hear from the forty-seven-year-old Charles Randall Boyd again.

The two KBI investigators followed up on Boyd's daughter's information concerning accounts of her father's last days on earth. The deceased had several credit cards in his name and they performed a check of credit card records. The charges showed that Boyd did travel from around Van Horn, Texas, in late July, 1995, up through Colorado into western Kansas, and finally to Kanopolis Lake campground in Ellsworth County. Credit card charges also showed that after Boyd was killed, there were charges in his name in Missouri and Arkansas. They checked with the different campgrounds in Colorado and learned that a vehicle with a Virginia license plate matching Boyd's and carrying two people checked into the Hasty Campground on July 24, at 9:07 P.M. The Colorado record also showed that Boyd and another individual with him paid cash for a two-night stay. This meant the two men would have left prior to 2:00 P.M. on July 26, otherwise they would have been required to pay for another night's stay at the campground.

The two special agents checked with various railroads in the western region of the United States and found that Lester Dykeman had been stopped in several states for trespassing on railroad property. Further, they found out that individuals stopped on railroad property are not always arrested, but usually are photographed, identified and sent on their way with warnings. Copies of photos identified as Lester Paul Dykeman were obtained, as well as photos of other trespassers, including Brad Foster and Robert Joseph Silveria. A photo lineup, with a picture of Brad Foster, was shown to Boyd's daughter. She identified the photos of Brad Foster as the person she last saw with her father, but could not be positive, because the photos were in black and white. She commented that if they were in color it would help her be more certain because of the other man's unusual blue eyes.

At the Double D Ranch, a deputy sheriff for Culbertson County conducted a photo lineup for the owner of the ranch, using photos he received from the KBI agents. The agents also learned from Salt Lake Police that Robert Silveria had an outstanding warrant for auto theft out of Cleveland, Mississippi. They notified the railroad police to be on the lookout for Silveria.

The KBI agents also traveled to Texas to learn more about Lester Paul Dykeman. They found a resident there who was able to provide the special agents with a fuzzy photo of Dykeman. They also came across some inconsistencies. For example, Boyd and Silveria hung out a lot together and they attended the Church of Christ. The officers learned that there was a card dated Sunday, July 23, with Dykeman's signature in the files at the Church of Christ. The "3" in the "23" looked like a "5" — the agents however, probably concluded that was just Silveria's handwriting and he meant to make it a "23". The director of the church required members to fill out cards each time they attended services so that a follow-up thank you note would be written to the attendees. There was no card signed by Boyd indicating he attended the services that Sunday, but there was one that he signed dated Friday, July 21. One of the residents at Double D Ranch told the investigators from Kansas that he had made plans with Dykeman and Boyd to be picked up after church services at one o'clock in the afternoon. He said the three of them were planning to drive into El Paso. He waited and waited, but the two men never showed up.

Another witness from the ranch recalled seeing the pair in El Paso on Friday, July 21 and supported the claim Silveria made to me that there was a third man with him and Boyd. The witness was told by Boyd and "Dykeman" that they were headed to Albuquerque, New Mexico where Paul Dykeman (Silveria) had a "brother" in construction. (The term "brother" is what FTRA members call one another.) That was the last time the witness saw the two men.

Even though it appeared strange that the two men would travel to Kansas through Colorado instead of taking the more direct and flat roads through Texas, the KBI agents sent flyers and a teletype stating that Lester Paul Dykeman was wanted for questioning in the murder of Charles Randall Boyd. They also followed the paper trail Silveria left behind when he used Boyd's bank and credit cards. They located the van Silveria sold in El Paso, but he still was one step ahead of them.

9

Another Day, Another Murder

"I watched, praying that the 'zigzag' man would pop up."

Robert Joseph Silveria, Jr.

During the next few months, Silveria hopped freight trains, traveling back and forth between Texas, Mississippi, California and Arizona. Then, during the end of the marijuana growing season that runs from late July to early October, when the cannabis plant leaves were still green, Robert Silveria returned to Vancouver, Washington. At Share House, from which he had long been absent, he was approached by a dealer peddling small nickel bags of bud in front of the rescue mission. All the money Silveria had gotten out of Charles Boyd's credit cards and the van that he sold were gone. The only thing he still had from that encounter was Boyd's identification, with his own photo glued on it, which Silveria used to establish a food stamp account in Vancouver.

Silveria didn't bother learning the dealer's name. What he found out about the dealer was that he was from Humboldt and had a summer home by the Klamath River, one of the most scenic spots in the northwestern states. Silveria would later describe the dealer to me as an aging hippie: long-hair, graying beard, medium height and stocky. He wore blue bib overalls that emphasized his roundness and, according to Silveria, made him look almost goofy. But what he carried in his maroon day pack kept anyone from laughing at him. And he kept that bag close to him at all times. Silveria noticed that the others in the mission knew the dealer well, for he had started coming around regularly in recent weeks to make himself available for any buys. What Silveria found most amazing about this "weed man" was that he knew absolutely nothing about trains. He was a perfect chump for a guy like Silveria.

Silveria told the aging hippie that he had just gotten his food stamps changed into cash and wanted to purchase one hundred dollars worth of weed from him. It's interesting that in that same period, while Silveria was making deals to purchase grass, back in Albany I was having Lincoln, my informant, wired up and making busts in the campsites where McLean was murdered. I was also completing the final steps needed to bull-doze the area by the Albany rail tracks.

The dealer led Silveria to an apartment where he picked up a whole bag full of marijuana that had been pressed tightly together in a trash compactor. Silveria exchanged his food-stamp money for the marijuana, giving the dealer the hundred dollars he promised him. The dealer asked Silveria if he was happy with the quantity he received and Silveria grinned and nodded. In truth, it was more than he imagined he would get. As they were concluding the transaction, Silveria and the dealer got into an animated discussion about train hopping. The more

Silveria talked about riding rails, the more interested the dealer became. After Silveria's purchase was completed, the two men headed down to the railroad yard. By then, the dealer had made up his mind. He wanted Silveria to show him the ropes on how to get to Roseville in a boxcar. Drug dealers prey on transients, lurking near rescue missions and soup kitchens looking for buyers, just as pedophiles are attracted to parks and school playgrounds where children can be found in large numbers.

Silveria told the dealer that they would probably encounter others like them at one of the jungles by the Vancouver rail yard, also waiting to hop a train to Roseville. The whole experience of finding a new way of getting to Roseville sounded like an exciting prospect for the dealer, especially the way Silveria presented it: new clients, great views and no cost to him — only profits. The dealer was enthralled and let himself be led by Silveria to a secluded spot by the Burlington Northern rail yard, where an FTRA member was waiting to hop a freight train with Silveria to Roseville. For the drug dealer, it was a lethal mistake. The transients had already made plans to lure the dealer to that spot and, once they got him on the freight train, to rob him. Silveria had no love for drug dealers. He actually hated them with a passion. In fact, he hated them more than anyone else, because he needed them to feed his rage-inducing habit.

Silveria and his FTRA companion charmed the dealer into feeling at ease. They assured him they'd show him the ropes and that he could count on the adventure of a lifetime. At the other end, they'd introduce him to other train hoppers like themselves — potential weed buyers. The guy must have been salivating, picturing his expanding marijuana market and the stories he'd tell his buddies when he got back. The trio smoked joints, drank beer and ate some food they brought with them in their backpacks. Their jovial camaraderie continued long after Silveria noticed a chain attached to a black wallet in the man's lower side pocket hanging from the bib of his overalls. Silveria could see only the top part of the wallet peeking out, but it looked "puffed out, like it might be holding a large amount of cash." Silveria didn't bring the wallet to the attention of the other FTRA train hopper. He wanted the contents all for himself.

It finally was time to board. They found an empty boxcar, threw their gear in and jumped on the train without being spotted by a rail officer. The train moved slowly, less than twenty miles per hour at first, then picked up speed to about sixty, passing through Portland, down toward Eugene, Oregon. The countryside was lush and green. They passed views of mountain peaks, valleys, redwoods mixed with pines, streams and waterfalls. The dealer frequently stood up to walk over to the edge of the open boxcar to take it all in. Silveria and the other train hopper remained sitting, smoking pot and shooting up heroin. The dealer himself did not shoot heroin. Why a street-wise guy like that trusted two druggies, who until then were perfect strangers to him, is something I still haven't figured out.

The three didn't talk in the cacophony created by the moving freight train, its cars rattling and rolling over the rails. However, I learned later what Silveria was thinking. His mind occasionally wandered to the dealer's day pack, the contents of which he was planning to split with the other FTRA member in the boxcar. He also thought about the loot in the wallet. His only problem was how and when to take action. He knew his train-hopping FTRA buddy was waiting for his lead.

It was still daylight when the train crossed over from Eugene to Klamath Falls, where it stopped briefly. A rail agent walking by saw the three men in the boxcar and came over asking for their identifications. Silveria and the other FTRA train hopper knew the rail agent, known in the FTRA as a *bull*, by his first name, Roger. They didn't bother pulling out any printed identification and simply rattled off their names, which the bull wrote down in a small pad. Silveria later told me that he identified him-self either as Brad Foster or John Plattner, he wasn't sure which, because during that period he used both names interchangeably. He also couldn't remember the name the dealer gave the rail agent. As for the name of the other FTRA member, Silveria refused to divulge it, keeping the group's code of silence.

Since September 11, security on the rails has gotten some-what tougher, but it's a far cry from being completely safe. I know this personally, because for a long time I myself have moved about freely, waking on and around freight trains in rail yards without being noticed or stopped. One of these times was after the Madrid train bombing. Smart FTRA rail riders still make sure they know the names of the different bulls in the rail yards they frequent. As for the railroad companies, the rail officer's action signified the company's policy of tacit permission to allow illegal rail riding on their trains. Many rail employees are even sympathetic with train hoppers, knowing that most of them can't afford any other means of transportation. I've spoken to officials who even denied the existence of the FTRA. One seasoned FTRA train hopper told me that with certain engines or cargo, the crew even warned them what they need to look out for and they in turn were careful to follow the instructions. These riders are the last ones to mess with the freight trains. They have no desire or intention of giving up their mode of transportation, which is also connected to their livelihood through the government food stamp allowance. As I have learned, once these tramps take up rail riding, it's in their blood forever. As Silveria said, "They may pull up a bucket with them into the boxcar, because they can't jump in and out of the cars like they used to when nature calls, but they'll keep on rid-ing." I have heard this confirmed many times. One old timer summed it up by saying, "I'll stop riding when I die."

On the day Silveria, the FTRA member and the unfor-tunate drug dealer were riding the rails, the whole process with the bull in Klamath Falls took several minutes. Soon the freight train with the three riders moved on towards Dunsmuir and then headed for Shasta Mountain. Coming out of the hills, the train started down the grade where it would soon cross Whiskeytown Lake and then Shasta River. Silveria knew the region well. Not only had he ridden these rails back and forth countless number of times, but he had lived in the area for a while. He even had a parole officer there whom he had gotten to know quite well. As the train crossed the first bridge, the dealer stood up, standing in front of the open box car door. Silveria shouted over the rattling noise of the moving train to the dealer, "Get away from there. There is no railing and the train will get shaky soon. It's your first time. Be careful." Silveria's voice rose higher. The dealer shrugged his shoulders.

"I'm not afraid," he shouted over the screeching noise of the rails. Then Silveria stood up. The box car moved side to side and he paused to catch his balance as he moved forward, taking wide steps towards the dealer. He shouted over the noise of the train for the dealer to sit down, that it wasn't safe where he was standing. But the man in the blue overalls remained unconcerned. He shrugged off Silveria's warnings. As Silveria neared him, the drug dealer turned his head slightly towards Silveria and shouted above the wheels' piercing screech as they moved over the rails that he wasn't afraid. Then he turned back to watch the view. Silveria continued to move closer, until he stood directly behind the dealer. Placing his right hand on the back of the dealer's shoulder Silveria said, "You gotta go over there and sit down, because the car could start shaking." Silveria pointed to a corner spot in the box car with his other hand.

The dealer glanced at the area to which Silveria pointed, but he didn't budge. He remained standing at the open box car door with his back to Silveria.

"How much longer to Roseville?" The dealer's voice rose again as he tilted his head slightly towards Silveria.

"Just a few more seconds," Silveria shouted against the wind blowing in his face.

"What?" The dealer was about to turn, but he was too late. Silveria tried to grab the wallet as he pushed the aging hippie, but he wasn't fast enough. The drugs and alcohol in Silveria's body slowed him down and that portion of the coveted prize escaped him forever. He leaned out and watched as the dealer went flying over the rail of the trestle, propelled by the force of Silveria's muscular arm. He continued watching as the dealer's body cleared the railing. He kept on watching from the moving boxcar as the dealer fell at a speed of about seventy-five miles per hour, his arms and legs spread out as he hit the water below. We'll never know what thoughts flashed through the dealer's mind. Those who have survived suicide falls from bridges have said that time slows dramatically at the end. The height that the dealer fell from was more than a hundred yards. That's like falling the distance of a football field. Thrown from such a height, the man would have been a dead duck for sure. To survive, he would have needed incredible luck to hit the water at an angle. But luck was not riding with him that day — Robert Silveria was. In all likelihood, the impact when he hit the water would have broken his neck and rendered him unconscious. Water would have rushed into his lungs as his body fell like a rock below the current.

Later, Silveria told me that he continued to stare from the moving boxcar at the spot where the dealer hit the water. He observed the ripple effect created by the fall. He said, "I didn't see the body emerge, although I watched, praying that the zigzag man would pop up and live to talk about his first train ride." Silveria kept looking down, but all he saw were boats. Beyond that, there was a freeway with cars speeding by. Everything looked serene and peaceful.

The train went over the trestle. Silveria turned his atten-

tion back to the interior of the boxcar where his FTRA companion was already going through the dealer's backpack. The
man stopped long enough to look up at Silveria with a big grin
on his face. "We have a small gold mine in our possession." The
bag was packed tightly with marijuana. The two accomplices
split the dealer's loot and when they were near Chico, California, another picturesque town along the route, they parted
ways. Afterward, Silveria threw the dealer's empty back pack
out of the boxcar and watched it disappear behind thick shrubs.
Then he sat down, leaned back and smoked a joint. Silveria told
me that neither he nor the other FTRA member in the boxcar
ever mentioned the incident again.

10

Catch Out

"I had let Satan make a hell's angel out of me"
Robert Joseph Silveria, Jr.

When Silveria and I finally spoke face to face, he told me that he still had the same weed on him that he had confiscated from the marijuana dealer he pushed from a moving boxcar into the Shasta River when he ran into FTRA member Paul Wayne Matthews in October 1995. He said he met this man under a bridge in Spokane, Washington, where train hoppers congregate to *catch out*. Matthews had been given the nickname Glassy, because he had only one eye. His older brother had shot him with a BB gun when they were young boys. His family hadn't heard from him in more than ten years, ever since he drifted out of their lives after his wife died.

Matthews had a daughter whom he hadn't seen in more than seventeen years. He spent his days riding freight trains from place to place, getting drunk. Occasionally he stopped at rail yards or was arrested for minor offenses involving alcohol. He did not live so much as he waited to die.

Matthews and Silveria first met at a mission in Klamath Falls, Oregon. Six months later, Silveria ran into him again in Spokane and both men headed to Havre, a town surrounded by the sharp curvatures of the Rockies in the plains of north central Montana. Matthews told Silveria he had food stamps to pick up in Havre and afterward he planned to continue wandering aimlessly up the Hi-Line through the state's rugged northern countryside into bordering states. It was one of the places in which he camped out. I learned from a police report that Matthews and a female affiliate were arrested when a police officer came upon their camp and found them skinning dogs they were preparing to cook over a camp fire. This practice of eating dogs is common when times are tough and there's no other food around for rail hoppers to eat. Rumor has it that this practice was brought to the rails by the original FTRA members, who had witnessed firsthand Vietnamese canine cuisine.

Silveria told Matthews he also had business in Havre, where he wanted to reestablish his welfare pickup. The train they caught, No. 48, was moving at a relatively fast speed. The men were pretty intoxicated, since they had been drinking a lot of malt liquor and beer in the early afternoon and continued drinking inside the open-door boxcar. The fact that they managed to pull themselves up into the boxcar indicated the tolerance they had developed for booze. Jumping trains requires skill. It's easy to slip under the moving wheels.

Unfortunately, the two men hit on a "junk" train, which took approximately eight hours just to reach Whitefish, a town situated in the middle of some of Montana's most stunning landscape and wilderness. There, a crew change occurred, which meant that the train would go no further that night. Matthews and Silveria would have to catch another train to continue their journey. It was getting dark and they were hungry. They were also out of booze, having finished off their last bottle of beer in the boxcar. They each jumped off the train. Then they crossed a bridge over the Whitefish river, looking for shelter. When none appeared, Silveria said, "Let's walk back to the bridge we just crossed. There's a camp down there and we can sleep there for the night." The campground Silveria pointed out was a natural for train hoppers and, in fact, was known among locals and police as a hobo campground. An abandoned fire pit and a four-foot section of telephone pole that someone had dragged over to use as a bench were evidence that others had been there before Silveria and Matthews.

The two men dropped their gear in the bushes and walked to a market a short distance from the main rail yard and their campsite to replenish their supplies. They bought packages of frozen hash browns, link sausages and eggs. They each also purchased a round jug of wine. The female clerk serving them asked Silveria for his I.D. She said he didn't look old enough to buy alcohol. However, there probably was a more pertinent reason. Silveria was filthy.

Typically, when FTRA rail riders travel, they wear two sets of clothing. Boxcars are dirty, so they put on an extra pair of jeans or pants over their clothes. When they arrive at their destination and want to go out in "social" settings, they remove their outer clothes and go out in clean attire. Silveria liked to travel looking soiled and being smelly, especially when he was setting up food stamps. He found that people in the welfare departments were happy to give him whatever he wanted just to get rid of him. That night, in the store, the look he affected backfired on him. Because he was wearing soiled clothes he'd

had on for more than two months, "stinking like a dog," the
clerk was diligently cautious. Silveria pulled out an Idaho identification card and showed it to the cashier. After examining the
I.D., she handed it back to Silveria and said, "No problem."

As they headed back to camp, Silveria started feeling as
though he wanted to kill Paul Wayne Matthews. Until then
they had been getting along fine. Did Matthews make a crack
when Silveria had to show his identification to buy liquor? Or
was it something else — a look, a laugh, a chance remark?
Whatever evoked that feeling, when the two men headed back
to their camp, crossing the bridge to reach it, Silveria was
already entering a zone where the desire to murder began to
itch him. His inner rage was boiling, threatening to break out
again. Silveria told me later that he had plenty of food stamps
on him at the time, which he had picked up recently in California and Oregon. Did he want to steal Matthews' identification?
Silveria already had about fifteen different pieces of I.D. on
him. This required him to keep careful accounting of the states
in which he collected food stamps, under what names he collected, and the dates when they were eligible for pick up in a
book that he carried with him. He had told me it wasn't his
intention to kill Matthews for the food stamps. He could just as
easily buy them off some train hopper. I believe Silveria had
reached a dangerous point where feeding his rage had become
synonymous with feeding his body and soul. No matter what he
did or how many times he killed, he couldn't satisfy the hunger
or desire for violence within him.

At the campsite, the two men started a fire using rotten
pieces of wood from the end of the telephone pole, as past
tramps camping in the same spot did before them. Then they
began cooking potatoes over the open flame. Silveria taunted
Matthews that he was a drunk who couldn't hold his liquor.
Matthews got irate and there was some shoving back and forth,

but then Matthews said, "This is all crap. Let's make peace."
The two men shook hands, but inside, Silveria was not satisfied.
He still wanted to fight. He leaned down over the campfire to
turn the potatoes. He waited for them to burn so that he could
get another rise out of Matthews. Silveria needed Matthews to
bring his inner rage to the surface, but Matthews was being too
nice of a guy. Finally, Matthews' patience started to wear thin.
"How the fuck can you burn those potatoes?" Matthews
looked at Silveria, puzzled.

 "How the fuck? How the fuck? I'll show you how the
fuck!" Silveria grabbed the frying pan by the handle. With long
rapid steps he moved towards the river bank, holding onto the
pan. "Here!" he shouted back to Matthews, who followed him
and tried to stop him. Silveria swung his arm back, then tossed
the frying pan like a Frisbee. Briefly it flew through the air and
then dropped down, sinking deep below the current.

 There was another shoving match, but then Matthews
announced, slurring his words, "I've had enough. I don't want
any food or anything." Plastered, Matthews looked over at Silveria and the bottle he was holding. "How much are you going
to drink of that bottle?" he demanded.

 "Probably the whole thing." Silveria took another swig
of wine, demonstrating his defiance.

 "Yeah," Matthews said, nodding his head, "you think
you're tough enough to drink that much and get on a train
tomorrow?"

 Silveria downed more wine. "Yeah, probably so."
Matthews shook his head and sat down on his sleeping bag to take
his boots off as Silveria walked around the fireplace. Standing over
Matthews, Silveria challenged, "Why don't you do something
about it?" In an instant Matthews rose to his feet and another
shoving match, which turned into a fistfight, ensued. After four or
five minutes both men gave up and stopped. Making friends

again, they shook hands. Matthews untied his boots, slipped them
off and crawled into his sleeping bag. He lay facing Silveria, who
was sitting across the campfire on the opposite side of him.
Matthews dozed off and Silveria watched the other man as he
slept. Then, lying on his own sleeping bag, Silveria continued
drinking the Thunderbird wine. The more he drank the less he
liked Matthews. He wasn't going to let Matthews disrespect him
and live to talk about it when he rode the rails or went to the missions. They lived in a small world and word traveled fast. He
stared at Matthews above the dying flames in the campfire.
Matthews had rolled over on his other side. The red glow of the
fire danced off the back of his head. Silveria didn't like men with
red hair, I later learned from another rail rider, because a red-
headed guy once assaulted his sister. The red light bouncing off
the back of Matthew's head must have been another teaser for Silveria in his agitated state.

Suddenly, Silveria heard the sound of a train. He looked
up and saw its headlight in the distance. Taking one last swig of
wine, Silveria jumped to his feet. He knew there wasn't much
time. If he was going to do it, he would have to do it now,
while Matthews had his back turned and wouldn't be able to
see what Silveria was doing. Besides, he appeared to be fast
asleep. Silveria picked up the four foot piece of telephone pole.
Carrying a pole that weighed at least eighty pounds, he walked
over to Matthews' sleeping area. The pole still had metal spikes
embedded in it, which once were used by linemen for climbing.
Silveria held onto a spike with one hand as he lifted the heavy
piece of wood up in the air. Then he slammed it down hard on
Matthews' head. The force of a four-foot piece of a telephone
post smashing against a man's skull has more than enough
impact to kill him instantly, but Silveria lifted the pole and let it
fall against the victim's head again and again. He kept pounding the pole against Matthews head until he saw the tip of

Matthews' skull break away and brain matter spew out into the fading amber glow of the campfire.

Then Silveria remembered the approaching train. Turning around, he saw it draw closer towards the trestle. Silveria carried the pole with the end covered in blood dragging along the ground. He quickly pushed it into the river so it would float, hopefully into oblivion. He ran back to the campsite. Picking up the two empty bottles of Thunderbird, he screwed the caps back on and began making his way back to the shore. Silveria threw the first bottle of wine as far as he could. It made a gentle splash going below the surface before reappearing again. Silveria then threw the second one. For a few seconds he stood there mesmerized, as he watched the bottles float with the current under a dim moonlight.

The sound of the train growing louder brought him back to his surroundings. He ran back to grab Matthews' backpack, which he tossed as far as he could into the river. Floating away, it bobbed with the current. It would only be a matter of time before water seeping in would replace the air inside and sink the bag to the bottom of the river. Silveria's work was not done. There still was the body of the victim to consider. Silveria looked up towards the sound of the approaching engine coming closer and closer. He pulled out Matthews' wallet from underneath the sleeping bag and moved it to the side on the ground, then grabbed the end of the sleeping bag with Matthews' body inside and tried dragging it towards a nearby ravine. However, the body repeatedly got stuck in a berry bush.

For a moment, Silveria thought Matthews was still alive, clinging with his fingers deep into the ground. Silveria tried pulling harder, but the sleeping bag came off. He grabbed the bottom of Matthew's pants, dragging the body by the leg of the pants to the ravine. Then he ran back to get the sleeping bag and covered the victim with the bag. The train was getting closer and closer. Time was running out. Silveria went back to grab his own gear and spotted Matthews' wallet, which he had left on the ground earlier. He picked it up, and although there wasn't much cash in the billfold, maybe ten or twelve dollars, he knew it also held a Social Security card that would be valuable to him later. He wasn't going to let something this useful to a rail rider go to waste. Adjusting his backpack over his shoulder, Silveria made a dash towards the trestle, meeting up with the on-coming Burlington Northern train that would take him to Spokane, Washington. He jumped onto the train and made himself comfortable as it sped away into the night.

The next day, a local resident was pushing his seventeen-month-old daughter in her stroller. Suddenly, the two family dogs that accompanied them sprinted down towards a ravine. They stopped when they reached the bottom, under the bridge, howling and sniffing.

The man tried calling the dogs, but they did not respond, continuing to appear agitated. Leaving his daughter in the stroller at a safe distance, the man walked down to investigate. When he reached his dogs, he saw that they were moving erratically in circles and yelping. A second later he looked down and froze. There was a shattered human skull and pieces of brain lying on the ground. Blood was splattered all around the area. Pools of it covered rocks, stones, grass and the ground. Looking around, he saw that the whole area was painted in blood. The madness that could create such horror was unthinkable to him. Pulling himself together, the man followed the drag marks in the grass to a piece of cardboard with a sleeping bag visible beneath it. He lifted the corner of the sleeping bag and saw the hand of the victim. Dropping the cover back down, he put leashes on the two dogs, went back to get the stroller with his toddler daughter and rushed home to telephone the police.

The Whitefish Police Department received the call at
around 5:25 P.M. Within minutes, Chief La Brie and two of his
officers got to the scene, soon followed by Flathead County
Sheriff's deputies and detectives. There had been another murder committed in the same hobo hangout about a year earlier.
Police wondered if they were connected. Since it was getting
too dark to see much, they decided to place security on the
scene and process the crime in the morning. Detectives roped
the area off and an officer stood guard for the night.

The following morning, Detective Mike Sward and other
detectives examined the crime scene for any evidence, taking photographs and video taping the area. They paid particular attention
to the end of the trail at a small incline where the body was found
lying in a ravine in pools of blood. There was no identification on
the victim. All the detectives could tell was that the victim was a
well-developed, well-nourished, adult Caucasian male, who
weighed about 140 pounds, was seventy-two inches tall and
looked to be in his forties. The victim had on white socks, but his
shoes were missing. His jeans and jockey shorts, still buttoned and
zipped up, were pulled down to the level of his mid-thigh, exposing the genitalia and buttocks. This led the detectives to believe
that the man had been dragged from the original spot where he
was actually killed with a blunt force to the head. They also found
a trail that stopped approximately thirty yards from the campfire,
which contained evidence of drag marks. Fly eggs had already settled within the victim's open head wound. Investigators marked
and photographed each pertinent item and spot, including the
uneaten package of link sausages and carton of eggs they found
lying on the ground. A short while later, the body and brain matter, including the skullcap, were transported to the Missoula crime
lab for further analysis. The autopsy showed the victim had a .20
alcohol level along with nicotine and caffeine in his system.

As Montana investigators began investigating Matthews' murder, Silveria was in a passport photo shop in Spokane, Washington, less than a thousand miles away, acquiring a laminated Idaho identification card under the guise of Paul Wayne Matthews. With his new ID card and Matthews' social security card, Silveria could apply for welfare in El Paso, San Francisco and Memphis, Tennessee, under Paul Matthews' name.

Meanwhile, the Whitefish detectives interviewed the employees at the market where Matthews and Silveria had purchased food the night of Matthews death, but got no good leads. The woman who had been on duty was not there at the time, which meant the detectives would have to return. Next, they sent out a teletype of the homicide to the western law enforcement stations describing the victim. They checked hospitals, but no leads developed.

A few days later, the police returned to Markus Food Mart to speak to Margaret Jones, the employee who might be able to help them with a description. This time she was at the store. Jones told the detectives that two hobo types had come to the store on the night in question. She recalled they looked like brothers, except one had an eye missing. She identified the photo of the victim as being one of them. She recalled asking the other man for his identification when he purchased the alcohol. Jones later came down to the police station and gave the forensic artist a description of the man who came into the store with the victim that night.

On October 31, a positive identification of the victim came in from the FBI office in Helena. He was identified as Paul Wayne Mathews, age forty-three. One week prior to his homicide, he had been arrested with Roy Allen Bell for trespassing on railroad property in Vancouver, Washington. An arrest warrant had been issued on October 25 for Bell and

Matthews for trespassing and failure to appear. On November 2, a composite drawing based on Margaret Jones' eye-witness account of the person accompanying Matthews shortly before his murder was released to the press. Soon the calls started coming in from people who thought they saw someone who matched the description of the victim, suspect or both. All had to be looked into even though they all led to dead ends.

By November, Silveria moved about freely on the trains between San Francisco, El Paso, Memphis, Havre and Little Rock, Arkansas using his new identity. Silveria also was using the identity of Lester Paul Dykeman, who was being sought for questioning in the murder of Charles Randall Boyd in Kansas.

At approximately the same time, the hunt for Matthews' killer spread across the states via teletype. A Burlington Northern agent questioned one of his transient contacts in Spokane, Washington about an Amtrak derailment in Arizona in early June of that year. He also asked about the homicide in Whitefish, Montana. "Dogman did it," the transient said, walking away quickly and looking around nervously. The agent tried to solicit further information, but the transient was too scared to continue the conversation and kept moving away, leaving the agent confused and puzzled. Was the hobo referring to the derailment or the homicide in Montana when he named Dogman? Regardless, the agent passed the information on to law enforcement officers investigating the case of Matthews' homicide in Whitefish, Montana.

Dogman's name stirred interest among detectives, because during the course of examining the crime scene, the Montana detectives had noted that on the side of a nearby train trestle was writing that was signed "Dogman, 1989." Suddenly, it appeared that investigators might be coming closer to the identity of the suspect.

On November 7, 1995, a Burlington Northern agent in Whitefish, Montana stopped a transient for trespassing in a rail yard. The man told the agent his name was Michael Kingston. After checking on Kingston's background, the agent learned that Kingston also went by the alias Hugh Ross. Further inquiry revealed that a Hugh Ross was wanted in Spokane for robbery and contempt of court. Ross/Kingston was arrested and jailed in the Flathead County Sheriff's Office detention in Montana — the same county where Matthews' murder had occurred. At the time that Hugh Ross was stopped, there were two other transients traveling with him. They were identified and released, free to continue on their course to Vancouver. The railroad agents also allowed them to take the gear and backpack belonging to Ross with them when they left.

On November 8, Flathead County Sheriff's Office Detective Mike Sward showed a photo of Paul Wayne Matthews to Ross, who claimed not to know the victim. Next, Sward showed Ross a photo of Roy Bell, who had been arrested with Matthews the week before Matthews' murder. Ross recognized the face in the photo as "Desert Rat" and said the last time he had seen Desert Rat was in Vancouver sometime the previous month. Sward asked Ross if he also had a nickname. Ross replied he was known as Dogman and sometimes as Dogman Tony. This was one of those moments when invisible fireworks go off all around. Dogman was practically a legend. One cop I know thinks that Dogman may be responsible for more than one hundred deaths.

Sward then looked deeper into Ross' criminal history with Burlington Northern. He learned that Ross was a member of a train hopping organization, the Freight Train Riders of America, FTRA, and that he was being investigated by the FBI in connection with a train derailment in Arizona, because some papers were found near the derailment with the name, "Sons of the Gestapo," a name also tattooed on Dogman's arm.

A photo line up of Dogman and Desert Rat was shown to Margaret Jones, the Markus Food Market employee, to see if she could identify either of them as the men who were in her store on the night Matthews was murdered. She could not positively identify either subject. However, when Sward realized that the Flathead County jail held a "big FTRA fish" like Dogman Tony, he notified Burlington Northern officials and the FBI in an attempt to retrieve Dogman's belongings, which had been carried off by his two companions when the group was originally stopped. By then, however, it was too late.

Sward questioned Dogman again in the presence of an FBI agent. This time he used a form of behavioral analysis. Dogman shifted uncomfortably in his seat throughout the interview. He could remember clearly where he traveled except when Sward pinpointed specific events. Suddenly, Dogman's memory grew foggy. He even refused to divulge his real name and the fact he originally was from New York. Sward was interested in the FTRA, the existence of which he had only recently discovered. He asked Dogman Tony questions about the organization, but again, Dogman was evasive. Dogman even denied being a member of the FTRA and said they're just "brothers." Although FTRA members do refer to themselves as a brotherhood, Dogman knew a lot more than he said.

He did reveal that he did not like blacks and that he had many enemies, among them Bushman, who was after him because Dogman had told everyone that "Bushman hides in bushes and then leaps out and robs people." He never told the detective that Bushman was a black rail rider who hung out with the FTRA. When questioned about the swastika, other white supremacy symbols and the name "Sons of the Gestapo" on his arm, he claimed not to understand their meaning. He described the tattoos as something he got when he was incarcerated for two years in a Washington State penitentiary for something he "didn't do." He also denied involvement in the derailment of the Amtrak train,

stating that no one he knew was bright enough to figure out how
to do that. He explained you'd need to know the different features of lights and electrical changes. "Maybe it's terrorism," he
said. "You see a lot of strange things happening."

During the interview, Dogman moved back and forth in
his seat, at times crying that he was being blamed for something
he didn't do. It became obvious that when the nervous transient said, "Dogman did it," he was referring to the derailment
and not to the murder in Whitefish, Montana. In support of the
transient's allegations, investigators found papers on the
ground near the Amtrak derailment with reference to the Sons
of the Gestapo.

Later, a cop gave me a video of that interview in Montana with Dogman Tony. By his body language and demeanor,
I felt the guy was lying when he told Detective Sward that he
had no idea what the words, Sons of the Gestapo, tattooed on
his arm meant. By that time I had seen too many symbols relat-
ing to white power and white pride tattooed on FTRA riders to
label this a coincidence, and this group has been accused of
being associated with Aryan Brotherhood that has come to rule
the prison system in many places. Yet I heard many of them dis-
claim any association, insisting the tattoo means only what it
states and nothing more. Though I have seen and known of
black rail riders in and around the FTRA, such as Bushman,
New York Slim and L.A. Slim, it is plain that only the very
toughest minority riders survive in that racist climate.

11

A Deadly Downpour

"I got a little bit too carried away."
Robert Joseph Silveria, Jr.

Oregon had been bombarded with heavy rains and gusty winds for over a week in December 1995, when Silveria ran up to the first boxcar of a train that he thought was headed to Portland. There was another rail rider in the car already, an FTRA member Silveria recognized from the missions: William Pettit, Jr., over six feet four inches tall, with handsome features and a full mustache. His dark brown hair was tied in a long pony tail with strands of black and blue gypsy beads running down over his locks.

At the age of thirty-nine, Pettit was three years older than Silveria. Like Robert Silveria, he was a longtime transient. But unlike Silveria, he didn't travel light. He settled in the front half of the boxcar with a Coleman stove and a radio playing his favorite station. Against one wall was a mountain bike with blown out tires. His pack and roll sat on the boxcar's metal floor, pieces of broken boards scattered about.

Dropping his gear on the same side as Pettit's, Silveria parked himself in the front half of the boxcar near the other transient. He used Pettit's Coleman to cook macaroni and cheese while they waited for the train to take them to Portland. The steam coming out of the boxcar attracted a rail yard officer who drove over to see what was going on. The rail agent parked his vehicle several yards away from the open boxcar and sat there watching the two men for a while. Then, without getting out of his truck or speaking to the two men through a rolled down window, the agent drove away. Across from them was a stationary boxcar with closed doors. A man slept underneath it.

The freight train engine took off shortly after the rail employee left, pulling the boxcars behind it. A couple of hours later when it came into another rail yard, Pettit and Silveria suddenly realized that they had gotten into a boxcar sidetracked to Salem instead of Portland. They knew this meant that the boxcar was marked to be sent back to the factory. This kind of bad luck could strike even the most experienced rail riders. The rail agent who had watched them from his vehicle might have warned them, but he also might have told them that they were trespassing and needed to leave. Instead, he felt sorry for the two men, and allowed them to cook their dinner and shelter from the pounding rain.

Knowing they were not going to find a more comfortable or welcoming spot anywhere nearby, Silveria and Pettit decided to wait until morning before jumping another boxcar. Glow from distant street lamps bounced over a rustling creek several yards away from the open box car door. Both men were familiar with the area and knew that there was a fast food market less than two blocks from the rail yard, near the rail crossing yard office. Silveria had ten dollars tucked in each pocket of his black wrangler jeans. He asked Pettit if he wanted to drink some beer. "I have a little extra cash I can give you if you want to go out and buy some for us." Pettit agreed to do it and asked Silveria permission to also buy a pack of cigarettes with the money.

"Sure," Silveria shrugged. Covering up in a hooded jacket, Pettit climbed out of the boxcar, leaving behind his mountain bike and all his gear for Silveria to guard. Silveria knew he wouldn't be gone long, but it was enough time for him to search through Pettit's green canvas back pack to see what he had in there. Inside, he found the usual clothes rail hoppers carry, but he also saw a lot of identification cards bearing different men's names and social security numbers with Pettit's photo on them. Silveria carried phony IDs on him also, but wondered how Pettit obtained so many.

About fifteen minutes went by before Pettit returned with four bottles of beer and cigarettes. The two stranded railriders sat around drinking beer, listening to Pettit's radio and making small talk, watching the rain outside the boxcar die down. Silveria commented that Pettit had on brand new waffle stompers. Pettit told Silveria he paid $29 for them. It's not uncommon for rail riders to notice each other's shoes or boots — they tell a lot about the man. The kind of boots Pettit had on were the same kind Silveria wore — the black, steel-toe boots FTRA enforcers wear.

When they finished their beers, Silveria said, "I'm going to go out and buy some more for us." He still had the other ten dollars in his pocket. But first, Silveria headed towards a creek moving under a bridge beneath the rail yard. The spot was secluded and gave him the privacy to shoot a dose of heroin.

Meanwhile, Pettit sat inside the boxcar listening to the radio and waiting for Silveria to return. Silveria was gone a long while, at least three times as long as it took Pettit to buy the beer.

Finally, Silveria came out from beneath the bridge, crossing the rail yard, and headed towards the market. It was near closing time when he got there. He walked up to the refrigerator where the drinks were kept and pulled out not two, but only one bottle of beer. He had decided he didn't want to spend the entire ten dollars he had left on beer for himself and Pettit. He figured he might need the cash for something else. And besides, he already had a good high from the dope he just took. Silveria purchased a large bottle of the same brew Pettit bought earlier and returned to the boxcar.

"Let's just split this," Silveria handed Pettit the bottle of beer.

"All right," Pettit shrugged. They sat around making small talk and sharing the beer Silveria bought. When it was finished, Pettit wanted more beer, but he saw by his watch that it was late. There were only five minutes left before the liquor store closed. There was no way either one of them could make it to the store in time. Frustrated, Pettit became confrontational, insisting that Silveria should have bought at least one more bottle with the money he had. A shoving match broke out between the two men.

"Get out of here," Pettit insisted. "Find yourself another boxcar."

"Look, let's chill out," Silveria said and took a step back. "I'm not moving anywhere. This boxcar is just fine for me."

"Yeah, you're right. Well, it looks like we're both going to be here," Pettit said calmly, but Silveria was sure that the man was fuming inside. Silveria took his sleeping bag and dragged it all the way to the open boxcar door, distancing himself from Pettit. Later, Silveria told investigators that he knew Pettit could hurt him, but he made up his mind then and there that wasn't going to happen. *There is no way my name and social security number are going to turn up under Pettit's picture.*

Stepping deeper inside the boxcar, Pettit picked up his pack and unrolled his sleeping bag. Then, according to Silveria, Pettit did something strange. Carrying the bag, he walked over to Silveria and stopped. Holding up the sleeping bag and waving it like a Spanish bullfighter, he towered over Silveria. Silveria understood the challenge and without hesitation kicked Pettit in the face with his steel-toed boot.

The kick was so hard that he heard Pettit's nose crack as he pushed it back into the man's skull. Instantly, Pettit fell to the ground, not breathing. Watching him, Silveria knew that Pettit was not getting up. But that wasn't enough to satisfy his wild, beastly rage, which now took full charge. He continued kicking the already dead man in the head, ribs and jaw. Snorting like a wild animal, Silveria looked around and saw wooden boards lying nearby on the metal floor. He picked up a two-by-four and struck Pettit over and over again on the head.

As he pounded on the corpse the same words ran through his mind. He kept muttering, "Take a number and go to the mission. Take a number and go to the mission. Take a number and go to the mission." They were the words he heard months ago when he went to a mental health clinic in Vancouver seeking help.

The scene at the clinic rushed back:

"What do you want?" the woman behind the desk had demanded, glaring at Silveria.

"I've got this problem," Silveria started. He wanted to tell her so much. He wanted to tell her about his drug habit, about the people he killed and most of all about the beast living inside him.

But the woman, overwhelmed and in a hurry, snapped, "I've got problems, too. Everybody's got problems. Go take a number and sit down or better still, go to the mission. Deal with your problems there." When she turned her head in disgust, Silveria walked out humiliated, wanting to kill more than ever.

Now his thoughts returned to the scene around him. There wasn't much light in the boxcar, but Silveria didn't need it to know there was blood splattered everywhere. He could smell it in the cold, damp air. It was the damp smell of raw meat. He saw through the darkness that Pettit's face was deformed from the blows of Silveria's fury, and the Pettit he knew before, who so enraged him, was no longer there. Then Silveria started returning to reality, amazed by the rage that had exploded within him. Later he told me and other officers that when he calmed down and realized what had just transpired, all he could murmur was, "I got a little bit carried away." Everything was foggy one minute, and the next he saw another victim lying before him on the ground.

Silveria placed his hand near Pettit's blood-soaked face and then on the man's chest to see if he had been wrong and Pettit was breathing, but there was no air coming out and no upward and downward movement in Pettit's chest. Then Silveria recalled hearing the crack when his boot smashed Pettit's nose. Lifting Pettit's head, Silveria pulled a strand of gypsy beads from Pettit's ponytail. Next he wiped his hands against his clothes, still clutching the beads, and threw his and Pettit's gear out of the boxcar door to the wet ground below. Afterward Silveria took off William Pettit's shoes and shoved them in his backpack. Then he lowered the mountain bike down on the ground and climbed down himself.

Looking around, Silveria saw no human movement, just freight trains lined up in rows in a desolate area. Silveria picked up his own pack and walked towards the spot beneath the bridge of the nearby creek where earlier he had shot heroin. Because of the constant rain, the water in the creek was high and turbulent, flowing swiftly. Silveria placed his pack on the slanted ground high above the water level. For now he was safe. Even if a train came along and some lone rail rider got up and peeked out from a boxcar, Silveria was hidden by the ravine, the bridge and thick foliage.

His body aching from the force it took to act out his rage, he stepped down into the cold, raging water with all his clothes and boots on. He plunged his face, then his entire head into the icy stream, sinking below the surface of the cold water. Then suddenly, Silveria stood up on his two feet, balancing himself against the forceful current, letting the strands of beads he had pulled out from Pettit's ponytail slip from his hand and float away.

Silveria stared at his empty hand. Then he slipped out of his military style boots and began pulling off his clothes one by one, starting with his fatigue jacket, then moving on to a long sleeved polo shirt that he got in a mission in Eugene. He threw both of them into the creek and watched as they floated away. Unbuckling his belt, he held onto it while unzipping his jeans, pulling them off in the stream as he fought to maintain his balance. He let all his bloodied clothes drift away with the current. Finally, he leaned down and removed his socks, one by one. Standing there with the belt in his hand, totally naked except for a medicine pouch that hung from his neck, he crawled out from the creek and reached for his pack. Quickly he pulled out and put on a set of fresh clothing: a grey hooded sweatshirt and two pairs of jeans. He also put on two pairs of socks and an extra pair of low boots he had in his pack.

Afterward, he returned to the boxcar and confiscated more beads from Pettit's hair, which Silveria put inside the leather medicine bag hanging down his chest. Picking up Pettit's military-style jacket, Silveria pulled it over his shoulders. Then Silveria drew out of his backpack his own blanket and covered Pettit with it, wrapping the dead man in a wool cocoon. Pulling out a blue marker he used to draw tattoos, Silveria wrote the word "freedom" on the boxcar wall. Next Silveria got Pettit's bloody military blanket and used it to tie up the dead transient's gear.

When he was finished with these tasks he left the crime scene, pushing the mountain bike down the tracks with all the gear on top of it. A light but steady rain was falling. Silveria found another secluded area, near the tracks and the creek but some distance away from the crime scene. There he had some shelter from the penetrating rain and the wind. Sitting down, he went through Pettit's belongings, most of which were useless to anyone, such as the many identification cards with Pettit's photo on them. He threw these into the creek, but he kept Pettit's social security card and birth certificate. He also kept the new boots, which he later gave away to one of his FTRA buddies. To Silveria they were part of the spoils of war, which he felt he had to share to give the war any meaning. Some items he squirreled away under bushes in case he should ever come back and want to reclaim them.

The storm from which Silveria was seeking relief was hitting Millersburg, a tiny town sixteen miles south of Salem with less than 700 inhabitants. Then the town got another unwelcome surprise. On December 3, 1995, a body was found in a boxcar stationed in the railroad yard inside the hamlet's boundaries. The victim's head was flattened beyond recognition and covered up. The entire corpse was wrapped in a blanket. It was noted by investigators that the word "freedom" was written on the wall above the victim in blue ink and the dead man's shoes were missing.

The community was stunned that something so horrendous had occurred in a peaceful place like Millersburg. The first thought through anyone's mind was that some hobos got into a fight and this body was the end result. That was not far from the truth. The fight between Pettit and Silveria was started and ended over one bottle of beer, but the clash between these two transient titans might have happened over something else just as meaningless, because survival in their world is ruled by fear and mistrust.

The Linn County Sheriff's Department had the responsibility for conducting the investigation. The next day S.R. Fletcher, M.D. performed an autopsy on the body at the Fisher Funeral Home in Albany, Oregon. His findings revealed the victim had been murdered two days earlier, on December 1. A Southern Pacific Railroad computer tracking system determined the boxcar in which the body was found was part of a freight train that arrived in Salem, Oregon on November 18. The train left Salem on December 1, headed for Millersburg, where it arrived two days later. The victim, who had an arrest record, was identified by his fingerprints as William Avis Pettit, Jr. The responsibility for solving Pettit's murder fell on the Salem Police Department. The investigation was assigned to a forty year-old detective — Mike Quakenbush.

Solving the murder of a transient is tough. Most of these guys have been living apart from their families for a number of years. They also tend to move around a lot. Quakenbush located Pettit's father and stepmother living in South Carolina. The couple had lost touch with their son for a number of years and had no idea who his friends were or who he hung out with since he had dropped out to become a freight train rider. Quakenbush, however, did get a response to the teletype that he sent to police agencies to establish a travel history for Pettit and find out if any other police departments had similar homicides. Considering the number of teletypes that go in and out of police departments on a daily basis, his touched a rare chord.

Responses flooded in from a number of agencies, among them Flathead County Sheriff's Department in Montana, where Paul Wayne Matthew's shattered head had been found near a Burlington Northern rail yard, Detective Guy Yoshikawa in Salt Lake City Police Department in Utah where the murder case involving the young transient Hooter was still open and special agent Bruce Mellor, stationed at KBI headquarters in Topeka, Kansas. Personally, I think Mellor was the guiding force in providing direction to the other detectives and pushing them on.

Quakenbush wasted no time in contacting his counterparts in other places. One detective in Flathead County told Quakenbush that a murder victim in his area was beaten so hard that his brains were splattered on the ground. Yoshikawa called in and described that a victim in his territory who was stabbed and then beaten over the head with a board. KBI special agent Bruce Mellor told Quakenbush that his victim's head was smashed with a rock and then he was finished off with a blunt instrument.

Guy Yoshikawa and Bruce Mellor had already been in contact with each other and had phone discussions pertaining to their two open cases prior to telephoning Quakenbush. It was Yoshikawa who originally gave the KBI special agent, Mellor, Robert Silveria's name and his birthdate, which the Salt Lake City detective got from his county jail tracking system. Yoshikawa wanted to question Silveria, although he was not yet listed as an official suspect in James Lee "Hooter" Bowman's death.

When special agent Mellor first jotted down Silveria's birth date given to him by Yoshikawa, it didn't mean anything to him. He was searching for all the information about Lester Paul Dykeman he could find. But slowly more information was coming in.

Bruce Mellor recalls clearly the day he decided Silveria was behind the Boyd murder. It was a fall Saturday, about three months after Boyd was murdered. Mellor had gone to the KBI headquarters in Topeka, Kansas to catch up on some work, knowing that he would be alone, with no phone calls, pages or people coming in and out of his office.

Mellor opened the file on Charles Randall Boyd after finishing up some paper work on another case. He decided to review all the documents and information that had been gathered up to that time. He noted there were about fourteen different aliases collected. Among them was the name Robert Joseph Silveria, along with his birthdate. Detective Guy Yoshikawa had said that Silveria was the person he wanted to talk to about the murder in his city. By then, KBI investigators had obtained a description of the real Lester Paul Dykeman and it didn't match the man last seen with Boyd in Van Horn, Texas.

Mellor spread copies of the numerous identifications across his desk and studied them, his eyes roaming back and forth. Suddenly, he noticed something. All of the men, except for the "real" Lester Paul Dykeman, had the same date of birth. They each had a different social security number, but the birthdate listed didn't change. They also all had the same physical description, which did not match the real Lester Paul Dykeman, but matched the description Yoshikawa found through a tattoo belonging to Robert Joseph Silveria, Jr.

Mellor stopped reading. The twenty-year veteran at the KBI felt that the killer of Charles Randall Boyd was Robert Joseph Silveria, Jr. Further examination of records and interviews revealed that "Lester Paul Dykeman" had "freedom" tattooed on his neck. This revelation was another element that helped them identify Silveria and link the murders. From then on, the KBI special agent kept a look-out for teletypes on killings bearing similarities to the murder of Boyd. Another vital clue to finding Silveria was now in the possession of police. But one problem remained — finding the boxcar killer himself. Guys like Silveria don't stay in one place long. They can continue killing and acquiring new aliases for years, always staying one step ahead of the law. But this did not deter Quakenbush, Mellor or Yoshikawa from searching for the man. Silveria's second wife told me that about this time a local police officer came to see her and requested a photo of Robert, which she gave him.

12

Two Deadly Scorpions

"It's a dangerous group."
Robert Joseph Silveria, Jr.

Silveria was still in Oregon while the investigation into William Pettit's murder was escalating. He had arrived in Eugene from Klamath Falls at nightfall. He was looking for a train to hop that eventually would take him to Montana. Walking up towards the middle bridge in the rail yard with all his gear stacked on his back, he saw in the distance three men he recognized: Doc, Shaggy and Bam Bam. The latter was a Home Guard, one of the homeless who live and work in missions. They can be feisty and overbearing, but the FTRA call them pussies behind their back. As one soft core FTRA told me, "They can talk the talk, but can't walk the walk." Yet Bam Bam appeared happy to see Silveria, asking him where he had been.

The fourth man in the group was a stranger to Silveria. He looked to be no more than a kid in his mid-twenties, but he was exceptionally tall, towering over all the others. His blond mohawk accentuated his slender frame. Silveria noticed that the back of the young man's head beneath the mohawk was braided with strands of gypsy beads like Pettit's, only with shorter strands. This guy's hair was closely shaved on both sides above his ears and on one side, a tattoo of double lighting bolts was clearly visible. Some Elvis fans may take the tattoo to mean TCB, "Taking Care of Business," but in prison warfare it signifies a "hit" on a minority person. It's part of the Aryan Brotherhood pride in prison. One has to earn the double lightening bolts tattoo before it can be worn.

The blond kid's name turned out to be Mikey. He had a ten-inch knife in a sheath strapped to his leg. Silveria later learned that Mikey also carried a machete in his backpack. When Silveria walked up to the bridge, Mikey had just finished tattooing Bam Bam's forearm with a drawing of two crossed railroad tracks. The Home Guard was very proud and showed it off to Silveria. Silveria thought the men in the circle under the bridge appeared to have been drinking or involved in some other form of chemical recreation, but he wasn't sure. He was still feeling the effects of heroin he took earlier himself, but while he felt high, he also felt tired.

Bam Bam soon announced he wanted Silveria to be a witness to a business transaction between him and Mikey. "Look," Bam Bam said, "I'm going to trade a sleeping bag with Mikey."

Silveria, with his back and shoulders finally free from the gear he had dropped next to his feet, shrugged and said, "Okay."

Bam Bam was cautious. "Now look, I want you to witness this, because I don't want anyone to think this wasn't a fair deal." Stealing is often punishable by death along the rails and he didn't want anyone in the mission complaining to Silveria or his buddies that he cheated an FTRA member out of a good sleeping bag.

Mikey and Bam Bam were trading an old worn-out sleeping bag for a better quality one and Mikey was adding fifty dollars plus his old sleeping bag to make the transaction even. But there was a hitch. That night Mikey was riding to Roseville to get the fifty dollars, so he couldn't pick up his sleeping bag until he met up with Bam Bam in Vancouver.

The Home Guard asked Silveria where he was headed. Silveria said "Havre, Montana." Bam Bam and Doc then insisted that Silveria help out and ride with Mikey up to Vancouver since it was along the way. They told him that Mikey didn't know how to get back home and they couldn't help him, because they were on their way south to Roseville. When Mikey heard Silveria was going to Montana, he said he wanted to go there, too. Silveria looked down at his worn-out sleeping bag and told him to first pick up the new one he had just purchased from Bam Bam, because the one he had would not make it there. It was a nice way of Silveria getting rid of Mikey and stopping him from tagging along up to Havre. Silveria agreed to baby-sit the novice rail rider only to Vancouver. While the Flintstones are looked upon as a group promoting the oxymoron of anarchy without violence, the "Punk Rail Riders" have a reputation among the FTRA for violence and are rumored to be involved in prostitution. In Silveria's mindset, which was well known among many of his rail riding friends, he had no qualms about getting rid of "assholes" from the rails, such as rapists, pedophiles, drug dealers and anyone who challenged or threatened him. A ride with Mikey had best be as short as possible, in the interest of survival for both men. Having Silveria and Mikey in one box car was like putting two deadly male scorpions in one container.

While they were still standing with the group, Mikey asked Silveria if he knew where he could buy drugs. The young rail rider said he had gotten some earlier near the mission, but he wanted more. Silveria told Mikey where he could go to score, but warned him, "it's a dangerous group."

Then Silveria and Mikey separated from Bam Bam and the others. They walked towards a freight train headed for Vancouver. As they moved under a dark sky between freight trains parked along the tracks over uneven ground, Mikey bragged about the boots he was wearing. He had stolen them earlier in the day in a shopping mall. Silveria asked about the psycho monkey, a stuffed ape, attached to Mikey's backpack, which he had noticed earlier. Mikey told him, "I got it at a carnival I used to work at."

Silveria led Mikey to a gondola, a freight car that generally is used to transport grain and wood chips and is open on the top. Silveria didn't want to go into a boxcar with Mikey until his drug deal was completed. The gondola provided a more secure hiding place than a boxcar would, in case the drug deal went sour. In addition, Silveria didn't want to be alone in a boxcar guarding his and Mickey's gear where he could expose himself to possible robbery and assault.

The gondola Silveria found was stacked with aluminum cans. The two men spent some time looking for a piece of cardboard to protect their clothes and gear from the rust on the floor of the Gondola. When they couldn't find any, Silveria opened his backpack and pulled out a roll of plastic and they both climbed in with their belongings.

Then Mikey hesitated. He didn't want to go alone to make the drug deal. He even offered Silveria money just to go with him and leave both their gear hidden behind the high walls of the gondola, but Silveria said, "I'm not interested." When Mikey climbed out of the car, leaving his gear behind with Silveria, he was furious that Silveria refused to accompany him, but about one hour later, he was back announcing, "I got what I was looking for."

"Well then, let's go find a box." Silveria stood up and

began folding up his plastic roll and the two men left.

The boxcar they found was white with wooden floors. Both men rolled out their sleeping bags and got ready to settle in. Silveria wondered why Mikey had talked about getting crank at the mission earlier, but he hadn't seen him use it in the time they'd been together, nor had he offered Silveria any. At this point Silveria decided to leave Mikey to watch the gear while he went under a bridge to shoot up heroin. About an hour passed and Silveria started heading back to the boxcar, knowing the train was scheduled to leave for Vancouver. Suddenly, in the distance, he heard a man's voice calling out as if looking for someone.

As Silveria neared the train, a figure came out of the darkness and stepped toward him. The man, a Hispanic male, was about thirty-six or thirty-seven years of age, clean-cut hair, with a mustache and trimmed sideburns. He was wearing a camouflage army jacket. Aside from the way he was dressed, Silveria later said the man could pass for an office worker. He was carrying a piece of metal in one hand, but when he saw Silveria he pulled out a .44 Magnum and pointed it at Silveria's face. In good English with a slight accent, he told Silveria he was looking for a guy who ripped him off. Silveria recognized that the guy was Mikey. The guy asked Silveria where he was hiding. It was Silveria's turn to be annoyed at Mikey for placing him in this situation. Silveria knew that there was no way the dealer would have found their train unless Mikey told him they were going to Vancouver. Silveria knew he had to keep his cool. The guy wouldn't fire a hail of bullets into him just to make a point.

Silveria said nonchalantly, "Why would he rip you off? He could have made a mistake and given you the wrong money."

"I don't care what the reason was. I want my money." It was time to be practical. Silveria made a deal with the dealer that if he led him to Mikey, he would not rip Silveria's gear off.

The boxcar the dealer was interested in, the one with Mikey, was only three cars away. Silveria led the man with the gun to it. When the dealer jumped up onto to the boxcar, Mikey appeared to be fast asleep.

There was enough light from nearby street lamps for Silveria to see clearly what was happening inside the boxcar. He saw the dealer clobber Mikey with a piece of metal.

"Where's my money? Where's my money?" the dealer screamed. Silveria saw the dealer rip Mikey's medicine bag from his neck, still shouting and hitting Mikey with the iron bar. Mikey tried shielding himself, but managed to pull out his wallet, which the dealer grabbed.

"That's more like it," the dealer said. He threw the piece of metal pole he had used to beat Mikey on the floor of the boxcar and jumped out. Satisfied that he "got his," the dealer grinned at Silveria as he walked past him, counting the money he pulled out of the billfold.

Just then the train started to pull out of the rail yard. Silveria made a dash for the opened door. He jumped up and pulled himself onto the boxcar. Once inside, he walked over to Mikey and kneeled down beside him, touching Mikey's head with his hand.

"Man, what happened? Why'd you rip that guy off?" Silveria leaned down closer. Mikey was silent for a minute.

"Bullshit. You should have backed me up."

"The dude had a gun on me. Man, you shouldn't have ripped him off like that." Suddenly, Silveria noticed Mikey's ten-inch knife lying on the other side, by his head. He was surprised to see Mikey reach beneath his roll and pull out his machete.

"I'm wounded now, but one of us isn't going to wake up in the morning." Mikey stared fiercely at Silveria, tapping the machete against the wooden floor boards. Silveria leaned back and then stood up. He noticed that his gear had been moved. This meant that Mikey had gone through his pack when he was gone.

What did he pull out? Silveria wondered. Was his 9mm gun still inside the backpack, or did Mikey have it? Silveria thought about Mikey's threat. *He doesn't know who the hell I am, but he is about to find out.*

The train increased speed, pulling out fast, creating an ear-blasting cacophony. The boxcar swayed sideways. Silveria noticed the metal bar rolling back and forth near the boxcar door. Mikey continued tapping his machete against the floor. Every once in awhile, he looked up in Silveria's direction. Moving toward the edge of the open boxcar door, Silveria stared outside at the moving scenery and the nighttime landscape. Taking a deep breath he said, "Well, it looks like this train is going to Portland and..."

Mikey interrupted him, "My head is hurting right here, man..." Suddenly Mikey paused. He watched Silveria swiftly lean down and pick up the weapon the dealer had used on him earlier. His voice tensed. "What are you going to do?" Mikey looked stunned as Silveria moved closer, casting a shadow over him, shutting out the lights from the factories they were passing.

"I'm gonna clobber you with this pipe." Silveria stepped closer. All his hate and fury burst out. Raising his arm, he began beating Mikey's face. When he stopped, he leaned out of the boxcar and saw they were passing a body of water. Twirling the metal tube towards the stream, Silveria looked down at Mikey's bloody head. The boxcar rattled, shaking back and forth, causing the victim's body to vibrate with the roll of the wheels. Silveria thought he saw Mikey tapping the machete by his side again, mocking him as he had before. Furious, Silveria picked up one of the boards in the box car and began pounding Mikey over the head again.

Suddenly the words Silveria had been unable to forget began resounding in his brain. "Take a number and go to the mission," he kept repeating, striking Mikey's face again and again. Finally, he stopped. It occurred to him that Mikey might be dead. Silveria leaned down to see if Mikey was breathing. There were no signs of life. Silveria tried pushing Mikey's chest to revive him, but it was too late. Mikey's face was caved in from the force of the strikes and beatings. Only four days after murdering William Pettit, Robert Silveria had another bloody body with which to deal.

Quickly, Silveria went through Mikey's backpack and found the clip from his handgun that the younger man had pulled out earlier when he went snooping through Silveria's back pack. As the train moved towards Portland, Silveria threw out all of Mikey's belongings. Among them was the backpack, which Silveria couldn't keep, because too many people knew what it looked like. Covering Mikey with the sleeping bag, Silveria took the gypsy beads from his hair and his boots. When the train stopped outside of Portland, Silveria jumped off and spent a day laying low. The next day he hopped a train to Vancouver. Once in Vancouver, he went to the mission and saw Bam Bam, the Home Guard, sitting by himself behind a counter and glass windows. Silveria was surprised to find him there. Bam Bam had said he was going to Roseville. Bam Bam, seeing Silveria, pushed up the window and said, "Mikey was found dead."

"I don't know what you're talking about. I'm just here to use the phone," Silveria said nervously. He strode from the mission and walked two blocks to a public phone booth. Calling a cab to take him to a small airport near the railroad tracks, he hid out, waiting to catch out to Havre, Montana.

The Union Pacific Railroad police found Mikey's body on December 6 in the white boxcar on the east side of the Willamette River in Portland. The killer had removed the victim's shoes and covered up the head, which looked like a one-ton boulder fell on it, before departing. As in the other murders on the rails, the word "freedom" was written on the boxcar wall.

The victim was soon identified as twenty-four-year-old Michael Andrew Clites, from Hillsboro, a town twenty minutes away by car from Portland. He was described as six-foot-four inches tall, thin and heavily decorated with tattoos. He had an arrest record, had been married and was the father of a toddler.

When Mike Quakenbush saw the teletype come in on Clites' death, he realized the similarities between Clites' murder and Pettit's were too close to be ignored. Both were bludgeoned inside a boxcar, both had shoes missing and both times the word freedom had been written on the wall. The two murders appeared to be the work of one individual.

Quakenbush contacted Kerry Taylor, a Portland Police Bureau detective assigned to the case. The two compared notes and attended the autopsy. The Union Pacific Railroad computer tracking system revealed that the boxcar in which Clites' body was found was part of a train that left Eugene, Oregon the night of December 5.

Quakenbush and Taylor drove up to Eugene to interview transients in the vicinity of the city's vast network of rail yards. The detectives found a group of them huddled in a box car and showed the men photos of Pettit and Clites. One of the men told the detectives that he recalled seeing Clites at a mission in Vancouver, Washington on December 4. He had cashed a disability check for three hundred dollars.

Kerry and Quakenbush traveled up north again, this time to the Share House Mission in Vancouver. There the two detectives found Tom Alman, aka Bam Bam, who told them that he was teaching Clites, a newcomer, to ride trains, but that Clites had wanted to buy drugs. Clites left with another train hopper, Sidetrack, who had told the victim he knew where to score. Tom told Quakenbush and Kerry that Sidetrack returned afterwards to Vancouver alone without Mikey and when asked about him, Sidetrack said that the two of them had separated. The information they obtained from their new witness placed Clites with Sidetrack within one hour of the brutal murder.

At about the same time, Silveria too was in Vancouver. A friend of his, TNT, later told me that he recalls detectives coming to a camp in which he and Silveria were hanging out with a group of other rail riders. They asked for identifications and if anyone knew either Sidetrack or Robert Silveria. TNT said that Silveria gave the officers one of his phony identifications. He figured Silveria's clean-shaven and neat appearance and demeanor made him convincing. None of the other men there told the agents they were talking to Silveria. Rail riders don't rat on their members, but in confidence, some have told me that Silveria told them about the murders. They were his idea to keep the rails clean of scumbags and to attack before he got attacked. Now they claim that they didn't take him seriously, not even when, on moving boxcars, he pointed out spots where he recalled throwing out bodies. It wasn't until they read in the papers about all the killings that they realized what Silveria had told them was true. One rail rider, who didn't want his name revealed and was not a member of FTRA, but who has many friends in the group, said Silveria was a quiet guy, but also a mean drunk.

The investigation was moving ahead. Quakenbush was now looking for Robert Silveria *and* Sidetrack. He checked Silveria's name against the records of law enforcement divisions of Southern Pacific Railroad, Union Pacific Railroad, Burlington Northern Railroad and Santa Fe Railroad. He learned that four days before Pettit's murder, Robert Silveria was stopped and identified in a Southern Pacific Rail yard in Klamath Falls, Oregon. Quakenbush's immediate supervisor, Sergeant Detective James Miller, told the detective that he learned from the Oregon Adult and Family Services that Silveria had applied for public assistance in Eugene three days before Pettit's murder.

This information was significant because of its reference to Silveria's movements. Klamath Falls is 225 miles south of Salem, Oregon and Eugene is about sixty miles south of Salem. It became apparent that Silveria was in the Salem area around the date of Pettit's murder. Still thinking that he was looking for two different men somehow connected to the crime, Quakenbush put out another teletype in mid-January to various railroad police agencies requesting that, should any of their agents have contact with Robert Silveria, Jr. or Sidetrack or any of the other aliases listed, they contact the Salem Police Department.

To his dismay, Quakenbush learned that someone fitting the description in his teletype had been stopped and released in Roseville, California on January 13. One month later, on February 13, Silveria was in Colton, California, where another violent confrontation would take place. This time, Silveria played a secondary role in the murder.

Colton and Fremont are hundreds of miles apart. Fremont is in the San Francisco Bay area; Colton is northeast of Los Angeles and part of the Bernardino and Riverside metropolis, located inland between the San Bernardino and San Gabriel Mountains. Railroads played a significant factor in the development of both towns, but it was in Colton in the late 1800s that two transcontinental rail lines crossed each other's tracks for the first time: Southern Pacific and the California Southern railroads, a subsidiary of the Santa Fe Railway. Colton was actually named after a Southern Pacific official. It was in Colton that Virgil Earp, the former marshal of Tombstone, who is responsible for many of the feats attributed to his younger brother, Wyatt Earp, made history again. He was elected Colton's first city marshal in 1887. Today the city remains an important distribution and shipping point. It is also popular with rail riders making connections in Southern California. This is what brought eighteen-year-old Quincy Dear from Fremont to Colton and a world of trouble.

Quincy was sitting in the middle of the tracks, slumped over, his head facing west and his feet on the tracks, pointed east, when a Southern Pacific engine pulling a series of four locomotive engines ran him over. The engineer and conductor each saw a form from the distance, but they thought they were looking at debris, which is common for engines to encounter en route. It was shortly after two o'clock in the morning and Quincy had on dark clothing, which added to the problem of visibility. As the train neared the object, the conductor saw it wasn't debris. The conductor shouted, "Plug it," meaning stop the engine. By that time the engineer also realized that the object they saw was a person crouched between the tracks. Although he pushed on the brakes it was too late; the so-called "light load" of four locomotives he was carrying made it impossible to stop. The train was going at the legal speed limit of thirty miles per hour, but being hit with that kind of force is equivalent to being thrown off the top story of a three-story building. According to the engineer, the person on the tracks did not move or react to the approaching train. What no one knew at the time was that the man on the tracks was already dead.

Within minutes of the accident, police and paramedics arrived and the latter pronounced the victim dead. Railroad officials also came to the scene. The coroner arrived shortly afterwards to remove the battered body. Quincy's severed right bare foot was found lying a few feet from the tracks. His body had been thrown off the tracks by the oncoming freight train; there were deep lacerations on his skull and back; blood was found in both ears. Police at first thought the death a suicide.

At the autopsy the coroner determined that no alcohol or drugs were in the victim's system. The victim measured five feet and nine inches and weighed about 141 pounds, with brown hair and eyes and a fair complexion. Quincy's identity was learned through his fingerprints. It turned out that Quincy had past scrapes with the law and was well known in the Fremont Police Department. Colton Police found out that the teenager's father was deceased and the whereabouts of his mother were unknown. His next of kin, his stepmother, had been Quincy's legal guardian since the boy was a toddler. They notified her of his death.

Quincy's stepmother did not buy the story that Quincy was suicidal. She told police he had been riding the rails for only two months and she would have his friend, Jared, who was traveling with him, call the Colton police. The next day, Colton investigators received a telephone call from Jared. Like Quincy's stepmother, Jared insisted Quincy was not suicidal and that he didn't drink alcohol, but occasionally smoked marijuana. He told them he and several other riders were sleeping in a boxcar when a railroad police officer woke them up and told them to get out. Looking around, Jared saw that Quincy was gone, but his gear was left behind so Jared thought his friend must have gone out for a walk. He took Quincy's gear so that the railroad police wouldn't confiscate it and found a ditch where he slept through the night. At six o'clock the next morning, Jared awoke and started looking for Quincy. He said he ran into several transients who told him Quincy hopped a train to Bakersfield the night before. Jared told the police that he got on a train to Bakersfield to look for Quincy, but he never found him. It wasn't until he got back to Fremont that he learned Quincy was dead. The account Jared gave the police did not ring true to any of the investigators.

I felt Jared was not telling everything he knew to the police. Most likely, he was afraid of the members of the FTRA. First, he claimed he had assumed his friend took off for Bakersfield without his gear, based on what some transients told him. Even a novice rider would have thought that was suspicious. When somebody gets run over by a train or murdered on the tracks, the news spreads almost instantly. Jared was sleeping not too far away in a ditch. The idea that he couldn't hear the sirens of police and ambulance wasn't plausible. With all the commotion going on in the area, why hadn't he woken up?

Colton police investigators soon learned that Quincy had informed on Cowboy, an FTRA rail rider, about food stamp irregularities. Food stamps are the mainstay of FTRA existence. I believe Quincy, who had a mother to turn to and was still living at home, didn't have the street smarts to understand the dangerous game into which he stepped. Nor did he know what a vicious bunch these FTRA guys can be. He must have felt at ease around the FTRA rail riders, because as one man said, Quincy, Jared, Cowboy, California Spud and Silveria were near the railroad tracks cooking plants or seeds with gypsum weed, which produces a hallucinogenic state. Cowboy and the others walked Quincy to the rail tracks and it was alleged by "hostile" witnesses that Cowboy killed the teenager with a machete. Quincy was left on the tracks to be run over by the train to make it look like an accident or a suicide. Afterwards, Silveria, California Spud and Cowboy went to a mini market behind a bridge. There, Cowboy used a faucet behind the store to wash the blood off his hands and the machete. Afterwards, the men divided the items they had found in Quincy Dear's backpack. Silveria kept the boy's BB gun, which could have passed for a real weapon, and some other items.

Today Cowboy is still out there riding the rails. Two softcore FTRA members, with whom I met not long ago in Merced, California, told me Cowboy was down in Texas keeping warm. After Quincy's death, FTRA were swarming all over the Roseville rail yard. Mike Quakenbush figured he would have another chance now that he knew the alleged killer used the rail yard to change trains and that it would be just a matter of time before either Silveria or Sidetrack would pass through

Roseville again. To make certain that the rail yard police in Roseville were vigilantly looking for the "two" men he wanted to question, every week or so Quakenbush phoned the railyard police to check if they encountered anyone identified as Robert Silveria or Sidetrack or any of the aliases the wanted men were using: Brad Foster, Lester Paul Dykeman, Paul Wayne Matthews and Charles Boyd. They were getting closer, but not close enough.

13

Closing In

"God will forgive me for everything."
Robert Joseph Silveria Jr.

On Sunday, February 28, 1996, it was raining heavily outside the Roseville soup kitchen and Robert Silveria was back in town. Unfortunately for Mike Quakenbush, the people he was counting on in his search for the killer of Clites and Pettit, the rail security agents, didn't know that Silveria was there. Jenny Taylor, however, noticed him. As one newspaper reporter described him, "Silveria was ruggedly handsome, six feet tall, 180 pounds and appeared to be well-fed and in good shape." He was soft spoken and, like many train-hoppers, easy to converse with. Jenny, a blond-haired homeless woman living out of her old green car with her dog Daffodil, was short and busty, with a smoker's raspy voice. Her manner and face reflected her life on the hard edge. Silveria started the conversation using the "didn't we meet before" opening when he and Jenny waited in line at the Roseville soup kitchen. Jenny didn't remember the meeting he was talking about, but said she did notice him around town.

"I saw you once with Bobby Joy," she told Silveria, referring to a young woman staying in one of the FTRA safe houses in Roseville run by a woman known by the moniker of Forty-Pounder. Safe houses offered transients temporary escape from brutal weather conditions and a place to hang out with others and make contact with old friends. Forty-Pounder's place was one of a half dozen tiny bungalows lined up around a small parking lot. It was hidden from the street and could be reached only through an alleyway.

When Jenny had seen Baby Girl and Silveria, they were sitting very close together by the White Methodist Church on Washington Boulevard and Main Street counting food stamps. At the time she thought the two appeared to be a couple, because of how close they were, but she didn't say anything to Silveria about it now. Their exchange was light and jovial. Jenny didn't want to break the moment with questions that were none of her business. Silveria asked Jenny if she liked his new boots. "Yeah, they're nice," she told him, unaware that they had once belonged to Michael Clites, one of Silveria's recent victims. Silveria mentioned he was heading to the Roseville Post Office area to catch a train out of town. Like typical rail riders, Silveria was loaded down with heavy gear, in this case his huge pack and a smaller maroon backpack. Jenny said she was going that way to pick up her mail and offered to give him a lift.

After they finished lunch, Jenny led Silveria to her vehicle. It was cold and drizzling when Silveria threw his gear into the back seat of Jenny's car. "Why are you leaving town?" she asked, as they drove towards the post office. Silveria explained that he had been investigated for a murder that occurred in Vancouver on the Burlington Northern Railroad tracks. He claimed the sheriff's office there took his fingerprints and plaster casts of the boots he was wearing at the time. But neither the fingerprints nor the boot casts matched those found on the homicide scene and they had to release him.

"I need to get back to clear some more things up," Silveria told her.

Jenny dropped Silveria near the post office and parked her car nearby. Climbing out of her vehicle, she started walking towards the white post office building when she saw Soda Pop, whom she had met at the mission. He was coming out of Duffy's Liquors, waving and shouting, "Hey, Sidetrack." He was accompanied by Forty-Pounder, with whom Soda Pop lived, and Baby Girl. Silveria looked up at the mention of his name and crossed the street towards them. Jenny paused to rummage through her handbag for her mailbox key, looking up occasionally to watch Soda Pop, who she knew was an FTRA member. Then she stood there briefly watching as the four people walked down the street in the opposite direction.

The same day, late in the afternoon, Jenny was driving down Washington Street on the other side of the Roseville railroad tracks when she spotted Silveria walking under a wide culvert with a large pack. She was surprised to see him by himself. She pulled her car to the side of the road and waited for him to approach.

"Where are you going?" she called, leaning toward the passenger side with the window rolled down.

"I don't know where I'm going." Silveria leaned down, grinning at her weakly through the open window. Jenny invited Silveria to hop in. For the second time that day Silveria got into Jenny's car, placing his pack in the rear of the car next to her cocker spaniel. Jenny noticed that his mood appeared subdued and no longer peppy as it was earlier at the mission.

"Are you all right?" she asked.

He told Jenny that he had been at Forty-Pounder's for a while and that she, Soda Pop and others there warned him that the word was out on him and that he was wanted for questioning in three homicide investigations up north. He insisted to Jenny, "I didn't do any of them. I'm being set up." Jenny drove around for a while with Silveria, listening to him as he unfolded his problems to her. She finally found a desolate spot and parked the car where they could have some peace from the noise of moving traffic and she could be free to focus on him. It became obvious to her that he was a deeply troubled man.

Silveria told Jenny he planned to turn himself in up north for the murder of a guy found bludgeoned to death in a boxcar, even though he didn't do it. "There's nothing to hide," he told Jenny. He said that one day, coming from a mission, three guys approached him and asked where they could buy some drugs. Silveria said he gave them a name of a dealer and the directions as to where they could find him, but he didn't go with them. Later he heard through the FTRA grapevine that he was being described as the last person seen with the victim, who turned out to be one of the three men who approached him earlier. Silveria claimed it wasn't him, but another guy, who went with the young victim to buy the drugs. Silveria also told Jenny that the victim had been beaten beyond recognition.

"Well, honey, what are you going to do? You can't run for the rest of your life," Jenny said and looked sympathetically at her passenger. "You got to go and straighten your life out," she added gently.

Silveria's story changed at this point. "I didn't do it all by myself," Silveria repeated extensively and insistently. He told Jenny that it wasn't fair that the cops had singled him out. "There were three guys in the boxcar when the victim was killed," he said.

The couple sat talking for several hours. Silveria breaking into occasional sobs, while Jenny tried comforting him, but all she could advise him to do was to go and clear his name. During the course of the evening, not once did Jenny feel she needed to get away from Silveria. Even though she noticed a gun in his backpack, the thought that he could do her bodily harm never crossed her mind.

"I'd be lying if I told you I ever felt afraid of him," she told me later. "It was quite the contrary." The two moved to the back seat where they had sex. By then the grey dismal sky had turned dark, casting a deep shadow over the car.

After they finished, Jenny realized that it had been a long time since either of them had eaten. She offered to take Silveria out to dinner and he seemed pleased by the invitation and accepted. But first, Jenny drove Silveria to her storage facility where she pulled out some warm clothing for him to take up north where the weather was more severe. The homeless woman, who had so little herself, also gave him canned food to take with him for the trip and five dollars. Then they drove down to a small restaurant where she bought them both dinner. Afterwards they sat talking for a couple of hours before she gave him a ride to the railroad tracks. Before they parted, Silveria told Jenny that there was a contract out on his life. She asked him why and he told her that it was because he would not rob and kill people for his group in the FTRA. She said he told her he had been an FTRA member, but that he quit because he did not want to rob and kill people. Jenny asked about the handgun she had seen in his maroon daypack earlier. Silveria shrugged, claiming that he had it for protection because of the contract on his life. At about two o'clock in the morning, before he took off to catch out, he turned to Jenny and said, "You're one of the nicest people I have ever known."

In the early hours of the morning, Jenny watched as Silveria jumped aboard an outbound train heading to Vancouver. It was not until she returned to her car that she noticed he had left his maroon daypack behind in her vehicle. She was relieved to find that his gun was no longer there. Figuring she would see him again, she took the backpack to her storage unit and locked it up with her other possessions.

Less than two weeks later, Silveria was back in Roseville. A black rail hopper, New York Slim, was walking past the railroad tracks near Silveria's camp, heading towards the Roseville mission when he saw Silveria stumble out of his campsite looking dazed and disheveled. New York Slim would later become a media personality along with Dogman Tony, appearing in a film documentary and in a magazine article on train hopping. It was attention that would be brought on in part by Silveria's infamy. But that day he was concerned not only by Silveria's appearance but by his aggressive behavior.

As New York Slim drew nearer to the camp, Silveria eyed him, his features twisted in torment. "I never killed fucking nobody in my life," he hollered at the black train hopper. "I never killed fucking nobody in my life." His voice rose higher and higher. Maybe Silveria had heard that New York Slim was passing around a story that one time he and Silveria got so stoned that Silveria wanted to kill the local bull in Klamath Falls and steal his white truck, but New York Slim stopped him. By then, many of the seasoned rail riders were avoiding being alone with Silveria. New York Slim, whose six-foot-six frame gave him an advantage few rail riders could best in a fight, did the same. He strode silently past Silveria, totally ignoring him, even though in the past the two had hung out together. He didn't need someone else's problems. He had plenty of his own.

New York Slim continued walking, increasing the distance between Silveria's shouts and himself until he could no longer hear the echoes of the ghosts in Silveria's mind cry out. Later in the day, New York Slim encountered Soda Pop in the

Roseville mission and told Soda Pop how he had seen Silveria, who was acting weird. Soda Pop told Slim he did well to move on and not stop. He said Silveria tried to get Soda Pop to go with him alone to a secluded area, but there was "no way" he was going to go anywhere alone with Silveria.

There is no doubt that Silveria now saw his world caving in. He knew by then law enforcement agencies across the country were looking for him as a suspect in homicides and that members of his own group, the FTRA, were spreading the word that Sidetrack had crossed the line, falling into the deep end of madness.

The following evening Silveria went to the home of Forty Pounder, whom Jenny had seen meeting up with Silveria the afternoon Jenny dropped him off near the post office. Forty-Pounder was a pretty but chunky woman, who had a preference for flowing, loose fitted dresses hanging down to her ankles. The lines etched in her forehead confirmed a hard life. When Silveria walked into her safe house, he followed FTRA custom and signed a flag hanging on the wall. Sitting down by the door, he looked to Forty-Pounder to be spun out, wired, as if he was high on methamphetamine. He talked fast. She didn't say much to him. There was another infamous rail rider in her home that night, who few people ever see, but many talked about. Bushman had ridden the rails with some of the deadliest FTRA members. He was a short, black train hopper with smooth features. He himself was wanted for questioning in Texas along with Dogman. Although Bushman and Dogman were rumored to be rivals and therefore unlikely to join together in crime, information from FTRA members can be twisted and misleading. There were also rumors that he was one of the members of the Death Squad.

You wouldn't think that a guy like Bushman could be afraid of anything, but that night Forty-Pounder noticed that he looked troubled by Silveria's presence. Later Bushman pulled Forty-Pounder aside and told her he saw Silveria pull out a handgun from his backpack. "I don't like the idea of a gun in the safe house," he said. "Silveria doesn't look stable to me." Forty-Pounder agreed with Bushman that something needed to be done to protect and respect the sanctity of the safe house. Bushman took Silveria aside and talked him into leaving. The FTRA handle an individual they think is "51-50" (police code for someone crazy) by isolating him from the rest of the group. Silveria was being shunned by his own brotherhood of train riders. Meanwhile, the law was closing in on him. Silveria didn't return to Forty-Pounder's safe house again. He remained in the campground when he was in Roseville. Yet the irony of it was that no one was going to turn him in. If he wanted to ride the rails until a younger enforcer came along to eliminate him, he could have. He was protected under the unwritten law of the FTRA.

14

The Cry for Punishment

"I know I am an animal. I know the cops will
treat me as an animal. They better because I'm not
well. I will kill again and again."
Robert Joseph Silveria, Jr.

Maybe some men are born under a "testy" star. It seems to be true in Silveria's case. Isolated for years from his family, he slowly isolated himself from the Brotherhood that over the years had come to be his other family. His rage — a wild, hungry beast gnawing inside of him — was wearing him down. At the same time, haunting images of faceless men covered in blood, whose trinkets he carried in the Indian-leather pouch around his neck, followed him like shadows. He later told people that after the murders his hands hurt for days. According to Silveria, when the killings were over he sat and read the Bible trying to find salvation. It never came. He was stuck in a nightmare that no booze or drug had the power to obscure.

On March 2, 1996, the evening before his thirty-seventh birthday, Silveria, who knew by this time that the police were looking for him, did something that betrayed his inner turmoil, an act that was a sure way to call attention to himself. Typically, rail riders hide from the rail police. They may not always be successful, but they don't go out walking on or near railroad property in the open. But that's just what Robert Silveria did.

At nightfall, Silveria left his camp and wandered down towards the Roseville Southern Pacific Railroad yard, crossing the tracks with a stuffed backpack over his shoulder and moving with determined steps. Every hardcore freight train rider knows the bulls' names in the rail yards he travels through. He knows which guys to avoid like the plague and which ones will give him a break. In California, the railroad special agents are commissioned peace officers and given authority under the governor. They are covered by the laws of arrest and search and seizure, which are just as binding on railroad police officers as they are on public officers, except the former work for private companies.

Around the same time, an old-time Roseville railroad police officer, Billie Metcalf, only three years away from his retirement, was driving a Dodge Ram police truck in the vicinity. One hour later he would be signing off to be replaced by the night shift officer, but first he wanted to check the area out. He had been in contact with Mike Quakenbush and received a flyer from Bruce Mellor that fit the description of a man he had stopped on January 13, 1996. It contained Silveria's name and his aliases. In checking his own notes, Metcalf saw that the name of the man he had stopped was Lester Paul Dykeman, one of the aliases for which he was asked to be on the lookout.

He and Quakenbush had spoken numerous times when Quakenbush called the Roseville Security Office to remind the

officers how important it was to stop the man who called himself Robert Silveria, Sidetrack, Lester Paul Dykeman or Brad
Foster.

During this period, Mike Quakenbush, Mellor, Yoshikawa and Flathead County Detective Mike Sward in Montana
kept in touch, discussing their cases with each other extensively.
Mellor and Quakenbush had already traveled to Montana to
interview Dogman Tony to no avail. But they did not make a
connection between Silveria and the FTRA even though
Yoshikawa was aware of the existence of the FTRA and Mike
Sward learned about the group from some internal reports that
a Burlington Northern security agent gave him. Part of the reason for this was Mellor, a senior member of the group and a
strong guiding force, who was unaware of the FTRA. In addition, there is only one north and south line running through
Kansas and Boyd's murder had nothing to do with the rails. As
a result, the focus rested on catching one man.

The four detectives on the lookout for Silveria, in particular Mike Quakenbush and Bruce Mellor, did not have enough
for a warrant for Silveria's arrest, but they wanted to get him
into custody for questioning. They learned there was a warrant
out for Silveria in Cleveland, Mississippi for auto theft and one
for parole violation in Plumas County, California, which could
be used to stop him. Meanwhile, Quakenbush was still looking
for Sidetrack and still thinking he was a different individual than
Silveria. Quakenbush hoped one or the other might answer
some critical questions about his case. Mike maintained peri-
odic contact with Metcalf, hoping one or the other of his suspects would be stopped when passing through Roseville. And
then came the critical moment that would turn events around.

Looking out his car window, Billie Metcalf recognized
Silveria as the same man he had stopped less than two months
before, who might be the same man Bruce Mellor and Quak-

enbush were interested in. Metcalf drove his Dodge Ram alongside Silveria and brought it to a halt.

"I believe I know you. What's your name?" Metcalf said through the rolled down window of his truck.

Silveria walked over to the driver's side of the truck, looking up at Metcalf with his sharp, blue eyes and replied, "My name is Dykeman."

That's all Metcalf needed to hear. He jumped out of his truck and stood face to face with Silveria. He told Silveria that he wasn't sure, but he thought there was a warrant out for Silveria's, alias Dykeman's, arrest. "Please accompany me to my office so I can check it out." When Metcalf said this, Silveria was not standing on railroad property. If he wanted to, he could have said "No" and walked on. There was nothing Metcalf could do to him legally at the time and Silveria knew this.

Instead of objecting, Silveria said, "Yes, Mr. Metcalf, I would be glad to go with you." Later he would reveal that there were doubts running through his mind when he walked around the truck to the passenger side of the vehicle. As he walked, he reached into his backpack and pulled out his gun. For a moment he felt the stirring of rage inside him. His fingers itched to pull the trigger. Perspiration beads crowned his forehead. It crossed his mind that maybe a goon stick would be better, because it wouldn't make as much noise and attract attention. He also could use his buck knife. He knew he had to decide quickly, while he still had the advantage and an easy escape route. The urge to kill was overwhelming. But then something stopped him from pulling the trigger. "It was God," Silveria would later tell me. He said he knew there and then that he had to make peace with the Almighty.

I feel that Silveria's decision to resist his temptation to kill did not spring up suddenly that day at dusk, when Billie

Metcalf stopped him, but developed gradually. However, with the help of God, it was the most critical element he would ever embrace to free himself from the self-imposed curse that had haunted him for so long.

A few moments later Silveria dropped the 9mm to the ground and kicked it under the Dodge Ram truck. With a far-away look in his eyes, Silveria said, "I *will* this to you." Puzzled, Metcalf looked at him. He watched Silveria closely as the man put his pack in the rear of the vehicle and climbed into the passenger side of the truck. The agent thought Silveria's comment was strange and Metcalf noticed a glazed, hypnotized look in the man's eyes.

"Buckle up," Metcalf ordered gently. "It's company policy." Silveria put on his seat belt, the railroad policeman stepped on the gas pedal and the two made small talk as Metcalf drove the six miles back to his office. Silveria told him he was coming from his camp along the river by Sacramento Street when Metcalf stopped him. This was quite a distance and Metcalf thought perhaps the man was just tired. Otherwise, Metcalf recalled later, Silveria's demeanor was calm and non-threatening.

Once they arrived at Metcalf's office, the rail yard officer asked Silveria if he was thirsty. Silveria said, "Yes." Metcalf got him a soda and asked Silveria to sit down, pointing to a chair by his desk. He explained to Silveria that he would have to make a telephone call, "In fact," he added, "I have to make a couple of telephone calls." Silveria shrugged and said that was fine with him. The first phone call Metcalf made was to Detective Quakenbush, informing him that Lester Paul Dykeman was in Roseville. He asked if Salem had a warrant for Dykeman's arrest. Quakenbush told him there wasn't one in Salem, but he thought there might be one in Mississippi that was extraditable. Quakenbush was heading out to Yuba City the following day, less than forty-five miles north of Roseville. The detective told Metcalf, "I'll get there as soon as I can to interview Dykeman, but it will probably be a couple of days."

After hanging up, Metcalf turned to Silveria and asked if he had ever been to Mississippi or had anything going on there. Silveria shook his head and said, "No."

Then Metcalf went one step further. "Is it true that your name is Robert Joseph Silveria?"

Silveria nodded and said, "Yes." He told Metcalf that he had purchased the name Lester Paul Dykeman for food stamps from a man in Oregon and that he was using the name Dykeman rather than Silveria because of child support payments he couldn't afford. Metcalf phoned the Roseville Police Department and asked them to run Silveria's name. He found that there was a felony warrant on him from Plumas County, California and Metcalf asked Roseville Police for a transport.

Then Metcalf turned to Silveria. "There is a warrant out for you and I am placing you under arrest." He said a transport unit he requested was coming in from the Roseville Police Department. Silveria appeared to take the news calmly.

"Now, stand up, empty your pockets and put all of their contents on my desk." Silveria complied. After handcuffing him, Billie Metcalf read Silveria his Miranda rights. He also pulled out Silveria's backpack from the back of the truck and gave it to the evidence officer. He knew from previous experience that cops and deputies liked to book people, but not their packs. Sometimes officers get lazy. They don't like going through someone's backpack or bag, because it entails documenting everything they find and that's extra paperwork. In Silveria's case, the potential for a crime investigation gold mine made it worthwhile.

Within ten minutes of Silveria's handcuffing, two black and white units from the Roseville Police arrived, one of them a

K-9 unit with a dog in the back. After Roseville police officers picked up Silveria, he was transported and booked at the Placer County Sheriff's Department in Auburn, a short distance from Roseville. His backpack, which contained some evidence of the killings in Oregon, was left behind in the evidence locker at the rail yard.

The buzz over Silveria's arrest created as big a stir along the rails, in hobo jungles and safe houses as it did among law enforcement. Rumors spread that it was a shock for FTRA groups to hear or read that Sidetrack was suspected of committing a multitude of unexplained murders. Or so they said when questioned. But I think their unease was created by the fact that Silveria exposed them and their lifestyle. Food stamps are the mainstay of the group. Traveling through different states and collecting them is how most of these homeless transients survive. The portrayal of Silveria in the media as the "Boxcar Serial Killer" who went around killing his "own kind" for shoes and food stamps was disconcerting. His FTRA buddies knew Silveria killed and they fully understood that he was not unique in that regard. One guy, a rail riding buddy of Silveria, told me that occasionally guys got thrown off moving boxcars just to see the expression on their faces.

The media probably picked up its cues about Silveria from the officers interviewing him and I think that part of the problem was that we didn't quite understand how deeply his troubles ran. Silveria was so calm when he spoke about the murders and sometimes he was so matter of fact when he described how he killed someone and took his shoes and I.D. for food stamps that we didn't understand the deeper madness behind the actions, even though he talked about his rage. One day, years after Silveria was locked up in Oregon State Penitentiary, I met with Roseville Police Officer Mike Allison at his station. Mike, a tall, broad shouldered guy with dancing blue eyes, was a detective at the time of Silveria's capture. When Allison was involved in investigations, the Roseville Police Department was located in the hub of downtown. The department later moved to a large, fort-like modern structure on the outskirts of town. Meeting Allison at the new police headquarters, he was dressed in the full uniform of a motorcycle cop. Our meeting was brief but very productive. As we stepped out of the new Roseville police building into the sunshine, still talking about Silveria's case, Allison suddenly paused and turned to face me.

"One time he wanted to show me his rage and what happened to him," Allison said.

"What do you mean show you?" I inquired.

"Silveria said, 'Let me show you what happens to me when I get into that state.'" Mike leaned closer. "He said, 'Just go to a safe spot away from me where I can see you, but I can't touch you, where you'll be totally safe and I'll show you what happens when I get into this rage.'" Mike paused, nodding at my dumfounded expression.

Quickly I asked, "Did you videotape it?"

"Nah." Allison shook his head disappointedly. He explained that the powers that be, in this case the jail commander, were worried about liability issues.

"Typical, liability fears," I said and shook my head.

"But," Allison continued, "they could have placed Silveria in a padded room where, as you said, he could have been observed through a video camera. I would even have had in there a department psychologist or psychiatrist, someone from the DA to observe him from a monitor. He wanted us to understand him and the changes he went through from Dr. Jekyll into Mr. Hyde."

I left Mike Allison, thanking him for all his help. His information about Silveria wanting someone to see his rage from a safe vantage point kept ringing in my mind. It was interesting that he singled Mike out to stand in the distance to watch him change into a beast. Mike Allison became heavily involved in interviews with Silveria during the week-and-a-half Silveria was incarcerated in Placer County, before Mike Quakenbush had Silveria extradited to Oregon. Quakenbush didn't meet the prisoner until the third day of his arrest, because Silveria's thirty-seventh birthday and second day of captivity was spent in an infirmary going through detoxification. Robert Silveria told Mike Allison later that he actually went through detoxification about a month earlier in Vancouver and hadn't touched any heroin since. Silveria, when we spoke, told me the same thing and recalled coming out of the tremors telling the nurse that he killed people. "Don't worry," she said. "It's just the drugs leaving your system. You'll be all right."

The same day that Robert Silveria was locked up in the infirmary, KBI special agent Bruce Mellor telephoned Placer County Sheriff's Office. He got Detective Bill Summers on the phone. Bill is a twenty-seven year veteran in the department whose commanding presence is dictated by a deep baritone voice plus an approachable and relaxed manner. Mellor's purpose in telephoning the department was to draw attention to the importance of one of newest prisoners, Robert Joseph Silveria, Jr., and to solicit help in his own case involving Charles Boyd's murder. Mellor briefed Summers on his case and asked him to check Silveria's personal property for any mementos he might have kept from the homicide. Summers promised the special agent that he'd look into it and get back to him.

After learning that Silveria was being held in the Placer County Jail based on a warrant from the Plumas County Probation Department, Detective Summers telephoned the agency. They informed Summers that Silveria was still on probation and subject to search and seizure. That's all Summers needed to hear to have the go-ahead to follow up on Bruce Mellor's request. He went down to the Southern Pacific Rail yard and retrieved Silveria's backpack from the evidence room. At the time, Summers had no way of knowing that the backpack he was handling belonged to one of Silveria's victims, William Pettit. He would learn that through the killer's own voluntary admission.

Summers rummaged through the backpack, which contained a series of different identifications. Among them were items Bruce Mellor was hoping he'd find. It included a series of documents pertaining to Lester Paul Dykeman, the alias Silveria used when he met Boyd in Texas and traveled with him to Kansas. They included a U.S. Postal Service routing slip to verify Lester Paul Dykeman had applied to receive mail, general delivery in Texas; a yellow Arizona Department of Economics and Security identification card in Dykeman's name; a State of Idaho resident card for Dykeman; an Arkansas food stamp identification card for Dykeman; a food stamp program identification card for Roseville in Dykeman's name; Dykeman's social security card; and an Oregon food stamp identification for Lester Paul Dykeman. Summers made an inventory of the items in the back pack and then phoned Mellor in Kansas the same day and told him what he found. I can only imagine the elation Mellor must have felt when he heard Summers inform him Silveria's backpack held Dykeman's property.

Mellor told Summers to seize the evidence pertaining to Dykeman and that he would be coming down to interview Robert Silveria, Jr. himself. Mellor also informed Summers that Mike Quakenbush would be driving down to Placer County after he finished his business in Yuba City. Quakenbush wanted to interview Silveria about a homicide that occurred on the railroad tracks in Salem and Mellor suggested Summers check with Quakenbush's department for any additional information on the case.

When Bill Summers finished talking to the KBI special agent, he telephoned the Salem Police Department and was told that Quakenbush already was driving down to Yuba City for a court hearing and then would proceed directly to Placer County Jail to interview Robert Silveria. The Salem Detective Sergeant requested that Bill Summers assist Quakenbush and that, in the meantime, he would telephone Quakenbush himself and tell him to get in touch with Summers personally when he arrived at the Placer County jail.

Bill Summers quickly saw the magnitude of interest Silveria's arrest was drawing. I doubt, though, that he envisioned the fifty hours of overtime he would be putting in during the first week of Silveria's incarceration alone. Summers informed his superiors of the growing interest in Silveria and received from them the green light to assist the other agencies in their homicide investigations in any way possible. Next, he phoned the Roseville Police Department to let the investigation division know about the interest Silveria was generating from other law enforcement agencies and to inquire if they had any homicide pending involving transients that might be connected to Silveria. It turned out that the detectives in Roseville Police Department had been looking into the death of a forty-five year-old Hispanic male, Juan Lara, whose naked body was found floating near the rails in Dry Creek off Vernon Street in Roseville on December 23, 1994. It was believed at first Lara was bludgeoned and stabbed to death, but an autopsy revealed the cause of death was drowning, due to multiple blunt force traumas. Roseville Police Detective Michael Allison set an appointment through Summers to interview Silveria about Lara's death.

The following day Summers received a call from the Monroe Police Department in Louisiana about a case they had dating back to the summer of 1993. Monroe is in the northeast area of Louisiana, an area known as a sportsman's paradise and part of a rail system where the south meets the east. A fair-size railroad yard is located close to the downtown area. The crime

in which Monroe Police were interested was originally discovered by a thirty-eight year-old transient searching for a piece of
cardboard in a parked boxcar sometime before sunrise.

Interiors of boxcars are typically filthy and dusty. Hobos
use cardboard to sit on and spread their sleeping rolls over
them. This guy pulled himself up into a parked boxcar that
appeared empty. Moving his flashlight over the floor, he saw the
fully-clothed body of a white male spread across the floor on a
piece of white cardboard. Blood was splattered and smeared on
the walls and pooled around the man's head on the floor.
Jumping out of the boxcar, the transient walked the tracks for
three-quarters of a mile to the rail yard office to report the body
he found on the property.

Police were quickly able to identify the victim, a forty-
two-year-old white male from Illinois by the documents found
in his wallet: a veteran's ID card, VA patient data card and some
medical forms from the VA hospital in Alexandria, Louisiana.
The wallet contained no money, but inside the pocket holding
the wallet, police found a watch. They later learned the victim
had an arrest record in Baton Rouge and Shreveport, Louisiana.
The victim's next of kin, his mother, was located living in Palatine, a charming historical village of approximately 50,000 people about thirty miles northwest of Chicago's downtown area.
She was notified of her son's death through the Palatine Police
Department.

The coroner determined the victim died of pulmonary
hemorrhage from numerous severe blows to the back of his
head with a blunt object. Investigators found two sets of bloody
shoe prints. One of them appeared to come from a military
boot and was found in several places in the box car. Another
print with ridges going straight across the sole was found only
near the door. The body was believed to have been there for at
least a few hours before its discovery, but already insect larvae
were found on the victim's face. A scraping was done, in order

to help determine the time of death by analyzing what stage of development the larvae were in.

Summers now was asked to look into the possibility of Robert Silveria being involved in the homicide and told that he would be forwarded information on the case to assist him in interviewing Silveria. Summers received a similar request from the sheriff's department in Missoula, Montana, who learned from Detective Mike Sward that Silveria was being held in Placer County. Their local records show that Missoula City Police had contact with a Brad Foster, one of Silveria's aliases, traveling with other transients on June 7, 1995. Missoula had records showing that both Dogman and Silveria were in the vicinity when "Cadillac Man," a forty-nine-year-old transient, was murdered. There were two types of blood found, but when DNA tests were run they didn't match Silveria or Dogman. This is particularly interesting since two days earlier, Silveria was ripping off a drug dealer outside of Tucson, Arizona. The speed with which Silveria traveled from place to place and the distances he covered in short periods of time continue to amaze me.

The list of crimes in which Silveria was a suspect was growing. The crime the Missoula County Sheriff's Department was interested in involved the murder of "Cadillac Man," which had occurred several years before. The man was found stabbed with a folding knife near a transient camp, the broken blade still embedded in his chest when he was found. The right side of his forehead was crushed with a rock. His killer buried him in a shallow grave with dirt and bushes laid over him.

Summers suddenly found himself not only scheduling and coordinating the activities of other agencies coming into Placer County to interview Silveria, but also being asked to be the front man for other departments. The Roseville Police Department, because of its proximity to the sheriff's office, also received requests for preliminary interviews from other police

departments. Even though many of the requests for preliminary
interviews met with dead ends, such as the cases in Monroe,
Louisiana and Missoula, where those murder cases are still open
and listed as unsolved, it required extensive time and energy
from investigators. Although conclusions about Silveria could-
n't be drawn, it doesn't mean that Silveria wasn't involved in
those crimes. There simply was not enough physical evidence to
link Silveria to the crimes. If Silveria said he didn't remember
and there was no physical evidence linking him to a crime, there
was nothing investigators could do, even if the crime displayed
his "modus operandi."

Accompanied by Bill Summers, Mike Quakenbush got
the first crack at interviewing Robert Silveria. He arrived at the
Placer County Jail from Yuba City on March 4 around five
o'clock in the afternoon, but he didn't get to speak to Silveria
until seven o'clock in the evening. First, he and Summers
briefed each other, comparing notes and examining evidence
Summers found in Silveria's backpack. Then came the moment
of truth, when the suspect, Silveria, and Quakenbush, the
detective who for the past several months intensely searched for
him, had their first face-to-face meeting.

Quakenbush later told reporters and others that Silveria
looked nothing like he had imagined. He was surprised how
physically strong and healthy Silveria appeared—not at all like
the emaciated, unkempt transients he had seen hanging around
rail yards.

Mike got another surprise when he asked Silveria if he
had any other names that he went by. Silveria said, "Yes, Sidetrack." It was then Quakenbush finally realized that the two
men he was looking for were one and the same person and that
the killer was sitting right there before him in the holding cell.

It was Mike's perception that Silveria at first thought the
detective was interested in his food stamp scam, but soon realized he was being led up another road. He was told there was

a witness in Salt Lake City who could identify him and people
who saw him with Charles Randall Boyd in Texas and Kansas.
Then he was told there was a witness who could identify him in
Montana and another who saw him get into a boxcar with
Michael Andrew Clites. Silveria also had on him items that
linked him to the different killings, as well as items belonging
to his victims.

Silveria appeared to the officers in the room to be
relieved to have it all come out in the open. That first interview
with Quakenbush and Summers lasted until midnight. Summers filled the role of the second detective, acting as a scribe
and taking notes, even though the tape recorder was going.

The interviews with Silveria went on over a six-day
period. The detective was anxious to secure a flawless case. Preliminary interviews by other agencies typically lasted one hour
or less, but if in that time there was enough information involving their cases for them to go on, they returned the following
day or the next time there was an open time slot. The second
interview varied in time. It could last one hour to two-and-a-
half hours or more. Summers made sure that Silveria received
appropriate breaks and rest periods. From the beginning, Silveria was not only cooperating, but he actually appeared to be
enjoying the limelight. My guess is that after all those years hiding in the dark shadows of bushes and boxcars, it felt good to
be noticed and feel so important, even if the honor was dubious. Then again, maybe he thought he was communicating to
us the hell he had been through.

The challenge for investigators talking to Silveria was to
establish his credibility in crimes he admitted to committing so
that his confession would stand up in court. They also had to
make sure he wasn't confessing to other people's crimes,
although Silveria repeatedly refused to name names or implicate
others. When Silveria was interviewed, the detectives were
required to read him his Miranda rights or remind him that he

was still under the Miranda rules applied in an earlier interview. Mike Quakenbush also asked Silveria to voluntarily sign the Miranda waiver.

Silveria talked freely of the killings in Oregon, providing Quakenbush with intimate details that only a killer would know. Silveria later told me that he saw Mike as his younger brother. For some time after Silveria said this, I understood him to be referring to an actual younger brother, of which he has two. Now however, I have come to understand the meaning of his remarks differently. He was referring to a brother the way such a term is viewed within the FTRA. The organization is basically masculine — very few women ride the rails. The group is viewed as a brotherhood and they refer to each other as "brothers." I think Silveria transferred his concept of the Brotherhood to the cops interviewing him. He also wanted the burden of his conscience taken off his shoulders. He had made up his mind the day he was brought in to talk freely and to turn in all the evidence against himself.

Some of the details he revealed were horrifying even to seasoned police officers. He spoke of bludgeoning his victims repeatedly to stop their bodies from jerking with the swaying motion of the boxcar floor beneath. He also identified some of the items in the Polaroid photos Mike took earlier in the evening as belonging to the murdered victims.

At one point Quakenbush left the interview room briefly to make a telephone call while Summers remained behind with Silveria. Suddenly Silveria, who had his head down pensively, looked up at Summers and said, "You know, I once tried to get help in Vancouver." Summers was taken back. Silveria continued talking without being prodded. He told Summers about the day he went to a mental health clinic and told a female working behind a desk that he had "problems" and wanted to talk to someone about them. He recalled how he was seeking help to stop the killings and the heroin addiction, but the gov-

ernment employee was not in the mood to listen. He repeated
how she told him, "I have problems too. Everyone has problems," and ordered Silveria to take a number or go back to the
mission and deal with his problems there. Silveria said that after
the episode in the mental health clinic, his rage grew fiercer and
he wanted to kill even more than ever. Silveria then told Summers how his rage spilled out and he murdered Paul Wayne
Matthews in Whitefish, Montana.

When Quakenbush returned to the holding cell, Silveria
asked Summers to leave the room temporarily. The two detectives paused, glancing at each other. Silveria explained he
wanted to talk to Quakenbush in private about the murders in
Oregon. Although we later spoke of that time, Silveria's
thoughts at that moment still puzzle me. Did he think that any
confession he made about a murder to one cop would be kept
a secret from the other cop? I think Silveria was too smart for
that. Maybe he just felt comfortable talking to different detectives about different things. During the interviews, at times, he
told the officer with him to turn the tape recorder off and then
gave the "okay" when to turn it on again. He was very nervous
talking about the FTRA, particularly about the death squad, the
group that he and a small group of other FTRA riders formed.
He revealed nothing about the group when the recorder was on
and provided only the most minuscule information when the
recorder was off. He just wasn't going to snitch on anyone. I
don't know if it was an honor thing or he was just looking out
for his own skin. Maybe it was both.

The investigators tiptoed around him. They wanted to
keep Silveria happy as long as he kept talking about his crimes.
Yet Quakenbush did question Silveria about his lifestyle after
the detective got the information he needed for his investigation of the murders in Oregon. He was seated in the interview
room with Roseville Detective Mike Allison on the other side
of the small plastic table. Dressed in an orange prison jump suit,

Silveria was chained to the chair, his back to a wide-open window where intrusive sounds from the parking lot below occasionally muffled the conversation between the three men. Leaning back in the chair with the soles of his running shoes pressed against the wall, Quakenbush asked Silveria, "Why did you live like that? Why did you prefer dumpster diving and living in a world that's so unsafe?"

Silveria eyed Quakenbush calmly. "It's for peace of mind. I like the violence."

As they spoke, Silveria provided Quakenbush with graphic details about Pettit's last moments. He told Quakenbush and Summers about killing Michael Clites and taking the beads that Clites and Pettit wore to hold their hair back in pony tails. He spoke about keeping the items he put in his leather medicine pouch as mementos. "It allows me to be closer to their spirits," he said. Serial killers often retain possessions of the victims as their souvenirs of conquest.

The interview with Silveria finally ended when a medical technician was called in to take vials of blood and hair samples from Silveria. Summers also snapped photos of Silveria's tattoos.

The following morning, Quakenbush and Summers were back fishing for more information, but this time, other investigators were there and wanted time to press their cases with the prisoner. The national total cost of interviewing Silveria and investigating his crimes was becoming huge.

Summers was doing a well-coordinated juggling act as officers from around the country made their way to Auburn. Depending on the number of agencies showing up or on the particular extradition hearing, the interviews rotated between the Placer County Jail and the Placer County Sheriff's Office, located less than one mile apart. In the sheriff's office, Summers allocated a room directly across the hall from a conference

room, which he used as a waiting room for incoming investigators, as well as a working office for the visiting investigators.
I learned months later that in the first two weeks about twenty-
eight agencies sent investigators in pairs to interview Silveria. I
was one of them. Of course, I was unaware as I made my way
to the jail to talk to the serial killer of the strange bond that
would develop between us.

   Many other detectives telephoned Summers or the
Roseville Police Department requesting that Summers interview the prisoner on their behalf and the frenzy didn't stop
there. The media picked up on a press release issued by the
Placer County Sheriff's Department about Silveria's capture.
Press releases are frequently used by law enforcement to gain
the public's interest and help. But in this situation it was also a
matter of public concern when a high profile case such as Silveria's falls in a local jurisdiction. It didn't take long before
reporters were calling in from all around the country inquiring
about Silveria. It was the headlines and Silveria's photo in the
local press that attracted the attention of Jenny Taylor, the
woman who had once offered Silveria her sympathy.

   Later, I found Jenny with the help of Roseville Officer
Mike Allison. She was no longer living in her car but, thanks to
an SSI check, had moved into an apartment in a fairly new complex. Her car was parked between covered wooden posts in the
complex parking lot, still in working condition. When Jenny
opened the door, I was shocked. That Jenny was small, buxom,
attractive, with a hard edge about her was not a surprise to me,
but seeing her with plastic tubes attached to her nostrils was.
Behind her was a small oxygen tank that she wheeled through
narrow passages in the apartment lined with a clutter of boxes,
furniture and other items Jenny had collected over the years.
Jenny's blonde hair was gone, replaced with gray strands. Her
personality, however, was warm and cheerful. She still had her

dog, Daffodil, who competed for visitors' attention by pulling noisy toys out of a basket on the floor near a comfortable upholstered chair facing a television set. There was also a raucous parakeet in a nearby cage desperately attempting to pull up the door to the cage with its beak to get out. A sense of spirited energy filled the small apartment. Jenny graciously invited me to come in and sit down on her "TV" chair, while she sat across on the couch.

"I still pray for him," she said. "But I'd be lying if I said I ever felt in danger when I was with him. I always felt safe around the FTRA, even though I knew they could kill in a heartbeat." However, the idea that Silveria could be a serial killer was mind boggling for Jenny when she first saw the headlines. It was especially disturbing, she said, to read that he killed to obtain shoes and identification cards for food stamps. Reading about Silveria and his crimes also made her realize that she had in her possession something that could be of interest to the police. Jenny had rushed over to the Roseville Police Department to report that she had Robert Silveria's backpack in her possession. Detective Michael Allison, who had talked to the homeless woman in the past about crime in the area, interviewed her and accompanied Jenny to her storage unit to pick up the backpack.

Jenny shook her head, "You know, I put Sidetrack on a train to go up north to Washington and what does he do?" Jenny didn't wait for my reply.

"He comes back to town and then he walks openly right by the rail yard. How stupid can you get? Jenny shook her head, again. Then a sheepish smile crossed her impish face.

"You know, we had sex together in back of my car."

I said nothing. Sometimes even cops find it awkward to pry too deeply into personal relationships.

"You know, later I was told that he was planning to kill me that night too, so maybe having sex with him that night saved my life. Do you think so?" Jenny looked up with wondering eyes, noisily breathing through her plastic tubes.

"I never heard of him killing a woman, so I can't say, but it's possible." I mused, though I was puzzled by her revelation.

She nodded. "Yes, I think having sex with him saved my life, because I was told later that he said he was going to kill me, but changed his mind," she went on.

"I also bought him dinner." Then she paused. "How stupid can you get walking in the open like that? I put him on that train. I stood there watching him jump the train and then he comes back. I pray for him and think a lot about him." As if talking to herself, she repeated, "But I was never afraid of him. Not for a moment. I'd be lying if I said I was. Then I saw his photo on the front page of the Auburn Journal and read about him killing all those people." Jenny shook her head sadly. "It's hard to believe he would do that."

"But he did," I said firmly.

15

Jail House Snitch

"I didn't do it when I was on drugs. Somebody else did it."

Robert Joseph Silveria, Jr.

A talkative inmate, George Schlichting, who was well known to area law enforcement, was locked up in a cell next to Silveria's in the "B" tank of the Placer County Jail. From his vantage point, Schlichting was able to view the news broadcasts from a television set up against one wall facing his quarters. The two men discussed the broadcasts through a vent. Silveria told me later that from his cell he could only hear pieces of the broadcasts, because his cell was around the corner, away from the television monitor. The way the cells were situated gave Schlichting power and control. It made Silveria dependent on Schlichting to learn what was being said on the news about

him. This dependence grew as all the channels and news broadcasts were picking up on the story of the exploits and capture
of the Boxcar Serial killer.

After years of running and hiding in and out of boxcars,
Silveria found himself the center of attention — not just on television, but also among law enforcement. This newfound noto-
riety seemed to satisfy an inner yearning for celebrity and
confession and led him to open up more and more, admitting
even to murders that were unknown or unsolved. A good
lawyer would have put a muzzle on him, but at the time, Silveria wasn't interested in talking to any lawyer. He had a need to
spill his guts, so several days after his capture, Silveria informed
Summers and Quakenbush that there was a black book in
which he kept records of all his killings hidden in his old camp
in Roseville.

The following day, Silveria was taken handcuffed to
accompany the officers to his former camp to help them look
for the infamous black book. Chief Deputy Bob Kindler from
Klickitat County, located on the southern border of Washington State, was scheduled to interview Silveria when suddenly
Summers and Quakenbush decided to take Silveria to his old
camp to help them find the ledger of which Silveria had spoken.
If they found the book, they would have in their possession
extremely incriminating evidence against their prisoner. Kindler
understood the importance of their mission and agreed to conduct the interview with Silveria during the transport itself.
There had been a series of homicides involving train hoppers
and transients that occurred in Klickitat County about which
Kindler wanted to question Silveria.

On the drive Silveria readily admitted to the chief deputy
that he knew about the homicides committed by his FTRA friends
in Kindler's jurisdiction, but he agreed to talk only about the one
he had done. The murder he told Kindler about had happened

two years earlier. Silveria had met an older transient in a bar in Pasco, Washington, where rail riders like to hang out. The older man was loaded with money and was buying rounds of drinks. The topic of conversation circled on train hopping and Silveria bragged how well he knew the trains. He promised the older rail rider that for several more rounds of drinks he would show him the right train to hop to Vancouver, where the man wanted to go. The man took him up on it. After a few more drinks, Silveria and his bar companion jumped the train Silveria pointed out. They smoked a few joints while they waited for the train to start moving. Silveria also did heroin, which he had picked up for sixty dollars in Pasco. The train began to travel through the night. Then the freight train unexpectedly stopped for about ten minutes at a bridge crossing. Looking out the boxcar, the old timer suddenly realized they had taken a wrong train and that they had traveled northwest towards Wishram in Klickitat County, instead of southwest to Vancouver. He turned livid and cursed Silveria, "I'm going to stay on the train regardless where it takes me and you should get lost." Then he made a fatal mistake, the same mistake many of Silveria's victims made. He turned his back to Silveria. In a flash, Silveria pulled out his oak goon stick, striking the old man over the head with all his strength. The man fell to the ground, dazed. He tried raising himself, but Silveria kicked him, shoving him out of the box car with his steel-toed boots and the goon stick. Standing there watching, Silveria was satisfied that he had taught the man a lesson. Suddenly, he remembered that the older man still had all that cash on him. Silveria jumped down from the boxcar and went after him, again.

The man was still alive when Silveria approached. He was sitting on the ground holding his bloodied head with both hands, as if covering his head would stop the excruciating pain he felt. Grabbing the man's arm, Silveria pulled him over to the side of the tracks, dragging him like a rag doll. In spite of the victim's loud cries to let him go and leave him alone, Silveria began striking the older man's head with his full might, holding the axe handle tightly in his hand. He could hear the cracking sound the goon stick made when he smashed it against the train hopper's skull. Fresh blood poured out and splattered with each blow from Silveria's axe handle. Finally, Silveria noticed the old-timer go limp and watched his body roll over on the ground. Silveria stepped forward and leaned down. Blood and grease covered his hands as he pulled out the wallet containing the cash and food stamps from the man's pocket. Then, grabbing the victim's backpack, Silveria jumped back into the boxcar.

Just then the train started to move. At first it traveled slowly. After crossing the trestle, it picked up speed, leaving the body of the old rail rider behind, exposed to wild animals and scavengers, while the train rolled towards some of the most beautiful sights along the Columbus River.

Silveria told Chief Deputy Kindler he wasn't sure he killed the rail rider and that he might have still been alive when he was left by the side of the tracks. Other FTRA members have said the same thing to me after describing a fight in which they pushed someone out a boxcar door. In Silveria's case, though, he admitted to attacking first, whereas the others typically claimed to be defending themselves. Yet Angel, a close FTRA friend of Silveria's with a similar ferocious reputation, told me that FTRA members have been known to throw men out of moving boxcars just to see the expressions on their faces when they went flying out.

Silveria finished telling Kindler about the old transient he had attacked. Kindler asked about another incident just as their group, which consisted of Summers, Quakenbush, Kindler and several other officers, arrived at the Southern Pacific security office. The office was not far from Silveria's former Roseville camp. With members of the rail yard police accompanying them, Silveria led the group underneath a bridge near a creek. A thorough search revealed nothing that proved to be of any value. The officers would have to be satisfied with another notebook of Silveria's they had in their possession. That one listed the different dates and names for Silveria's food-stamp pick-ups. Silveria kept the ledger of the victims, in order to help him track his food stamps allotments. Next to the names, he listed the cities and dates on which he was eligible to pick up the food stamps, which he sold for drug money once he got them.

On their return, Kindler talked to Silveria about another murder and robbery in Wishram, Washington, which Silveria had mentioned to Kindler in his preliminary interview. After they finished discussing it, Kindler had to leave. Summers had the tape-recorded interview transcribed and booked into evidence. A copy of the tape and the transcribed interview was mailed the following week to Chief Deputy Kindler.

It was late at night when Silveria was transported from the Sheriff's Office back to the Placer County Jail. There he was given a break, dinner and time to talk to his neighbor, George Schlichting, through the vent.

"Hey, where did they take you?" Schlichting paused, listening for Silveria's response, pressing his ear up to the vent. He waited while Silveria climbed up to the second bunk to speak to him. Silveria sighed, obviously feeling the toll of the day.

"I'm kind of strung out and tired, but let's talk in the morning. I just want to go to sleep now," Silveria said. The following day, Silveria's mood picked up. He and Schlichting talked into the early morning hours. Schlichting made every effort to endear himself to Silveria. Each night the two prisoners lay on the upper bunk of their cell beds talking to each other through the vents, jumping to the lower cot whenever they heard someone approaching. There was no one else in the cells next to them, which made them feel comfortable in their privacy. While Silveria was being interrogated by investigators who came in from different parts of the country, the deputies were also questioning and taping Schlichting's reports on what the alleged Boxcar Killer said to him. Everything he learned from Silveria, he passed on to the Placer County Deputy Sheriffs. Silveria told Schlichting that he killed four people in Montana, although in the end only one was confirmed, Paul Wayne Matthews. He allegedly told Schlichting that he killed people because he wanted things they had for his medicine bag. I assumed when I first heard this that Schlichting was referring to the leather pouch Silveria wore around his neck.

Soon, Schlichting's assertions began to grow wilder. He told the deputies that Silveria put things in his medicine bag so that he could pray for his victims, because they were bad people, especially the drug dealers. Schlichting's revelations carried some credibility with the Placer County authorities. Before they had taken Silveria to his old camp in Roseville to look for the black book listing Silveria's murder victims, the deputies confirmed with Schlichting that indeed such a book existed. At first, Schlichting's reports were helpful, but as time passed, the conversations between the two prisoners yielded only a few bits of information.

About the sixth day of Silveria's incarceration, KBI special agents Bruce Mellor and Galen Marple took a plane to Sacramento and then drove to Auburn to conduct a custodial interrogation. The agents read Silveria his Miranda rights and had him sign a Miranda card. Afterwards, Silveria talked a lot to Mellor, the prime interviewer. Silveria sobbed when he recounted the killing of Charles Boyd. He admitted using the name of Lester Paul Dykeman when he met Boyd in El Paso and at the Christian ranch to which Boyd talked him into going. He spoke of making a stop at Boyd's daughter's house in Kansas and he described the campground and roads leading to the Kanopolis State Lake campground. Silveria told the agents that originally he planned to steal Boyd's wallet and go off on his own, but Boyd made several homosexual advances at him. Silveria said this enraged him. Silveria described how after the crime he sold the Plymouth van in El Paso. All that Silveria confessed to could be corroborated by witnesses: Boyd's daughter and the person who ran the Double D Ranch. Silveria also had left a paper trail with his signatures using Boyd's name. During these talks Silveria did not bring up Arkansas Bobcat, who he now insists was there with him and Boyd. Although no proof surfaced, it does make sense that a third person entered the picture when Silveria and Boyd left El Paso, because why else would they have traveled to Albuquerque, instead of going directly to Kansas from Van Horn?

At around six o'clock that evening, when Detective Mike Allison returned from picking up Silveria's maroon backpack at Jenny Taylor's storage unit, he got additional news. Detective Bill Summers phoned and said Allison could now talk to Silveria. Allison and his supervisor, Detective Sergeant Halley headed to the Placer County Sheriff's Office. By then it was too dark to see the rows of mountains in the distance that provide a soothing view from the entrance to the tall, rectangular, white brick building. Allison brought the maroon backpack with him.

Summers came down to greet the two officers and led them upstairs to the second floor where Silveria was seated, chained behind a table in a small interview room facing the door. Summers told the Roseville officers that Silveria had already confessed to several homicides. "He's given intimate details of each killing that only the murderer would know." Regarding the Lara homicide, one in which the Roseville Police Department was specifically interested, Silveria only indicated that he might know who did it.

As Allison reached the open door to the interview room where Silveria was, he set the maroon backpack down in clear view of Silveria. He turned in time to catch Silveria sitting up and studying it. "Hey, that's mine," Silveria said loudly from across the room. Later that day, Silveria admitted to the Roseville investigators that, although the backpack was his, the items inside belonged to Clites and Pettit, his Oregon victims and the boots he was wearing the day he was stopped were taken from the body of Michael Clites. But it wouldn't be until the following day that an affidavit for a search warrant was granted to search the backpack for trace evidence: hair, blood, fibers, fingerprints, saliva and semen — anything of an evidentiary or forensic value that might link Silveria to his crimes. However, as far as the Roseville detectives were concerned, that evening they were more interested in what Silveria had done in their own backyard.

Detective Sergeant Halley and Detective Mike Allison advised Silveria of his Miranda rights, which he said he understood. He also gave the two detectives permission to record the interview. With the recorder on, he told them that a cellmate in an adjoining room kept asking him about a Roseville homicide involving a guy named Lara, letting the detectives know he was aware his neighbor was snitching on him. One of the officers told Silveria that Lara's family wanted Silveria to tell the police about the homicide so that the family could understand what happened. And as far as the Roseville detectives were concerned, they wanted to close their investigation into Lara's homicide and needed his help.

Silveria began to talk about the specific location where Lara's body had been found floating naked. He accurately described the area in detail as the Roseville officers listened intently. Although Silveria didn't recall Lara's full name, perhaps because the Mexican dealer gave a different name to the transients, his physical description of the victim was precise. When the detectives showed Silveria a photo of Lara, he identified him as the victim. Silveria described the victim as a Hispanic male, about five-feet-five inches tall, somewhat stocky and with hair that looked like it was starting to grow back in after being shaved off. The victim was an illegal alien who made his living transporting marijuana on the railroad tracks. "We all would go to him to buy small amounts of weed," Silveria told the detectives. He said Lara lived in an orchard at one end of the railroad yard under a bridge and that he had seen him around the Roseville mission and around town riding his beat-up bicycle. Normally Lara came into Roseville on freight trains several times a month, but he had gotten into some trouble with the law in Sacramento and had been hanging out in Roseville for a number of weeks before his death.

Silveria still wouldn't tell Halley and Allison who murdered Lara, but he now admitted to being present when it happened. He told the detectives the killer was an old FTRA friend with whom he sometimes rode. Allison asked Silveria to describe the incident and tell them the whole story. Silveria's account began when he said Lara sold Silveria's FTRA friend weed, which the Mexican dealer had picked in Kansas City fields where marijuana was being cultivated in the wild. Most likely he stole the buds before they were ready to be harvested. "You could smoke all you wanted and it would not get you high," Silveria said. His FTRA friend became furious after paying Lara seventy dollars for the weed. Typically, Silveria explained, this FTRA friend of his robbed people for drugs, but this time, the guy had the money on him to make the purchase from Lara. When Silveria and his FTRA buddy started smoking the grass, the Mexican scurried off. The two men sat at the hobo camp drinking bottles of beer and smoking pot and waiting to catch out and jump the next freight train to take them both up north. But when they smoked the grass, all that happened was they both got headaches. The FTRA friend got up and told Silveria to watch his gear. He then pulled out his blade and began sharpening it, telling Silveria he was going to get his money back from the Mexican.

According to Silveria, when the FTRA friend became satisfied that his knife was sharp enough, he left the campsite, walking some distance to the Vernon Street Bridge looking for Lara. Then he turned around to return to the area below the campsite. Afterward he looked up at Silveria, who was sitting on a higher plane overlooking the lower ground, which was covered with thick foliage and where hobos sometimes hid to sleep undisturbed. Their friends knew where to find and wake them when it was time to go to the higher ground and get ready to catch a freight train.

The FTRA friend shouted to Silveria, "Can you see the Mexican from where you're sitting?" Silveria stood up and stretched his neck. He saw Lara hiding in the brush below near a tree and pointed him out to his FTRA buddy. Lara tried to make a run for it, but the other man, who was much taller and larger, outran him and grabbed him. Then he pulled Lara towards him.

From the distance, Silveria saw his FTRA friend smash a rock against Lara's head. "I lost sight of Lara when his feet gave way under him and he disappeared behind the thick shrubs, but I could see my FTRA friend." Silveria said he watched his friend's hand go up and down repeatedly in a stabbing motion. The officers asked if there were other witnesses. Silveria said that there were other people in the vicinity of the campsite whom he had seen around before, but he told the officers he didn't know them by name. He also said he wasn't sure if they saw anything. Silveria said that he watched his friend drag Lara around for a long time. Then he thought he heard a splash, most likely from the victim's body being tossed into the creek.

A short while later Silveria's friend returned to the camp, wet and covered in blood. He was carrying a rock, which he put in his pack. He took off his jacket and shirt, which were drenched in blood, and burned them in the campfire. He changed into new clothes and threw his old wet socks down on the sand bank and left them there. He took his blue Levis and wrapped them in a plastic bag in which he and Silveria had brought their beer earlier and shoved the bag with the Levis inside his pack. Afterward he turned to Silveria and said, "I got the money. We better get out of here." When they got to the tracks, Silveria's friend asked him to let him know if "this makes the paper." He said he was going "back home." Despite his rush, two hours later they went back to the crime scene to check on the body, because Silveria's FTRA friend kept repeating, "I wonder if he's dead." By then it was nightfall.

Silveria insisted to the detectives that he was not involved in the murder. "All I did was watch the gear the first time that my FTRA friend went in and assaulted Lara." According to Silveria, that was all he did the second time, too, when his FTRA friend went inside the brush area and returned with the man's clothes.

The news of the murder had spread all over the tracks, for the area where Lara was murdered is also a very popular spot to hang out and catch out. No eyewitness ever came forward, despite a flyer asking for information under a photo of Lara that was posted around town. I know the place where Lara was murdered. I had been to the camp myself and hung out one warm winter afternoon with some of the FTRA, drinking beer and liquor with them, to learn more about what makes them tick.

It is my opinion that it would have been impossible for the other train hoppers Silveria claimed were there not to know or have seen what was going on. I would guess that in addition to Silveria and his FTRA friend, the others in the campsite also shared the bad marijuana. There probably was a lot of cursing going on and complaining about the bad weed, which would have made the FTRA buyer of the weed even angrier, because the dealer made him look bad in front of the others in the group. What Silveria described was an enforcement scene, FTRA style. When Lara sold the bad weed, he signed his own death warrant. First, he sold it to the very men who carry out enforcement within the FTRA. Secondly, if Lara wasn't stopped, he would have continued to sell bad weed to FTRA rail riders. Finally, the FTRA member who bought the weed would have been humiliated by the group if he didn't take care of the problem. In their world, to save face and eliminate the problem of a dealer selling bad weed to his "brothers," the enforcer had to kill Lara. Afterward, the victim was left naked, stripped of his dignity as a sign that you don't mess around with the FTRA.

Silveria told the two Roseville detectives that he saw his FTRA friend again four weeks later hiding in his camp "up north" in Vancouver where he had access to food stamps. He told Silveria he knew that he was wanted for other similar types of incidents. The detectives asked Silveria if he assisted in dragging the victim's body or any other part of the assault, but Silveria continued to deny involvement, claiming all he did was watch his FTRA friend's gear.

As the interview continued, Silveria revealed to the two detectives that he witnessed this particular FTRA friend commit other homicides, but that most of them were north of Roseville. He specifically saw him "do one" in Wishram, Washington. The detectives tried again to solicit the name of Silveria's FTRA friend, but all he would say was that he was one of the people who "trained me to do what I do." Allison and Halley each asked him specifically if it was this friend who trained him to kill and rob. Each time Silveria said that was true, but he wouldn't give up the name. Then Silveria asked for the tape recorder to be turned off, because he didn't want to jeopardize his safety.

The detectives already knew that Silveria and Dogman were acquainted. When Dogman was being interviewed in Flathead County by Mike Sward about the rail track derailment and the murder in Montana, he threw out the names of Sidetrack, Crazy Angel and a woman named Cricket in a non-related incident. The police felt this was to draw attention away from his own activities. The incident to which he referred had to do with a situation where Silveria and Crazy Angel threw some riders off a boxcar. Dogman said that "doesn't happen unless something went wrong to cause it" and he believed that it was Cricket, an older female with curly hair, who instigated trouble. There really appeared to be no reason for Dogman to talk about the group, unless he wanted law enforcement to go after them and leave him alone. In that case, he was not a good friend to Silveria, any more than he was to Bushman.

With the tape recorder shut off, Detective Allison told Silveria that they already had a pretty good idea who his friend was and that it was Dogman who murdered Lara. They only wanted Silveria to confirm it. Silveria's jaw dropped. He looked very surprised. "How did you know? I mean, how do you know?" Silveria looked at the two investigators questioningly. Halley and Allison immediately took Silveria's comment as admission that Dogman was the friend to whom Silveria referred. Allison asked Silveria to describe Dogman to them. Silveria described him as a white male, in his late thirties or early forties, with long black hair and a dark mustache. He said Dogman had bad teeth, was about six-two and wore several dog-choker chains around his neck with numerous tattoos on his arms.

Halley asked Silveria if he knew the type of shoe Dogman was wearing on the night of the murder. Silveria said he thought that he was wearing boots, or "waffle stompers," with a star pattern on the sole, but he wasn't positive. Silveria's interview continued until 9:30 P.M. During that period he was shown a booking photo of Dogman, taken during Dogman's arrest in November 1995, which they got from Detective Sward of the Flathead County Sheriff's Office.

Silveria identified Dogman in the photo without hesitation, but he refused to say Dogman killed Juan Lara. Eventually, the detectives would learn that Dogman was incarcerated at the time of the crime and couldn't have killed Lara, but that night when the Roseville Officers questioned Silveria, they were certain that somehow he confirmed that Dogman did it with the statement "How did you know?" This miscommunication may have occurred because Silveria had difficulty at times structuring his sentences. He related accounts in his confession choppily, which made it difficult for detectives to understand him at times and he was asked frequently to go back and explain things. Silveria was not deliberately trying to mislead the detectives, but he had been a heavy drug user and drugs damage memory and impair brain function. Additionally, shortly after he first started riding the rails, Silveria was sleeping under a bridge and viciously beaten by a group of men wielding clubs. He survived, but it gave him a Darwinian outlook on life — survival of the fittest — and the clubbing may also have had an effect on his speech patterns and communication skills. He also was involved in many other brutal fights, during which he may have suffered lasting injuries.

Since it was late, the detectives wanted to end the day's session. Saying it would be his last question, Detective Allison

Lt. William G. Palmini, Jr. and Robert Silveria, Jr. at the California Placer County Jail.

At left, Silveria's moniker, incorporating FTRA symbology.

At right, Silveria's black rag and concho. The button on the upper left signifies his membership in an FTRA "death squad."

A typical boxcar, the transportation of choice for Silveria and other FTRA members.

The body of James "J.C." McLean, discovered in a transient camp in Albany, California.

The body of William A. Pettit, Jr., discovered in a boxcar in Salem, Oregon.

The body of Juan Lara, discovered in Roseville, California. Silveria has not admitted to participating in this murder, but has confirmed his presence during the crime.

SALEM POLICE DEPARTMENT

INFORMATION BULLETIN

HOMICIDE VICTIM/SUSPECT

On December 1, 1995 William Avis PETTIT, Jr. was murdered in Salem, Oregon. His body was found inside a railroad boxcar. Pettit had been a long time train rider. Investigation of PETTIT'S murder has revealed a suspect. In March of 1996 a Robert Joseph SILVERA was arrested for the murder of PETTIT. SILVERA is also a suspect in numerous other homicides of transients across the United States. SILVERA is also a long time train rider and goes by the name **"SIDETRACK"**.

Any person who knows SILVERA, AKA "Sidetrack" or the victim PETTIT is asked to contact Salem Police Department at 503-588-6050. Please ask for Detective Mike Quakenbush. All calls can be made collect, and the callers can remain anonymous.

Other train riders may still be at risk from people who are associates of SILVERA and still riding the trains. Any information concerning PETTIT and SILVERA will be kept confidential. The source of the information will not be released without the person's permission.

SILVERIA
ROBERT   JOSEPH
DOB: 03/03/59
RACE: WHITE
SEX: MALE
HEIGHT: 6'01
WEIGHT: 180
EYE COLOR: BLUE
HAIR COLOR: BROWN
PHOTO DATE: 03/14/96
PHOTO NUM: 705826

WILLIAM
PETTIT

The teletype sent by Mike Quakenbush of the Salem, Oregon, Police Department to police across the country requesting information on Silveria's whereabouts and warning rail riders of the risk posed by the "Boxcar Serial Killer."

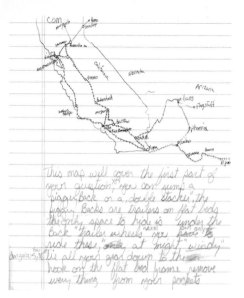

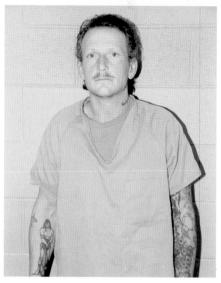

Map drawn by Silveria indicating that he could have indeed traveled, via a "hotshot" train from Arizona to Albany in time to have comitted the McLean murder.

Robert Silveria, Jr. at the California Placer County Jail. Currently he is incarcerated at the Oregon State Penitentiary, known as O.S.P., where he is serving a life sentence for the murders of William Pettit and Michael Clites.

Lt. William G. Palmini, Jr. performing as Elvis. Tanya Chalupa is at right. This photograph hangs on the wall of Silveria's cell.

asked Silveria about the FTRA and his ties with the group. Silveria wouldn't talk about the organization and asked the officers not to discuss it with the media. He looked nervous and
repeated to the detectives, "Say nothing to the media about the
FTRA." Of course, the discovery of the existence of the rail riding organization or a "rail gang," as the police started calling
the FTRA, was one of the hottest discoveries to to result from
Silveria's arrest in Roseville.

16

Lies and Revelations

"That old black gentleman killed there was my
doing."

Robert Joseph Silveria, Jr.

The following morning, the Roseville detectives were back talking to Robert Silveria. Detective Sergeant Halley asked Robert if there were other homicides in Roseville in which Silveria was involved. Silveria told them there might have been one in the "B" yard a couple of years earlier. He recalled being out of heroin and trying to find a victim to rob or "roll" for some money.

Silveria had climbed up on the boxcar where a man was sleeping. Other than the man being white, Silveria remembered nothing about him. Shining a flashlight in the man's face, Silveria told him, "I'm a police officer. I need to see your I.D." The man groggily pulled out his wallet.

At that moment, Silveria attacked him ferociously, first smashing his face in with the flashlight and then repeatedly striking the victim in the head with his goon stick. Silveria described the axe handle as having leather wrapped around the base and "North Dakota 38 Special" carved on the handle. He said he made axe handles as weapons for himself and for other FTRA brothers. After the crime, as usual, Silveria wrote the word "FREEDOM" in blue marker on the inside of the boxcar above the door.

As Silveria came out of the boxcar, he cut his leg on one of the metal straps hanging by the door. Moving swiftly away from the scene, he said he examined the victim's wallet under the first light he encountered and found a couple of hundred dollars and a food stamp card for San Francisco. Silveria burned the wallet, but kept the contents for himself. That night he jumped a train to Eugene, Oregon.

Silveria hung on to the axe handle he used as his murder weapon, sanding it down to remove the blood imbedded in the wood. He carried sandpaper specifically to remove bloody finger prints from his murder weapons. He also used battery acid to burn off the blood-soiled fingerprints.

Allison told me that Roseville police had no records of this boxcar murder in their files. Later, when I got to know Silveria, I wondered if he was confused about where the incident happened. Was he making this up? Did he dream it? Silveria also told several of the investigators that in 1993 he was involved in a murder of an older couple in Havre, Montana. As he told the story, he became very upset and cried. He also said there were other homicides that occurred in Keddie, California in the early 1980s that were related to the homicides in Havre.

Silveria was asked by the detectives to draw a picture of the inside of the house in Havre. He did, but his emotional outburst had made Halley and Allison suspicious. They thought his demeanor and body language were different from the times when he spoke of other killings and he wasn't as consistent or clear with the details. They stopped the interview to give the agitated Silveria a break. In the meantime, they contacted the Havre Police Department by telephone to obtain their hold-out information to see if Silveria was telling the truth. What they learned affirmed their suspicions. The details Silveria gave the detectives turned out to be "published information" and nothing that he said came close to the information held back by police.

When Silveria's break was over, the two detectives, Halley and Allison, confronted Silveria with what they had learned from the Havre Police Department. Silveria grinned sheepishly and said that he had been lying. He told the detectives that he couldn't stand to think about all the terrible things he had done and even felt guilty about things he had nothing to do with, so he made up his involvement in the incident to stop the questions and rest his mind.

Not taking any chances, Summers telephoned the Plumas County Sheriff's Office in California to let them know that Silveria had confessed to a murder in Havre, which was connected to a mass murder in Keddie, a picturesque resort town in Plumas County, but had recanted. Nevertheless, a team of three men, Detective Larry Rives, Detective Hitch and Assistant Sheriff Rod Decrona came to interview Silveria at the sheriff's office. Decrona had been acquainted with Silveria when he was a detective sergeant in the department. Silveria had lived in Quincy with his first wife.

Detective Hitch remained hidden in a room monitoring the interview by video. Summers and Quakenbush came to talk to him, going in and out frequently. While Decrona and Rives were questioning Silveria, Quakenbush came in and sat there for about ten minutes, listening. Silveria said he was "recalling a dream" about committing the homicides when talking about the murders in the resort town of Keddie, which had involved four victims. The interview did not bring the Plumas County group closer to solving the killings and they returned home. Afterwards, Detective Hitch checked with the Corrections Department to get a profile of Silveria's criminal record. He found that at the time of the Keddie murders, Silveria was in custody for auto theft and therefore couldn't have done it. Later, Silveria gave me his explanation for lying.

"I gave the false confession to bring around the officers from Plumas who knew me and knew I wasn't the horrible person that I was being made out to be. I wanted to talk to someone from law enforcement that could understand me."

However, Silveria apologized for lying to the two detectives, Allison and Quakenbush. Then, to further clear his conscience, he told them he was going to make it up to them. He told the detectives that he wanted to provide them with information they didn't have that involved a 1994 murder in Tallahassee, Florida.

"That old black gentleman killed there was my doing," Silveria said, as he voluntarily confessed to a killing to which no one previously had connected him. Those listening were surprised. Just how many people had Silveria killed?

Silveria said he met fifty-two-year-old Willie Clark in Tallahassee, Florida, when Silveria jumped off a CSX freight train. The first thing Silveria did was hide his roll pack in an area protected by heavy foliage. Then he walked towards the Amtrak station, to a place where many of the homeless hung out. Silveria claimed he was traveling alone at the time. Willie Clark was stretched out in his Levis, sitting under a tree in a popular hobo drinking spot, drinking wine. He wasn't a big guy, only five feet and six inches tall. His nose looked like it had been bashed in pretty badly in a fight. Over his graying Afro he wore a gray wool knit cap. A gray-specked beard formed a semi-circle on the lower half of his face.

"Hey, tramp. Where you headed from?" Clark called to Silveria.

Silveria paused, then, turning around, he walked towards Willie. "I'm coming from Mobile," Silveria said.

Clark grinned. "That's a rough neck part of the woods you're coming from," he said, referring to the FTRA goon squad that rides the southern rails and hangs out in the abandoned ice house in Mobile. "What are your plans to catch out again? Only one train comes through here a day."

Silveria told him he was looking for the welfare building. Willie nodded that he had been there himself. Silveria then introduced himself as Tim Williams. Willie Clark smiled and said, "Just call me Old Man." Neither one of them seemed to want to know much more about the other.

Clark offered to show Silveria around the area and Silveria agreed. Giving Silveria the survival tour, Clark pointed out where the best places were for dumpster diving. He also took Silveria to the welfare building where Silveria applied for food stamps under the name Tim Williams, using a social security card he claimed he purchased for twenty dollars at a Fort Worth flee market. While Silveria was standing in line and filling out the forms, Clark waited for him outside by one of the picnic tables. Silveria was informed that it would take four to five days before he could get his food stamps. When he came out and told this to Clark, the black man said that he had a check coming from the Salvation Army for ringing the bell at Christmastime and they might as well both go there so Silveria could check out the mission. The two men walked the six blocks from the welfare office to the Salvation Army headquarters, lodged in a three-story building. Silveria had an ID made with Tim Williams' name and his own photo. He was told to go to the thrift store and get any clothes he wanted. Meanwhile, Clark filled out forms to get his overdue check.

When I learned of this admission, I asked myself, why did Clark wait so long to collect his check? Did he pull out enough from the till to keep himself going without the money? Or was it because somebody raised questions that he may have pocketed the donations and he wanted to wait until things quieted down? Clark had a long prison record and had served time for murder in Arizona. Silveria himself was leery of Clark's intentions and wondered why the old man was being so helpful to him. They waited an hour for Clark's check to come through, but the staff was friendly, asking Clark to come back next year. However, one of them jokingly said to Silveria to watch out for Willie, because he would get Silveria into trouble. When Clark got his check, he and Silveria examined it carefully. They noted, making disparaging comments, that it showed a tax deduction, which reduced the net amount from $300 to $245.

The next day, Silveria accompanied Old Man to cash his check. Silveria waited outside with the old transient's gear and his own backpack. When Clark came out of the bank, he had the cash in his hands and was hopping with joy. He kept counting the money as he walked with Silveria down the street, spreading the bills. Showing the many singles, fives and tens, he waved them back and forth like a fan. As he watched the other man, Silveria became increasingly irritated by Clark's behavior until Silveria was filled with jealousy. Clark was too gleeful to notice the dark mood coming over Silveria. He was too busy imagining how he would spend the money.

Finally he put the bills away, thumbing them in his wallet like a deck of cards. The next step, they agreed, was to get some meth and some needles. All the while, Silveria had his handgun tucked in his waistband. Clark led Silveria around the block from the mission and the Salvation Army building to an area lined with abandoned, graffiti-tagged apartment buildings. As they walked down the street, Silveria noticed he was the only white face around. It was hard for him not to wonder if Clark was leading him into something dangerous.

Suddenly, two large black men strode out of one of the abandoned buildings. Though Silveria is six foot tall, these guys looked huge to him. What's more, they headed in his and Willie's direction. Silveria pulled back his jacket, moving his hand close to the handle of his gun. The men glanced at the gun, then kept on walking. As he and Clark were about to walk up a wide set of concrete steps, several other guys came towards them and asked what they wanted. One of the men had a handful of crack, but Silveria told him he was looking for some heroin. The man said he'd be right back. Silveria's eyes followed and he wondered how he was going to make them victims. Clark pointed to a building and led Silveria up the stairs into one of the abandoned town houses. Pipes stuck out of walls and the whole place looked in shambles, but Willie and Silveria scored, picking up heroin, crank and some needles. Soon they left the building, heading back to camp. On the way, Clark stopped off at a grocery store. He asked if Silveria wanted anything. Silveria said, "Only a soda." Willie purchased a bottle of liquor for himself and a soda for Silveria.

They walked back to the Amtrak station. Clark was hoping a certain female in whom he was interested would be there and became disappointed when he saw that she wasn't. In fact, the only one there was a cranky, old homeless man who complained loudly that others were taking his aluminum cans. Silveria wanted to go off and shoot up in private, but Clark objected. "You junkies are all the same." The comment rubbed Silveria the wrong way. Suddenly, it became a matter of respect. Silveria recalls thinking, "I'm gonna kill that dude for talking like that."

Willie Clark drank most of the whiskey, giving Silveria only a few swigs. Silveria didn't need much to drink to get high, as he was feeling the effects of the heroin he did earlier in the day and the mix of crank and smack was triggering his rage. After drinking most of the liquor, Clark slid down under a tree and fell into a deep sleep.

Now, as he talked, Silveria described details about the park to the detectives, in order to demonstrate to them that he had been in the area and knew what it looked like. "It was located in Tallahassee near a major highway, across the street from a row of restaurants, near the capitol and a railroad trestle." Silveria drew a map depicting the park and its surrounding area. Then he continued describing the events that took place.

It was rapidly growing dark and Silveria was growing more and more angry at Clark's attitude. Silveria left the spot and walked over to a dumpster. This time he was looking not for food, but for a weapon. It didn't take long for him to find one. Inside the dumpster were materials from a fence that had been broken down and taken apart. Silveria found a four-foot piece of metal that was once part of a gate post and still had concrete attached to it at one end. There was also concrete inside the pipe. Silveria took it out of the dumpster and carried it back on his shoulders to the spot where Willie Clark lay sound asleep.

Silveria walked up to the sleeping man and hollered, "Hey, are you gonna get up so we can go check the dumpsters?" Willie didn't move. By now it was totally dark with very few lights around the park. Hanging on to the post by the mortar part, Silveria swung the forty pound piece of metal like an axe down on Clark's head, crushing it. Clark's foot jerked. The involuntary motion of Willie's foot made Silveria think the man was still alive. Again and again, Silveria swung down on Clark's head with the metal, concrete-filled pipe. He continued striking his victim's head, first on the top and then on the side, until the top portion of his head separated from his face and pieces of his brain matter were on the ground, seeped in blood. Finally satisfied that Clark was dead and could never be identified, Silveria rushed over to some ivy bushes and shrubbery about thirty feet away. He flung the murder weapon deep into the foliage. Then he returned back to the spot where Clark lay dead. His head was unrecognizable. Pulling out the blanket Willie was lying on, Silveria covered his head. Moving around, away from the covered up head, Silveria knelt down besides the lifeless body. He pulled out his buck knife and with it cut off the belt holding the victim's money. He also pulled out Clark's buck knife with a gold-top handle, which he took as a souvenir, as he had taken other men's hunting knives numerous times before. Then he ripped open Willie's back pocket to get to his billfold.

All of Silveria's actions were done with precision and swiftness. Once he was through with the victim and had taken all he wanted, Silveria got out. Quickly, he moved to an area in the park that was well lit. With bloodstained hands, Silveria examined the billfold he took from the dead man. He found Clark's food stamps, social security printout, social security card, bank card and another old bank card. Wrapped in a plastic paper were another black man's identifications, which Clark kept for a friend. Then Silveria dug a hole in the ground by the corner of a nearby bridge and placed all the identifications and documents he found in Clark's wallet in a bread bag he had gotten earlier from the grocery store where they bought the booze and the soda. Burying the items, he then covered the spot with rocks. He figured when he got back to the area he would dig the bag out. Silveria went to the place where he had hidden his own gear when he first arrived in Tallahassee. Picking up his belongings, he walked to a secluded spot to wait for the next train out, careful to avoid any others that were passing by. He finally hopped a freight train that made its first stop in Mobile, Alabama. Its second stop was Jackson, Mississippi, where Silveria got off.

A week later, Silveria was back in Tallahassee. When he walked past the spot where he had murdered Clark, he saw yellow ribbon barricades around the area, which read, "Crime Scene — Do Not Cross." The body had been found.

As soon as he'd finished his session with Silveria, Detective Allison telephoned the Tallahassee Police Department, relaying the information he and Quakenbush had received from Silveria. Detective Jeff Johnson, who handled the case back in 1994, confirmed that Silveria's description of the incident was very similar to the homicide he investigated. Detective Johnson said that the details Silveria provided about the victim's belt and pocket were not released to the public. That was the hold-out information. The county gave Willie Clark a pauper's burial. The man was an ex-con whose family had disowned him many years ago when he was sent to an Arizona prison for murder.

Detective Jeff Johnson requested that Allison obtain a recorded statement from Silveria. Silveria was brought back to the holding cell for another interview on Willie Clark's murder in Tallahassee. He was advised again of his Miranda rights prior to the new recording, which was sent to Tallahassee. When Detective Johnson traveled to Salem, Oregon to interview Silveria personally, Silveria continued to be cooperative and open, in spite of the possibility that he was facing death sentences in Oregon, California, Kansas and now Florida.

17

Sealed Fate

"I used a source which has no culture and is not civilized.

> Robert Joseph Silveria, Jr.

There were six of them at the campsite in Barstow, California that fatal night, including Kelly, a thirty-one-year-old from Nevada. Kelly had a history of arrest for prostitution and petty theft. Females who travel with the FTRA will frequently trade sex for money. They will do a "mule train" and for a twenty dollar bill, raised by the men pooling their cash, they will satisfy four to five men, one at a time. The campsite was used frequently as an illegal dumping ground and where the group sat around drinking beer that night, there was a discarded mattress and sofa. Typically, most jungles where rail riders wait and hide to catch out do not have such amenities.

Kelly was accompanied that night by Michael Allen Brandolino, a forty-four-year-old from Kansas, a young rail rider named Gordon Russell Coffey, originally from North Carolina, and Michael "Cherokee" Hampton, an FTRA rider who was half Native American. There was also a man traveling under the name of Jack Caines.

The group was waiting to jump a train to Las Vegas. Most of the people around the campfire, except for a local Barstow man, had previous criminal arrests. Hampton's arrests involved assault, battery, vandalism and spousal abuse. Coffey had a record for arson, vandalism and habitual driving while impaired, which is a felony. Members of the group had been at the same campsite about five days earlier on December 18. As is typical for most of these "jungle" encounters, the group got rowdy after a few drinks, "shouting jibes back and forth" and "yelling and carrying on." It's not unusual for FTRA members to get in each other's faces around campfires to see who is the toughest and can withstand the heat, but Brandolino inadvertently overstepped the boundaries. They were drinking wine and beer and around dusk an argument erupted. Everybody there was pretty drunk, which may explain why Michael Brandolino didn't pick up the vibes around him. He said something about the Washington Redskins, which was taken out of context and interpreted the wrong way by Hampton. Maybe Hampton was just looking for an excuse to pick on Brandolino. Maybe he knew about the double lightening bolt tattooed on Brandolino's neck, partially hidden by longish brown hair. The tattoo alone might have been enough to fire Hampton up.

Whatever the stimulus was, Hampton got into Brandolino's face and wouldn't budge. There was more shouting back and forth. Then Brandolino made a contemptuous comment about Indians, which enraged Hampton even more. He took it as a personal attack on his heritage. Hampton's fury intensified, drawing Coffey and Robert Silveria, using the alias Jack Caines, into the Indian's corner. Suddenly Brandolino found himself outnumbered. There was more name calling, shoving and bullying. Coffey and Silveria forced Brandolino into giving them five dollars for beer, which was nothing short of strong arm robbery tactics, despite the seemingly negligible amount of cash involved. Five dollars is a lot of money among transients. Brandolino tried leaving the camp, but Hampton, Coffey and Silveria wouldn't let him go. They continued taunting him. Brandolino suffered from epilepsy, a condition that had been worsening in recent months. His poor health and smaller physical stature made him an easy prey for taller and bigger men like Hampton and Silveria. He was outnumbered three to one.

Brandolino announced, "This is my camp that you're all in. You all have to leave." This is an old FTRA rule. The owner of the camp has the right to throw out those who disrespect his camp, just like McLean in Albany had that right to throw Silveria out, because he disrespected his hospitality. There is only one problem with that rule. The owner of the camp needs the "might" that goes with the "right." Silveria glanced at Cherokee and Cherokee glanced back. With crooked grins on their faces, they motioned to one another, *let's kick some ass. STP*, thought Silveria, *time to start the party*. Silveria unleashed the first punch, slamming the victim's face with his fist. Hampton and Coffey jumped in. They all thumped on poor Brandolino, using goon sticks on his head, chest and abdomen, smashing him with their fists and kicking him with their boots. Rail riders typically wear heavy, military-style boots. Many of them have steel-plated toes built into the boot and being kicked with one of these can legally constitute the use of a deadly weapon.

For about three hours, Hampton, Coffey and Silveria assaulted Brandolino, using him as an outlet for their anger and aggression in a campsite just a stone's throw from a major free-way and only a matter of yards from the box-like homes and businesses facing a busy street. Despite the proximity of civiliza-tion, Brandolino was trapped in a wasteland ruled by the law of survival of the fittest in which he was the weakest link. Still, he wanted to survive and perhaps get revenge on his attackers. Lying wounded and bleeding on the ground during a break in the assault, he saw his assailants drinking and laughing at one end of the campsite. Brandolino took that moment to try to make an escape. He rolled over, rose halfway and tried to get away. I assume that he was too weak and injured to stand and run for the highway and therefore was forced to crawl. Unfor-tunately for Brandolino, he didn't get far before somebody noticed he was missing and dragged him back. Brandolino tried to fight back, threatening to call the police, but his attempts were feeble. To keep him from escaping, Silveria and his rail rid-ers hogtied the bloodied Brandolino. Then they poured water on him, laughing that it was gasoline and that they were going to roast him like a pig. The fright and pain Brandolino had to endure during the hours of his nightmare were horrific. Silveria and the others had punched and kicked him hard enough to cause broken ribs and other internal damage, which the coro-ner would later note. Brandolino suffered excruciating pain at the hands of men he invited into his camp. He was the victim of a hazing that progressed from cruel to evil to deadly.

Kelly and the lone Barstow male in the group who did-n't participate in the beating sat horrified as they watched the assault on Brandolino while they waited for the train to arrive. They were too terrified to leave or say anything that would fur-ther enrage the violent trio.

Silveria, Hampton and Coffey realized they had gone too far with their "patsy" when he began shaking from an epileptic seizure; blood flowed from his nose and mouth from the beatings and his eyes rolled back. The three stared at each other trying to figure out what to do next. They didn't think Brandolino would make it and they didn't want him found in that state before they had a chance to make their escape. He might live long enough to identify them to the police. The best thing to do was to kill him. The two witnesses watched the three men drag Brandolino some forty yards towards the rails. Silveria snickered that the victim was about to meet up with Uncle Pete — short for a Union Pacific Railroad train. The plan was to place Brandolino on the rails and have the train cut him in half. But then Silveria and the two others changed their mind. The walk to the rails might get them noticed and attract attention. The rails were also too close to the nearby houses. It was decided that they were better off killing him near the campsite and burying him under a tree.

The Nevada woman and the Barstow man watched the three men untie Brandolino and lay him besides a tree stump. They watched as Silveria held the victim's feet down while Coffey sat over his chest and Hampton kneeled over the victims head. They couldn't tell what was actually taking place, but shortly afterwards they saw Hampton, Coffey and Silveria burying the victim in a shallow, makeshift grave, where he was eventually found. Silveria placed a rock there to serve as a headstone for the victim's grave. One of the men was heard to say, "Dead men tell no tales."

When the freight train arrived, Hampton, the Barstow man and Kelly jumped into an open boxcar, fleeing to Las Vegas, a place far away from the maddening scene of the night. The other killer, Coffey, who worked in a nearby fast food chain with his wife, went home. It's hard not to wonder what thoughts went through their minds that hellish night. Was the alcohol enough to help them sleep soundly?

No one knew what happened to Robert Silveria, known to the group as Jack Caines, because he separated from them. Kelly told police later that she ran into him in Las Vegas with Hampton and the Barstow man in a bar, days after arriving in Las Vegas herself.

Keith Libby was called to the scene to head the investigation. At that point he had spent only four years on the police force and one year in the investigative division in Barstow. When Libby and his officers got there, they mistook Brandolino's hand, sticking out from beneath a layer of branches, for a red scarf before realizing that it was part of the decomposed hand of a man and a red sleeve. San Bernardino County Deputy Coroner Dick Ebel also arrived to examine the deceased. Ebel saw that rigor mortis had come and gone. The body was mushy and cold to the touch. It had been raining on and off and at night the temperatures dropped into the low thirties. All of these conditions affected Brandolino's decomposing body. Dick Ebel estimated that death occurred two to three days before the body was discovered. The deceased was fully clothed, dressed in brown corduroy pants, a flannel shirt and a sweatshirt. He had on socks and one leather boot. The other boot was found a few feet away. Ebel noticed a small hole on the right side of the dead man's head and numerous old abrasions on his face that could have been caused by falls or beatings. It became apparent that Brandolino was laid on the ground, covered with tree branches and leaves in a makeshift shallow grave. Dirt had been thrown over him, covering his entire body.

The rock placed near the top of his head, it was determined, served as a headstone. No blood was found on the rock, but investigators did find a bottle of Dilantin, a medication for epilepsy seizures, lying on the ground nearby among empty beer bottles. Visible high above this scene, thirty yards up an incline, was what appeared to be an abandoned transient camp containing a mattress and bedsprings, a portion of a fifty-five gallon drum used to contain fires, pieces of chair frames and a beat-up couch.

Those investigating the area where Brandolino's body was discovered thought that the victim may have been beaten to death and his body hidden in the shallow grave. But they also didn't discount the possibility that the deceased stumbled and fell during an epileptic seizure and hit his head against a rock and died. Other transients with him at the time, seeing the consequences of his fall, may have been too scared to call authorities and took it upon themselves to bury him out of respect. One of the officers recognized the victim by the Aryan Nation lightning bolts tattooed on the left side of his neck and recalled that he had been arrested for drunkenness a few years back. Tats, as the convicts and parolees refer to tattoos, provide a lot of clues about an individual. Their popularity has spread to mainstream society, but in prison culture they play a significant and meaningful role in communicating three main things about the person: who he is, what he's done and where he's been. They identify the individual's racial or gang affiliation, time spent in prison and a few other personal notes, as well as where they did time. In California, for example, a tattoo that looks like the star-shape on top of a navel orange signifies prison in Orange County, while the northern star stands for Northern California. Popular symbols included clock faces without hands to signify doing time or a laughing face next to a crying face, which stands for the mottoes "play now, pay later" or "my happy life, my sad life." Prison tattoos are all done in the color blue, which may turn black or purple depending on exposure to the sun and skin pigment. Tattoos have also become popular among women parolees who have adopted their own symbols. The double lighting bolts tattooed on Brandolino's neck had to be earned before they could be inked in. They signified that the wearer had assaulted, in a prison gang fight, a minority person or killed a member of a minority group.

An autopsy found that Brandolino had traces of Dilantin in his body. The postmortem also revealed a blood ethyl alcohol level of 0.28 percent. But what struck the coroner were the multiple injuries over the upper body and the internal damage. And while a seizure may have been triggered by the beating, it wouldn't have caused the traumatic injuries that members of the coroner's office saw. The victim's injuries included several broken ribs and a lacerated liver. His head, face, neck, chest and abdomen were badly bruised. The man was beaten to death.

It takes effort for a cop to relate to a guy like Brandolino, but someone has to speak for the victim. Each crime reflects the ills of society and getting to the bottom is a search to root out the evil that breeds among us. The responsibility of police investigators is to step in and clean up messes created by others, solve riddles and put together pieces of puzzles through clues left behind. For the coroner's office, the Barstow police and the San Bernardino sheriff's office, their first task was to figure out whether Brandolino was murdered or whether he fell to his death during an epileptic seizure. The entire area was secured and marked off by yellow and black crime scene tape that ran to the fence along the freeway and along the rocks and shrubs by the river bottom. This served to keep onlookers out and evidence intact. Libby had all the items around the grave marked and gathered for evidence. One of the officers found a welfare application form with Hampton's name on it. It was located several yards away, near the campsite where the group originally sat. At first Libby didn't think he'd need it. Different transients were always coming and going in the area, but then he said, "Take it."

"Wow," Libby said and shook his head, recalling to me how close he came to screwing up when we both stood on top of the ridge overlooking the spot where Brandolino was murdered. I sympathized with him. I know only too well how easy it is to overlook an important clue that may, at first, appear meaningless. What counts is that Libby's judgment was sound and he used the information on the welfare application form to list Hampton's name in a law enforcement network computer file.

Authorities found in Brandolino's pocket a series of identification cards from Arizona and Minnesota, dating back to 1994. They learned that Brandolino also applied for food stamps in Barstow on November 30 of that year and received medication for his epileptic seizures from the local health department around the same time. When questioned by investigators, the staff at the Barstow health department remembered Brandolino's visit. He stood out because of the black and blue marks on his face. The health department staff had asked Brandolino if he was beaten up by someone, but he insisted that he suffered from bad seizures and that he fell down numerous times, hitting his face and head against the ground. The detectives also found records that Brandolino had been arrested by their department for public intoxication in 1989. They were able to locate living family members of the deceased, which included an uncle and a father. The victim's family, however, was unable to handle funeral arrangements because of financial difficulties and Brandolino was buried by the county.

Brandolino's death shared front-page headlines in the local newspaper, the *Desert Dispatch*. Almost four weeks after Brandolino's death, twenty-eight-year-old Gordon Russell Coffey was arrested in Barstow on suspicion of the Kansas native's murder thanks to Michael Dwayne Hampton's uncontrollable temper. Kelly, the Nevada woman he traveled with from Barstow, charged him with assault and battery a few days after their arrival in Las Vegas. When she filed the charges against Hampton, Kelly told Las Vegas Police about the Barstow incident. Hampton was arrested for assault and remained in custody until he was released to be extradited to San Bernardino county where he was charged, along with Gordon Russell Coffey, in the homicide of Brandolino.

The two witnesses who sat and watched Brandolino's torment and murder provided instrumental testimony in the trials of Hampton and Coffey. They also assisted in the construction of a composite drawing of the third suspect, Jack Caines (Silveria) who at the time remained at large. The Barstow Police Department continued to be on the lookout for him long after the trial of the other killers was over and long after all the evidence and objects were cleared from the crime scene. Even though Hampton could have provided law enforcement with Silveria's rail name — Sidetrack — he didn't. It continues to amaze me how these violent FTRA train hoppers adhere to their code of silence, but at the same time think nothing of torturing and violently killing one of their own. Hampton and Coffey were found guilty of second-degree homicide.

Barstow police continued to look for the third man, Jack Caines, believed to be a train hopper from Missouri or Wisconsin. After Silveria was arrested and his capture made headlines across the country, one of the witnesses to Brandolino's murder came forward and told Barstow investigators that the photo of Silveria in the newspaper resembled Jack Caines.

Roseville Detective Mike Allison showed Silveria a photographic line-up that was mailed to him by Libby. Silveria identified Cherokee, but not Coffey. By then, all the culprits were locked up behind bars, including Silveria.

The savage method by which Michael Allen Brandolino met his death illustrates the unbelievable cruelty that sometimes takes place in FTRA camps and how easy it is for one of the members, in this case Robert Silveria, to escape notice from police. Long after all the lawyers moved their stacks of files on Silveria into storage boxes, I decided to pay Barstow a visit, in order to learn more details about the murder of Brandolino and its perpetrators. I met with Barstow Officer Keith Libby at the police department. Libby, in his police car, led me to the area where the crime took place. I followed in another vehicle. Once we arrived and climbed out of our respective vehicles, Libby wasted no time in pointing out the crime scene.

"There it is. That's the tree where the body was found. The group was hanging out by those bushes over there." The area looked like a rugged crater next to a freeway. In the distance one could see the desert cut off by a range of mountains. Libby pointed to a tree located a few yards from the only large foliage growth in the area.

"Remember the double bolt of lightening the victim had tattooed on his neck?" I turned to look at Libby.

"Yeah, I remember." Libby nodded.

"Well, I found out recently from this expert on prison tattoos that you don't just get those tattooed, you have to earn them by killing or at least assaulting a minority." I saw a growing interest on Libby's face.

"Wow," Libby shook his head in disbelief. "If you remember, the fight started because the victim insulted one of the guys who was an Indian or rather half-Indian. It was a racial conflict." Libby's gaze turned back towards the lone tree that had served as a large cover for a makeshift grave.

"I guess so," I shrugged.

Libby and I stood around talking about the case that had baffled the Barstow Police. When he first read about Silveria's capture in the local Barstow newspaper, Libby wasted no time calling the Roseville Police Department.

Officer Keith Libby's call came in the first week of Silveria's incarceration. Mike Allison took the call, listened patiently and intently as Libby made his request. The young Barstow detective asked the Roseville investigator to check for his department whether Silveria was involved in a homicide in their jurisdiction in San Bernardino County, California. The victim, Michael Allen Brandolino, was a forty-four-year-old Kansas native, homeless at the time of his death in Barstow, a city located about 120 miles northeast of Los Angeles. His body was found on December 29, 1994, at 12:36 P.M. by a local man walking through an area frequented by transients near a dry river bottom known as the Mojave River, next to Interstate 15 and less than 900 feet north of a double set of railroad tracks. In the winter, when the rains come, the trees and bushes take on foliage, creating a woodsy appearance. The area lies on the outskirts of town, lined by low-income houses on one side and on the other side is the desert, with a mountain range that includes the so-called Elephant Mountain. Two men were tried and convicted of the murder, but a third was still at large, Libby explained to Allison. He asked Allison to check if Silveria could be that third man.

Allison traveled eighteen miles from Roseville to the County Jail in Auburn to follow up on Keith Libby's request. He eventually ended up making the journey on three separate days to see Silveria so he could finally close the files on the Barstow case. Allison, Bill Summers and their respective departments were more than willing to go the extra mile. During his first visit, after advising Silveria of his Miranda rights, Libby specifically asked if Silveria recalled any transient homicide victims in Barstow. Silveria thought a few minutes and told him "yes," he did remember being in a fight with several individuals while in a Barstow camp. He said the victim crawled away after they beat him. He recalled that the camp was located in a wooded area near a freeway and railroad tracks. Silveria provided Allison with enough information for him to report to Libby that it appeared Silveria was indeed the third man they were looking for.

Keith Libby sent Allison documentation on the case and a photo of one of the men convicted in the murder to see if Silveria could identify him, which would further confirm that Silveria was at the scene of the crime. That same day, after 5 P.M., Allison initiated a tape-recorded interview with Silveria for the Barstow Police Department.

The murder of Michael Brandolino clearly demonstrates that the kind of company a person keeps has its consequences. Then again, if the person is walking a tightrope heading towards death on the losing side of town like Brandolino, he usually doesn't think about where he is until it's too late. Brandolino's fate was sealed when he encountered Robert Silveria and a couple of his FTRA acquaintances. His last few hours on earth were unspeakably brutal.

All Barstow police had learned from witnesses was that a rail hopper, Jack Caines, arrived with Michael Brandolino and was the last unknown participant in the crime. It seemed to them that Silveria could have been involved and, once he was interviewed, Silveria confirmed many of their suspicions. He told Allison that he had been to Barstow numerous times. At the time of the crime he was traveling the rails with Cherokee, an FTRA rail rider who was half-American Indian, later identified as Michael Dwayne Hampton. Silveria knew him only by his moniker, Cherokee. Silveria was coming in from Salt Lake City and was headed to Colton to set up welfare in the town. They signed each other's vests with their symbols and rail names, a ritual when FTRA members ride together or cross paths. Sometimes they draw things on each other's jacket. Because of his artistic abilities, Silveria was frequently asked to draw on other members' vests. Silveria told Allison that he eventually gave his last vest to "Baby Girl" in Roseville, which Mike Allison retrieved shortly after the interview. There was another fellow traveling with them, too, a young rail rider from North Carolina, identified as Gordon Russell Coffey, who was a Barstow resident. He and his wife worked at a fast food chain near the rails. He and his wife also frequented the area down below the ridge, along with Brandolino, where they drank and hung out with passing FTRA rail riders. Silveria didn't know Coffey and couldn't recall his name when Allison questioned him. He did not recall Coffey's wife either, who was working at the time of the incident. I found that, with the exception of very minor variations in detail, Silveria's account matched that of the witnesses who later testified in court against Hampton and Coffey.

There were other twists and turns to the story which came out. Apparently, before Brandolino was so brutally murdered, a Minnesota physician had told him that if he didn't stop his drinking, he would die before Christmas 1995. The Minnesota doctor's predictions came true in an odd way. Brandolino did die, but he died that same Christmas, not because he was drinking per se, but because he was drinking with the wrong crowd.

One year and three months later, thanks to the help Barstow police received from Roseville, they were able to close their books on the Brandolino murder case. Silveria avoided standing trial for the Kansas man's murder, but eventually he had to stand trail in Kansas anyway for the murder of Charles Randall Boyd, whom he met in Texas and traveled with to Kansas.

Standing there at the strategic location overlooking the murder scene, to which Keith Libby led me, I gained a new perspective on the crime. Keith Libby broke in with his own thoughts.

"I was able to locate Brandolino's father someplace in New York." Libby stared ahead towards the tree where the victim's body was found. "At first his father sounded suspicions and gruff. He told me, 'I haven't seen or heard from him in years.' I explained why I was phoning. There was a long silence on the other end of the line. Then I heard a sigh. He thanked me for letting him know." Libby paused. "I remember his voice was quavering when he thanked me."

Soon Libby took off to follow up on a call. I ventured down towards the tree and the brush area where the crime took place. Retracing Brandolino's path, I walked over uneven ground, odd shaped rocks and pockets of debris. Though litter was strewn about the site, it looked to be a perfectly isolated spot for a rail rider to drink beer and wait to catch out on the next train to Las Vegas.

"A great place for renegades to party, but why the deadly screw-up?" I murmured, as the sharp whistle of a passing freight train rang out in the distance. Robert Silveria would answer that question when we finally came face to face.

18

A Strange Bond

"People don't realize how much the homeless go through every day just to get food and water. People telling me, 'Get off my property.' "
                    Robert Joseph Silveria, Jr.

Mike Quakenbush's background geared him to be disciplined. He was adopted as an infant in Germany by a career Air Force man and his wife. As a result, he moved around with his family frequently before settling on the outskirts of San Diego. After high school, he joined the Army and discovered his future career while serving in the Army's Criminal Investigation Division. He moved to Oregon to enroll in Oregon State University and after graduation got a job with the Salem Police Department.

While Silveria was being interviewed by investigators at the Placer County facilities, Quakenbush maintained close communications with his own department and with KBI agent

Bruce Mellor, gathering as much information and evidence as he could muster.

Around this time, Assistant D.A. Diane Moffat was told by the district attorney for whom she worked to be prepared for a special case involving a serial killer that was headed her way. A grand jury was also assembled for deliberation on the evidence Quakenbush gathered. Silveria provided physical evidence against himself, which we wouldn't have had in a million years if Silveria didn't hand it to us. The grand jury's decision in Oregon was swift and Silveria was handed over for trial. Quakenbush's next objective was to extradite Silveria to Oregon.

Two months after Silveria was locked down at the Marion County Jail to await trial, I received an unexpected telephone call from George Schlichting, Silveria's cell neighbor. In the beginning, according to Schlichting, Silveria was glad to have Schlichting talking to him, telling him about the references to him on the news. But Silveria had become disenchanted with the media, who dubbed him "The Boxcar Serial Killer." The title irritated Silveria. He was afraid no one would want to speak to him. Schlichting claimed Silveria insisted that he did not just kill in boxcars. Silveria also felt the media didn't explain accurately what he was really all about. He wanted George to telephone the television stations and relay a message to the families of the victims — to tell them on behalf of Silveria that he was sorry. Schlichting also claimed that Silveria, in letters and notes they passed back and forth, told him that he killed people because he wanted things for the leather pouch he wore around his neck, which he termed his medicine bag. He wanted to use the items in his bag to pray for salvation for the people he killed, because those people, especially the drug dealers, were bad.

I feel both men had reasons for cultivating communications. My guess is that Silveria was using Schlichting as much as Schlichting was using him. Schlichting wanted to ingratiate himself with the cops and later to get his own fifteen minutes of fame, making some money in the process.

Silveria's letters to Schlichting reflect his heated state of mind. There had to be some trust even if there was a hidden agenda behind what Silveria wrote, because he gave Schlichting written permission to talk to the media about their friendship and Silveria's behavior in the Placer County Jail. In one letter, he refers to Schlichting as "Brother George" and writes, "I don't know you, but I don't have to, because the spirits we both have are in a pattern of being close." Silveria also told Schlichting that he was glad he could not harm anyone anymore. As I got to know Silveria and was privy to his intelligence and cunning, I had no doubt that he saw Schlichting for what he was, a snitch to the cops. My bet is that Schlichting became a voice for Silveria to the outside world. Soon he sought out other voices as well.

After his arrest, members of Silveria's family, with whom he had lost contact in the preceding thirteen years, suddenly reappeared. He heard from his father and saw his mother. His first wife began corresponding with him. He sent her loving letters and drawings, rekindling their relationship. Silveria had remarried and had a second wife, who thought he was dead because she had not heard from him since 1991. They too reconnected and Silveria told her he was keeping a journal.

Meanwhile, George Schlichting was keeping his own notes on everything Silveria told him during their incarceration at the Placer County Jail. That journal fell into the hands of the Placer County deputies. He also made attempts to bait Silveria into revealing anything the cops or the deputies might find interesting. Silveria's letters to Schlichting at this time were compromising and reiterated what he told investigators. With Schlichting's urgings, Silveria expressed deep feelings and thoughts, such as in a letter dated March 5, 1996, in which he appears remorseful and provides his first known introspection:

"I, Robert Silveria, born in California, am a very different type of human being. I know I'm very sick and that I have a problem with life and all that's in the world. I know what I've done is very wrong and unkind to mankind. I know sorry can't bring back the life of others I put to rest. I can only say I know I've tried my best to end this madness. I know I'm willing to stand up and be a man about what I've done and help in any way to tell what I've done for the victims' families and friends. This testimony is in great sorrow from my heart to theirs. Might whatever sentence is given to me be what I deserve. I will talk and walk with the deepest regret for the things I've done. May God be with us all. Amen."

But in the same correspondence, after seeing a broadcast about himself, he added:

"I got to watch myself on TV. What a shock. If only I knew what was up with the way they come off with that. Bull shit — they never even said anything about all the things I told them [police]. They didn't have shit on me. My testimony is the only thing that helped these guys...I went to a polygraph testing and found that I might know something more."

Then in a letter dated March 8, Silveria writes:

"George — you ever been on a journey, but your journey one day stopped and it became a nightmare? Well my nightmare has become a tragedy...I started looking at the things I've done and it's very sick and horrifying to think I had to do something to someone and had to have someone else examine the contents of the brutal murder...I don't for one minute think you could take someone else's brains out and put it up on a table to examine the beaten contents of what's left of it. The only hope I hope for, is I can stop all these bad dreams and get them all out in the open..."

During their time as neighbors, George Schlichting posed a series of questions and jotted down Silveria's answers as they came through the vent. Today, Silveria denies Schlichting's claims and insists that Schlichting made them up based on television reports at the time.

However, the conversations reported to me do sound very much like Silveria based on his other correspondence. One conversation is especially chilling:

Schlichting: Robert, why?

Silveria: George, I didn't do it. When I was on drugs, somebody else did it.

Schlichting: Robert, how did it feel?

Silveria: I felt like so much weight was off my mind.

Schlichting: How many people did you kill?

Silveria: I think forty people. Every day I remember more. There's so many, I blacked out. I know my hand still hurts.

Schlichting: How many, Robert?

Silveria: I know I killed eighteen people. I know of twenty-two more that other people did and I've watched.

Schlichting: Were they men and women?

Silveria: It really doesn't matter. I killed people, George. Today, George, I think I found peace.

Schlichting: Did your victims say anything to you?

Silveria: The only thing they said was, "Why me?"

Schlichting: Are you glad you're in jail?

Silveria: Yes, because the killing stopped.

Schlichting: Do you worry about death?

Silveria: No, George. I won't let them have the pleasure.

According to Schlichting, Silveria also quoted a series of passages from the Bible. The selections Matthew 5:21-26,

Matthew 7:7-12, Jeremiah, 29:11-15, Romans, James, Corinthians 1 and 2 and Psalms address the act of murder and other personal issues with which Silveria was dealing at the time.

On a lighter note, Silveria expressed a hankering for Chinese food. I don't know if Silveria ever got his desired meal, but the demand for his time made the schedule around him so tight that one night Summers ordered pizza for the detectives waiting to see Silveria. Despite the seriousness of the discussions, the detectives and Silveria took pizza breaks. Another time, they got Kentucky Fried Chicken for everyone, including Silveria. Summers denies deliberately giving sugar or sugary substances to Silveria, as the inmate claims. He says they didn't know Silveria was on heroin. Silveria told Mike Allison that he was on heroin some time before his arrest in Roseville and a letter from Silveria to Schlichting seems to confirm this:

"I told Vancouver Police I was Robert Silveria. I was in a hospital and handcuffed. I was in D.T. (Detrimental Tremors). I was telling her I was on drugs and I might have killed some people. She (a nurse) laughed and said, 'It is the effect of the drugs wearing off.' I pleaded with her for help, but she said all beds are full. She gave me a ticket to the mission and $3... The police dropped me off at the mission."

Silveria asked Schlichting to pass on his letters to the outside world, particularly the media:

"My name is Robert Silveria. This letter will be read by a friend that doesn't want to be identified. First, please stop bothering my family. I have asked my friend to go to any news media he feels fit. Since my arrest, I have been in close contact with the Sheriff's Department. I have been truthful about the murders I have committed. I am helping the sheriff's department and other agencies to locate the bodies they have not been able to find. I used a source that has no real culture and is not civilized. Think about it. It's like getting kicked in the grill.

I will always control the weak. I'm the leader of my nation, the homeless of my nation. To each their own. Forget Mr. Nice Guy. I could have tortured others of your world, but I chose to torture my world because I preyed on the weak."

Later he wrote:

"If you had a gun, you could survive in the homeless world, but me I was with three to five people. I was with people that didn't back down from me, like you did George, last night. People always said I looked like the devil when I was beating the shit out of people. Sometimes, I wouldn't know they were dead until I came back to that state.

Even after Silveria was moved to Oregon, he continued to communicate with George Schlichting, sending him more letters. One of Schlichting's family members claims to have destroyed these in order to keep George from having any associations with Silveria. However, Silveria passed a series of handwritten letters and other writings, along with two drawings, to Schlichting through another inmate who was being released from the Marion County Jail where Silveria was locked up at the time, awaiting further legal proceedings in Oregon.

When the inmate got out, he mailed the packet to Schlichting. Schlichting wasted no time in contacting the media and getting his fifteen minutes of fame before following up on Silveria's instructions to phone me. I didn't know then, but it was my Elvis persona which made Silveria feel a bond with me. He even put up a picture of me a friend of mine had given him on his cell wall.

Schlichting called me on March 14, 1996, at the Albany Police Department, telling me, "I have letters [which would eventually be coined the 'Elvis letters'] specifically for you from Robert Silveria." While Schlichting was speaking in his rapid staccato, I hit the record button of the tape recorder attached to my phone and

grabbed my pen and a yellow pad, which I kept handy on top of
my desk. I wanted to highlight some points which I could review
in detail later without having to find the information by having to
listen to the entire tape.

Schlichting described his and Silveria's methods of communicating with each other via the vent. "He passed me a letter
that he wanted me to read to the news media...let's see," Schlichting paused. I could hear rustling paper in the background.

"Okay," Schlichting continued, "I got bunches of letters
from him, letters that I hid, because of what the sheriff department was doing, taking all my letters and not giving them back to
me."

"Oh?" I said noncommittally, knowing quite well those
letters could be used as evidence and that the police were within
their rights. I learned later that on numerous occasions, Schlichting's cell was searched and notes from Silveria were found by
deputies. These were turned over to Bill Summers. As Schlichting
talked to me it was clear that he didn't seem to understand the significance of these letters to law enforcement. His tone of voice was
complaining.

"And then they started giving me prints and stuff like
that," George said, referring to the Xerox copies he received. I
began to wonder if Schlichting was making demands of his own.

As George Schlichting went on, he bragged about the
televisions crews interested in him. "The news media always
came up and tried to talk to me." His voice sounded disappointed when he explained that the sheriff's department put a
notice on his booking packet that no media visits were allowed.
"And now they're just calling. Last night I was on Channel 3
and Channel 10. Channel 13 called me this morning, Channel
40 called me a little while ago." What Schlichting wasn't admitting to me was that he was responsible for stirring up the local
media in the Sacramento area by trying to sell the papers Silve-

ria sent him through another released inmate. Schlichting suddenly paused. I waited to hear what he had to say next.

I asked Schlichting if Silveria ever talked about McLean's murder. Schlichting said he'd have to go through his files and check, but what he really wanted that day was to talk about himself. He jumped to explaining how he had been jailed on a probation violation and that he wasn't locked down because he was in trouble, but for his own protection. He made it clear that he had a complicated relationship with different law enforcement teams in the Roseville/Sacramento area and had over seventy-five drug arrests.

I didn't have to say much to inspire Schlichting to go on. In fact, the only comments I made were grunts and an occasional, "Oh yeah? Tell me more." This was just to let him know I was still breathing at the other end and to keep him talking while I jotted down pertinent points. I felt if I was patient, he would begin talking about Silveria again and, though he darted back and forth in his recollections, I was right.

"Okay. When he first got in there, see, he never had a family. For twelve or thirteen years he hadn't talked to his parents, his uncle..."

The uncle to whom Schlichting was referring was a wannabe Hell's Angel. At one time Silveria was close to the uncle and claimed to have obtained much of his drugs in the early years from him, but since his incarceration, Silveria and his family had a falling out with the uncle.

Schlichting went back to his and Silveria's original conversation. "And I was the only one that was there (in the cell ward) and I introduced myself, see, that night on the fifth when they brought him at 12:30. I introduced myself," Schlichting continued, "and we started talking and that next morning when I woke up, he passed me a letter that he wanted me to read to the news media. Let's see…Let me find some of these letters." I heard the familiar paper rustling noise in the background again and then Schlichting began reading.

"'It's like being in a shoebox. How am I supposed to remember the horrible things I've done? Well, George, I've started looking at the things I've done and it's very sick and horrible… But…God will always be there to forgive us…'" George took a deep breath and then started reading from another sheet.

"He also says this. 'Rage, well, in my heart it's still there you know. I'm grateful I can't even think, but I remember what you said about the Bible, brother, from my heart. I can only say thanks, because I am sick and my only prayer is God will forgive me. …I don't know what I've done. I only know what I can do now.'" Schlichting stopped reading.

"Oh you know what? When he first came in there," Schlichting said, returning once against to the early stages of his talks with Silveria, "he wanted some pencils and some papers and so I gave it to him. And I even got in trouble. I think, I mean I even shook his hand. And I got in big trouble for that, because we were in lock down, you know, and we couldn't be out together."

George paused and then, as if he had suddenly managed to piece together why Silveria wanted him to talk to me, asked, "Are you that Elvis Cop?" There was momentary silence on the other end. Putting down my pen temporarily, I leaned back in my chair.

"Yeah, I am," I admitted. Immediately, Schlichting became chattier.

"Yeah, Silveria talked about you quite a bit. In fact, he kind of boasted about you." Despite the serious conversation, I grinned. Schlichting then spelled out my name and police address as Silveria had written it down in the instructions for him to contact me.

"And the phone number and then down on the right it says, 'will write book,'" Schlichting read from his notes. I shook my head at the other end of the line, saying that wasn't in the cards as far as I was concerned. Although I was fascinated by the FTRA, their customs and how Silveria had survived among them and I wanted to do more in-depth research on the group and crime along the rails, as well as on Silveria's life and personality, I tried to explain to George that it was highly unlikely that I would write a book.

That day, I wanted to draw Schlichting into discussing a subject that intrigued me. We turned to the symbolism in Silveria's tattoos. I asked George, "Did Silveria ever tell you the meaning of what looks to me like a peacock or a phoenix?" Instead of responding to my question, Schlichting went off on another subject.

"No state is going to put him to death. You know that, right?" Schlichting asked. Then he added, "He will be put to death by himself. He will kill himself. That was one thing he stressed to me. When this is all over, he said, in about five years, when this is all over, he will do his own thing. But then, I was telling him, 'Hey, if you're pretty much into the Bible, you can't do that.'" Schlichting paused, then continued, "Did he ever tell you that he was into the Bible?"

"Well, a little," I tapped my pen against a nearby coffee mug, after making a note to check whether there was a suicide watch on Silveria.

"And then he just says that one thing God won't forgive is him taking his own life." There was another pause and George said something else that I had heard before.

"Did he ever tell you that he tried to get help in Vancouver, Washington? It says so in another letter he writes me. He goes, 'I pleaded with them for help and to take me to the mental health. But all they did was give me a ride to the mission and three bucks. I jumped off a bridge. Then the bulls came and picked me up; they called the police and took me to a safe house.'" George added, "And it says, 'I told Vancouver police I was Robert Silveria. I was in the hospital in handcuffs, and I was having DT's in the hospital. The personnel called the mental health department and then the cops took four identifications from them.'"

"What year was that?" I prodded. I knew that detrimental tremors happened during detox.

"It was last year, when he jumped off the bridge and tried to get help," George replied. Then I heard the familiar sound of pages rustling in the background. A few seconds later, Schlichting became talkative again. "He wrote me on rage. It says, uh, okay, blah, blah, blah, about his rage, the black dots and all that. Then it says down on the bottom, 'Train Riders.' Okay on top it says, 'Train Riders, love your brother, Freight Riders of America.' It says, 'Sidetrack '96, Robert Silveria, Jr., 3-11-96.' He wrote that. And he was one of the kings of that world. He was one of the bosses. And the peacock stands for death."

So Schlichting had confirmed that the peacock stood for death, but what he failed to understand was that it also symbolizes resurrection. It is also the mythical phoenix that rises again out of the ashes.

Now Schlichting turned to another subject which fascinated me — Silveria's psychological troubles. According to Schlichting, "Silveria freaked out a few times in jail." I asked him what he meant by that. He said, "I mean, when some of these news people were saying that he was just a mass murderer...he would kick his door, punch the walls and after he was all done, he said, 'One thing George, my hands won't hurt tomorrow for killing somebody.'"

The difference between a mass murderer and a serial killer is that a mass murderer will kill a lot of people at the same time, whereas a serial killer, like Silveria, kills a lot of people one by one over a period of time. I didn't stop to educate Schlichting. I was more interested in what he could tell me about the one hundred pages of writing Silveria had passed on to him.

I agreed to meet him at a prescribed residence in Roseville to photograph or Xerox Silveria's writings. This would allow me to examine them and see if any new evidence about my case or any other cases that were still pending came to light. He gave me directions, in a typical Schlichting way, which by then I was getting used to, and added a non sequitur, "There were twenty-seven California police officers that talked to him."

"That's a lot," I murmured.

Suddenly, Schlichting veered off on another topic. "I met the devil when I met Robert Silveria."

"Yeah? Tell me more about why you feel that," I said, encouraging him to go on as if I were a psychologist.

"I'm serious. Did you know when he talked to them police officers he was staring at a white light all the time? He would not look at them, but he only looked at the light. He did not see the people asking the question. He put himself in a trance, where the person wasn't there. But they were asking him questions. And then there's his rage. He told me, 'George, you know when I went into a rage and I killed these people and I searched their bodies and I took something from them and put it in my bag? When I woke up, I realized I put something in my bag and my hands hurt really bad. So I'd write in my journal and then I'd read the Bible.' That's how sick he was."

19

Gathering Evidence

"I know, I'm stuck in this place till I die."
Robert Joseph Silveria, Jr.

The same afternoon that Schlichting called me in Albany, Mike Quakenbush telephoned Bill Summers in Auburn to find out about some documents Schlichting had in his possession from Robert Silveria. Quakenbush told Summers he'd had telephone calls from two reporters who said Schlichting was peddling Silveria's writings that came out of Marion County Jail. All Summers knew at that point was what he saw on TV. He told Quakenbush that the evening before when he watched one program, he saw a news clip in which Schlichting was being interviewed about Silveria's letters. Schlichting held the letters up for the television camera and Summers recognized on the bottom of one of the letters Silveria's "Sidetrack" moniker.

On May 16, the same day that Barry Galloway and I were heading up to Roseville to meet Schlichting to look over Silveria's papers, Summers called Quakenbush to give him an update on the latest turn of events involving Silveria's writings from Oregon. He told Mike that Schlichting had retained an attorney to represent him in civil court but not in criminal court and that an agreement had been reached between him, the attorney and Schlichting that the documents would be turned over to the Placer County Sheriff's Office. Further, Summers told Quakenbush that one of their deputies had already picked them up and they had the letters in their possession, ready to fax to him.

Meanwhile, Barry Galloway and I arrived at the house where George Schlichting told us to meet him. It was well before noon when a family member opened the door and told Galloway and me that George had phoned and left a message that we were to go to another location. We weren't happy about the change of plans, but what choice did we have, even if I felt it was not a good sign. The place Schlichting now asked us to meet him was his new lawyer's office.

We drove there quickly. Galloway and I parked the car and walked to the building, entering a very small waiting room, behind which was a narrow hallway lined with filing cabinets and leading to three rooms. One of the rooms was the lawyer's office, another was a storage office filled with filing cabinets, and the third belonged to a paralegal. George Schlichting was there, too. He and the paralegal were both in the lawyer's office. They were all too smug for my taste, telling me that the documents had been turned over to a sheriff's deputy, who had come for them one hour before we arrived.

"You can call the department and check for yourself," the lawyer said.

"Don't worry, I plan to," I said, irritated. Then I asked to see copies of the documents they had turned over to the

Placer County Sheriff's Office. They were reluctant at first, but then made copies of the documents and handed them to me. I examined them closely; strangely, not a single one mentioned my name or referenced the "Elvis Cop" as Schlichting had told me about two days earlier. In fact, I soon realized a lot was missing. There were only fourteen pages, which meant eighty-six pages had disappeared. Nevertheless, the small sample appeared to be genuine and contained information indicating that Silveria had killed individuals in the past and would continue to do so in the future. I told them I didn't like being lied to and they were in "deep shit." I used some more colorful words and finally said, "I'm not going to let you get away with jerking me around." The lawyer got huffy. He told Galloway and me to leave his office.

"Yeah, we'll leave now, but we'll be back and your ass will be in jail if you didn't turn over all the papers." I stormed out.

Galloway and I strode out to the parking lot towards our unmarked police vehicle, with choice words spilling from my mouth. Looking over at Barry, I noticed him grinning. "You were cool in there," he said approvingly.

Next, we drove to the Placer County Sheriff's Office in Auburn and met with Bill Summers. He showed us the original letters from Silveria that his deputies retrieved from Schlichting's office that morning. Summers said he thought he had all of them. I informed him that there were eighty-six total pages still missing. Then I told him about the so-called "Elvis letters" that were not in the pile, which could be evidence in my case.

Later, I returned to Schlichting's lawyer's office with Galloway. By then Schlichting was gone. There was no receptionist, so I walked right in. I leaned with one hand against the lawyer's office doorway, keeping the other in my pocket.

"We have a real problem, and…" I used a few expletives. Reluctantly, the lawyer admitted that he hadn't turned everything over to the Placer County Sheriff's Office. The final paragraph of the agreement stated, "I declare under penalty of perjury under the laws of the State of California that the forgoing is true and correct." When I read it out loud the lawyer looked to me like he was getting hot under the collar, although he maintained his composure. He said he would have to contact his client. Later I discovered that Schlichting had been offered $25,000 by a television show for the original documents. Not turning them over, I said, would be considered meddling with police business and tampering with evidence. The lawyer agreed to contact me on May 21, after consulting with his client.

When May 21 rolled around, I didn't hear from him. I telephoned the lawyer and got an answering machine. I left a message directing the lawyer to contact me regarding the Silveria documents. Early on, I had notified Mike Quakenbush about Schlichting's phone call and the missing documents. After talking over the latest development, Quakenbush, with whom I had been in close contact regarding Silveria's writings, called Schlichting's attorney as well. All he got was the same answering machine voice message I had. Mike and I began to discuss strategy over the phone. We decided we had to get a search warrant for Schlichting's residence and the lawyer's office. Mike came down to Auburn to work on the warrant. I met him at the Placer County Sheriff's Office and once again, Summers and his department extended their hospitality, letting us use their conference room for meetings and to write affidavits. Because of Silveria's pending trial in Salem, I let Mike take the lead in writing the affidavit, even though those letters could have been important in my investigation of J. C. McLean's death and other murders.

Barry Galloway, Kevin Horn and I spent three days with Quakenbush in Roseville working on the case. We also recon-

nected with Roseville Detective Mike Allison. I owe special thanks
to Lieutenant Ron Patton from the Albany police department,
who had a good understanding of the need to gather the evidence
in the way police work should be done. Since I had a lot of other
work to get out, he told me not to worry; he would handle this
part with the police chief.

Silveria had told me that he dropped the Albany murder
weapon in the creek near his encampment. While Galloway and I
were waiting for some important paper work to go through, Mike
Quakenbush and Kevin Horn went to the rail yards and visited Silveria's old haunts under the bridge and searched for the weapon.

While they were gone, Mike Allison brought over Forty-
Pounder and her live-in boyfriend, Soda Pop. Forty-Pounder
claimed to be very nervous about talking to us, fearing retribu-
tion from the FTRA, but Silveria's exposure and confessions
had shaken her up. She said she couldn't get over what she read
in the newspapers about Silveria going around deliberately
killing other transients for their identifications in order to
acquire food stamps. She told me in detail about Silveria's last
visit to her house and about Bushman talking him into leaving
when he saw Silveria's gun. Then she spoke about other gangs
along the rails and an anticipated war scheduled to take place
that summer between the FTRA and a Montana rail gang made
up of young and violent rail riders.

Checking on that tip with railroad security, I learned they
were already aware of the problem. Fortunately, like many rumors
that circulate among different factions, this one didn't materialize.
After a while, Mike Allison left to attend to another matter in his
department. I remained with Forty-Pounder, Soda Pop and Barry.
I wanted to learn more about the FTRA's conchos and bandannas, which I had first found out about from Silveria. Since they
lived only a short distance away, Forty-Pounder told Soda Pop to

go back and get his concho to show me. Within a half hour Soda Pop returned with both his black FTRA bandanna and his silver concho.

Wanting to make my interest in those items seem more friendly and not disclose my real intent of finding out more about the organization for official reasons, I said enthusiastically, "Boy, I sure would like to have one of those. I'm a collector and I'd love to have that." I pulled out a twenty dollar bill and placed it on the table. "It's yours if you want to trade." Soda Pop thought a while and said, "I had to go through a lot to earn that in the organization." But then finally, after looking over at Forty-Pounder, who appeared amused by my interest in FTRA memorabilia, he agreed to sell it to me for twenty dollars. "I'm no longer riding the rails anyway," he explained.

A few moments after the transaction, Forty-Pounder said loudly to Soda Pop, "Well, if he likes that so much, he will really like the flag I have," motioning towards me. Naturally, I asked her what she was talking about.

She explained, "I have a stars and stripe flag that I keep on the walls. It's common in safe houses for rail riders who pay a visit to sign their names on the flag with a waterproof black marker. It's very much like a guest book sign-in." I asked Forty-Pounder if it was possible to see the flag. She nodded and suggested meeting us in the park behind the police station, a half-hour after we got off.

"Okay, I'll bring the beer and you bring the flag," I agreed.

At 5 P.M. we all left. Barry and I climbed into my car and we drove around looking for a liquor store. We finally found one and I bought a whole case of Budweiser, enough for a small group, in case Soda Pop and Forty-Pounder brought along more friends. Then Barry and I returned to the park behind the police station. When we climbed out of our vehicle, we could

see Forty-Pounder and Soda Pop in the distance already waiting for us. Dressed in jeans, a black t-shirt, silver framed sun-
glasses and a baseball hat, with Barry dressed even more
casually, I carried the beer as Barry and I walked across the
lawn. If Forty-Pounder and Soda Pop were nervous about
being seen talking to the police, they probably felt safer with us
because of our appearance. No one would ever figure that we
were cops, dressed like that. I suddenly understood why Forty-
Pounder and Soda Pop agreed to meet us in such a public place.

Appearances aside, Barry and I were concerned about
carrying the beer in a park right behind the Roseville Police Station, because you're not supposed to drink alcohol in a park. As
we walked up to Soda Pop and Forty-Pounder, Barry and I
agreed that I'd do the drinking and that he'd just cover me.
Barry shared my attitude. We both wanted to get information,
but we figured we had better at least try to play by the rules. I
opened up the case, pulled out the beer and passed it to Forty-
Pounder, Soda Pop, but not to Barry. There were some other
FTRA friends of theirs watching us. After a while they came
over for a few minutes and I gave them some beer too.

Soda Pop explained, "I've had my last train ride and am
giving it up for good." Then Forty-Pounder left to go back to
the house, while I asked some general questions about train
hopping. She returned shortly afterwards with the flag she had
told me about earlier draped over her arm. When she unfolded
the flag, the FTRA signatures, some with doodles next to the
monikers, shot out like musical notes on a stars and stripes
music sheet. She said it contained Silveria's signature and Bushman's and other guys I had never met, but of whom I had
heard. I was impressed, wishing I could study the signatures.
The flag would provide information on the FTRA members
who had been in this area. However, I didn't think it could be
used as actual evidence in a courtroom, since it wasn't even

dated. Nevertheless, I decided that when I had time, I was going to study this group. I knew the flag would provide names to look into. I also recognized the flag's historical significance. Forty-Pounder said, "It was hanging on my wall on March 1, the last time Silveria signed in." I knew then that I had to have it. After the case was over, I would have it framed. A couple of beers later, I made my offer. Forty-Pounder bargained, but finally sold it to me. I showed the flag to Mike Quakenbush the next day and I could see he was impressed.

"You know, I need that for my case as evidence," he half-smiled.

"Bullshit," I grinned. "There's no way I'm going to part with the flag. I have a case, too; I'll keep it safe. If it needs to be evidence later, so be it."

A few days later, we were finally ready to make our move to rescue the letters from Schlichting and his attorney. Four agencies were represented in the action: Salem, Roseville, Albany and Placer County Sheriff's Office. Quakenbush couldn't believe that in California, in order to search a lawyer's office, you need a special master present, an attorney appointed by the court who oversees the search and makes sure that nothing is taken that does not pertain to what the search warrant covers. Nevertheless, we got the order and raided Schlichting's residence and the lawyer's office, looking for Silveria's letters. In the search we uncovered all the letters with the exception of the fourteen pages. Among those we didn't find were the ones written to me and, specifically, those mentioning Elvis. We did find copies of letters to nationally syndicated talk shows and one from a producer offering $25,000 for the original letters. We still don't know where the missing, so-called Elvis letters are. Some day I'd like to find them. At least we recovered most of the letters. I made copies of the ones Silveria wrote in prison. That night, reading them over, I was surprised by his continued openness. In one, he implicated himself in several murders and in another, he jotted down the places where he killed. Among them was scribbled "Albany."

20

Conference on a Killer

"I continued to live the way I did with the people who I thought were my friends, but they were gone in the very end."

Robert Joseph Silveria, Jr.

In June, three months after Robert Silveria's arrest, the FBI organized a three-day conference focused on him in Portland, Oregon. To me, it seemed a very smart move on the part of the agency. I was able to get both Barry Galloway and Kevin Horn permission to go there with me as part of a package deal, because both men were deeply involved in the McLean case. The conference generated tremendous energy. For me it was also something of a homecoming week. Mike Quakenbush was there, along with Wade Harper and many others I knew.

Among the cops I met at the conference was Bob Grandinetti, a retired cop I didn't know from Spokane, Washington. He

was credited with being one of the first cops to notice the existence of the FTRA. When Bob worked for the police, his beat
included downtown Spokane. He hassled panhandlers to keep
them out of the downtown area. That's when Grandinetti began
to notice that many of them wore bandanas. Most had black ones,
but some members wore red or blue ones, though these were
fewer in number. Grandinetti started talking to some of the guys
who wore the black bandanas. From these discussions he learned
of the existence of the FTRA. During his watch, there were a lot
of deaths reported on the rails, he said, which he was called to
investigate. He didn't buy the typical railroad company explanation that they were all "accidents."

It was the repeated appearance of dead bodies which
aroused Grandinetti's suspicions. Too many of the victims had
their shirts pulled up above their chests and the pants down below
their buttocks, indicating they probably were dragged to the
tracks. He started asking questions of the railroad officials, but all
that resulted were heated arguments. However, he did make
friends with some railroad security officers, who provided him
with books and information on the rail riders that the railroads
had developed. I sent him photographs of some of the things I
had in my possession.

One of the first nights there, Barry Galloway, Kevin Horn
and I went with Granadetti to the Airport Sheraton Hotel lounge
and sat for hours by a table next to an unlit fireplace exchanging
police stories and discussing the fact that Albany had the lowest
crime record in the I-80 Corridor. We told stories about how cops
chasing a subject sometimes had to ram them off the road with
their police vehicles in order to arrest them. Granadetti sat up and
said, "I like you guys from Albany. You're my kind of cops."

As the conference progressed, a lot of my thoughts and
insights on Silveria crystallized. For instance, during the workshops,
we developed a timeline for Silveria's activities and brought our
expertise and knowledge together to analyze his case from different

perspectives. One of the things I learned was that Silveria couldn't stand looking at his victim's opened eyes after he killed them, which led him to cover them up. Barry Galloway straightened up. "That explains why our victim had a folded chair placed over his head when he was found by his neighbors." I was proud of Barry and I would soon be very glad that Kevin Horn was there too, when a difference of opinion broke out between KBI special agent Bruce Mellor and our Albany group.

Mellor felt McLean's and Boyd's murders were too close to each other on the timeline. His idea was that Silveria heard the details about McLean's murder from another rail rider. Mellor had talked to witnesses who said that Boyd and Silveria left Van Horn, Texas, on Sunday, July 23, 1995. McLean was murdered July 22, 1995. Silveria couldn't have been in two places at the same time.

However, Kevin Horn checked with the Southern Pacific Railroad agents and was told that if Silveria jumped a "hotshot" priority train, he could have made it back in time. The trip would have taken him ten hours.

To this day, I have heard that Mellor continues to express the view that Silveria made a false confession in the Albany murder of James McLean. For a while, I have to admit, in the back of my mind I worried that he might be right. Today, my opinion is that Kevin was definitely right. Silveria now says he was coerced into the plea bargaining in Mellor's case.

In my correspondence with Silveria, I asked him if he knew of any hotshots from the San Francisco Bay Area to Texas. After a couple of months and several letters in between, he replied, in a letter sent to my post office box, that the answer was yes and he explained that it's done by hopping on a double stack flat bed freight car and riding above the axle of the wheels, which is very dangerous. He also stated in writing that it can be done only at night. Double stacks, also known as "pigs" or "piggybacks," are high priority trains. The knowledge Silveria possesses on the subject impressed me. He drew a map of California and the main railroads that run through the state. Kevin Horn and I used to think that Silveria most likely got away from the crime scene through Oakland, but I noticed on his map that he indicated the city of Richmond, which is even closer, and something Kevin and I didn't even consider at the time. He also drew a railway going all the way down to El Paso and to Arizona and suggested for more information we look up a web site where one can purchase a United States railroad map on a CD-rom.

      I believe Silveria could have made it to Albany on the night of Friday, July 21, and returned to Texas on the morning of Sunday, July 23. Another point that looks good for the Albany case is that one of Mellor's witnesses said that Boyd and Silveria or "Dykeman," as Silveria was known then, said they were going to Albuquerque, New Mexico on Friday, 21 at 4:30 P.M. to meet with Dykeman's "brother." This would explain why the two went through the Colorado mountains to get to Kansas, instead of taking the smooth and easy ride through Texas. Albuquerque is even closer to the San Francisco East Bay. And there is a direct rail route between the two locations which I have seen on the U.S. railroad map I obtained.

      Mellor felt he had evidence that Silveria was in church in Texas on July 23, because Silveria signed a church required attendance card. Again, this is not so clear to me. On the card that Silveria supposedly signed on July 23, the "3" could also pass for a "5," and the month of July is not in Silveria's handwriting. It appears as if someone else wrote in the month. There are some other problems that I see in the case, but I have come to feel they are moot points. The fact is Silveria did confess to killing Charles Randall Boyd in Kansas and James McLean in Albany.

      I believe that those of us in law enforcement can be territorial and overly protective of our cases, regardless of whether justice is served. And the irony is, in this case, the killer himself stepped in to make peace between us and to resolve our issues.

21

On Trial

"I know I've tried my best to end this madness."
Robert Joseph Silveria, Jr.

Barry Galloway and I were notified of a hearing on a motion to suppress evidence that was to take place January 6-7, 1998, pretty standard procedure for cops involved in a murder case. The prisoner talks and talks. Then he's appointed a lawyer and denies everything. The deputy district attorney for Marion County, Diana L. Moffat, was the prosecuting attorney. Moffat had fourteen years experience working for the D.A. in Oregon, with seven of those years in homicide. Silveria's would prove to be one of the biggest cases she had prosecuted thus far in her career. During the trial and negotiations, she worked eighteen hours a day, seven days a week. One section of her office became dedicated to paperwork on Silveria's case. For the defense, the Oregon court appointed Thomas C. Bostwick, a former prosecutor, and Noel Grefenson, a private attorney with Storkel & Grefenson. Moffat considers them two of the most outstanding attorneys in the state of Oregon.

In court, Silveria was polite and interested in everything. Moffat wanted to make sure that he never walked the streets a free man again or jumped another freight train. She didn't buy into the idea of an FTRA gang or the death squad and does not to this day. Silveria, in her view, is a sociopath who progressed in his killings and had no remorse for what he had done.

Thomas Bostwick, a native Oregonian and Silveria's court-appointed attorney, was born in Portland and received his law degree from Lewis and Clark University. During most of his career he practiced law in Salem. In 1976 he started working as a deputy district attorney and was a prosecutor until 1992, when he went into private practice in Banden, an Oregon coastal town. Later he returned to Salem where he handled defense cases for five years, concentrating on homicide. Because he had once been a prosecutor and was knowledgeable about how the office operates, he received a lot of death penalty cases, among them Robert Silveria's. Bostwick thought that Silveria was easygoing and a gentleman, unlike some of the difficult clients with whom he's had to deal. He felt they both got along. Like Diana Moffat, Tom Bostwick spent much energy and time on Silveria's case. He found the trial, paperwork and arguments extremely challenging.

The defense team of Bostwick and Noel Grefenson sought to suppress all the testimony Silveria gave when he was locked down in Placer County. They argued that Quakenbush, who spent six days with the prisoner, had coerced Silveria into a false confession. By then, Silveria had recanted everything he told the investigators in Auburn. Bostwick and Grefenson also advanced questions as to whether their client was given appropriate readings of his Miranda rights.

At this point, Diana Moffat started feeling the heat and pressure from her boss. There were a thousand other cases requiring attention. Also, a hearing with an appeal to suppress evidence would have broken the bank. Moffat was ingenious in solving the problem of the budgetary crisis. She decided to parade police officers from other parts of the country, in order to make her point as to how dangerous Silveria was. She made deals with chiefs and sheriffs that if they paid the plane fare for their officers to come and testify at the suppression hearing, she would cover the cost of hotels. She called around and many departments cooperated. Our chief, Larry Murdo, was not thrilled with covering the cost of airfare for Barry Galloway and me, but he realized the importance of it.

At the first day of the hearing in the Circuit Court of the State of Oregon in Marion County on January 6, 1997, Honorable James Rhoades presiding, the tables were turned in the suppression of evidence hearing. The investigators were called to the stand to be questioned, while Silveria sat at the defense table with his lawyer, as if in judgment. It took two days to fit everyone in. I appeared during the first day's session, flying up with Barry Galloway.

Silveria sat quietly at the defense table, dressed in dark slacks and a gray sweatshirt. The opening started with minor courtroom bickering between Moffat and Bostwick over Mike Quakenbush. Bostwick didn't want Quakenbush in the courtroom assisting Moffat. Unless Quakenbush was going to testify himself, he did not want Quakenbush there, because it might interfere with the recollections of the other officers. He moved that Quakenbush not be allowed to sit throughout the suppression hearing and assist the state, since he was heavily involved with Silveria's case from the beginning. Moffat argued that the State needed his assistance and that if he couldn't be there, then she wanted the private investigator for the defense not to be allowed in the courtroom either. Judge Rhoades ruled in favor of the defense, stating that it would be more appropriate for Detective Quakenbush to be excluded, but for future hearings it would be assumed that he would not be excluded. The investigator for the defense was permitted to remain. Silveria said, "Thank you, your Honor."

During the testimonies, it became apparent that several errors had been committed in not reading or reminding Silveria of his Miranda rights at the time some officers interviewed him. In one instance, confusion occurred when one officer concluded the meeting and then left, leaving his partner behind to watch the prisoner.

It also came out that during his time in prison, Silveria made a confession to a murder without being advised of his Miranda rights. The defense team pointed out that Silveria was videotaped without his knowledge more than once, although this is not illegal. He also complained that he was not read his Miranda rights each time he was interviewed. In the motion to suppress, there was also some question as to whether the defendant was experiencing heroin withdrawal when he was interviewed in Auburn.

The defense team consistently questioned officers as to whether there were any side effects of drug withdrawal visible when they interviewed Silveria. Every officer testified there were no such symptoms apparent. Roseville detective Mike Allison added that Silveria had told him that he had been a heroin addict, but that he hadn't used the drug for a while.

There were also questions about the arrest itself. Southern Pacific Railroad officer Billie Metcalf was asked about his right to stop Silveria on public property. It was also revealed that Silveria was not consistently handcuffed. On this subject,

Roseville Detective Sergeant Dave Halley recalled sitting in the interview room alone with Silveria, realizing that he was not armed and the prisoner was not chained.

Finally, I was called to the stand. I was sworn in, then asked to be seated. Next came the spelling bee when I spelled out my name for the court stenographer. Afterward, Moffat approached me smiling.

"Good afternoon, sir. Can you tell us, please, where do you work?

"Albany Police Department, Albany, California."

"And how long have you been a police officer?"

"Twenty-eight years."

The next questions focused on exploring my experience in police work, including how long I was in Albany (nineteen years), my position in the department at the time (detective sergeant) and how long was I in that position (five years).

Then Moffat came to the point. "On March ninth of 1996 did you have occasion to come into contact with the defendant who is seated here, third gentleman to my right?" Moffat looked over at Silveria. I glanced at him, suddenly recalling the intensity in his face that day.

"Yes, I did," I said and nodded.

"And where did you come into contact with the defendant?" Moffat studied me closely.

"In Auburn, California. He was in custody at the Placer County Sheriff's Department."

"Okay," Moffat said and asked a few questions pertaining to the time of the meeting. "And was anyone else present when you met with the defendant?"

I told Moffat about Barry Galloway coming there with me and that Detective Bill Summers of Placer County Sheriff's Department and Mike Quakenbush of Salem, Oregon introduced us to Silveria.

"Did Detective Summers and Detective Quakenbush stay with you?" Moffat continued.

"No, they did not." I shook my head. Next, Moffat inquired if we recorded our conversation with Silveria and when I answered affirmatively, she presented a taped copy of the interview as marked for identification purposes. Then Moffat turned her attention back to questioning me.

"During your interview with the defendant, was he advised of his Miranda warnings?"

"Yes, he was." I nodded, again.

"Can you tell me at what point in the interview that took place?"

"When Detective Bill Summers and Detective Mike Quakenbush left the office, I briefly advised Mr. Silveria of the nature of the investigation. I told him that I was going to be advising him of his rights as soon as I turned on the tape recorder, so he knew what was going to be happening. He indicated to me that he had been advised of his rights numerous times by other agencies. I subsequently started the tape recorder and advised him of his rights."

"And he indicated to you then that he did understand his rights and he wished to waive those rights and speak with you?"

"That's correct," I replied. Her next line of questioning focused on the homicide I was investigating, the murder of James McLean.

"And during your interview with the defendant, did he accept responsibility for Mr. McLean's death?"

Silveria's calm demeanor and self-acceptance of his deeds along with this cold matter-of-factness flashed through my mind. "Yes, he did," I answered firmly.

A few minutes later, Moffat covered another issue. "Was there anything about the defendant's physical demeanor that caused you to believe that he was suffering from some physical ailment or other malady?"

Once again I tried to be absolutely clear and concise. "No, there was not."

Next she touched on Silveria's state of mind. "Did the defendant's questions seem appropriate, as far as being oriented to space and time?"

"Yes, they were," I replied.

Moffat brought up my discussion with Silveria on his return to religion. "You engaged in some discussion with the defendant about the Bible and a religious discussion concerning scriptures and parables. Is that correct?"

I nodded. "It was exactly scriptures and parables. There was a discussion near the end of the interview on the ninth. Mr. Silveria had brought up 'cleaning the slate' and religion and the Bible. And I discussed the fact that occasionally I read the Bible and it was a good book."

Moffat picked up on Silveria's thought process. "So, to the best of your recollection, the defendant was the one who actually brought up the fact that he was attempting to clean his slate, if you will, and make it right with God?"

For a moment our eyes met. Perhaps we both were thinking of the horror of it all. After a pause, I replied, "That's correct."

When I finished testifying, I walked out the door. To my surprise, Moffat came out to compliment me, saying that the judge thought I made a very good witness. After we talked, I went back to the chambers where I had waited earlier, to pick up copies of the clippings I had xeroxed from Oregon files.

I saw Diana Moffat later during a break. She again told me that I had been a good witness. I was pleased to have been helpful.

Moffat continued to press her case during the two-day suppression hearing. She argued that the sheer number of confessions, in which Silveria knew the crime scene down to the minuscule details that only a killer would have known, pointed to his guilt. She also had obtained photos of him cashing checks and picking up food stamps under aliases in different locations. When Silveria was stopped and then arrested, it was found that he had twenty-eight monthly food stamp accounts at $119 per month. Quakenbush had told me that Silveria didn't use them all at once but traveled to different locations using five at a time when collecting the food stamps, raising around $600 a month. Judge Rhoades decided in favor of the State and Moffat won the round.

In a later plea bargain, Bostwick argued that Silveria was defending himself in some of the killings. In fact, Silveria never stood trial in any of the states that charged him. His family members believe that he plea bargained to avoid embarrassing them. He didn't want them to suffer through long arduous trials. One letter to Schlichting supports this to some degree. In it, Silveria expresses frustration and annoyance at the harassment his parents received from the media and others.

In the plea bargain, Bostwick also brought up the fact that Silveria was a heroin user. He considered using a psychological analysis of Silveria's state of mind, but then decided it wasn't necessary. Diana Moffat, on the other hand, ordered a psychiatric examination of Silveria. When I read it, I found the analysis pertaining to the murders of Clites and Pettit differed from what I concluded from interviews with Silveria and the police reports. For example, Dr. Frank Bennett, who conducted the exam, didn't bring up the point that Silveria was on heroin when he killed Pettit. In reference to Clites, Dr. Bennett again differs from the police reports that I have read and the taped interviews with Silveria that I have heard. I don't know if this is because Silveria told Dr. Bennett something different than what he told the police investigators. However, Silveria had been consistent in his statements throughout the ordeal of investigation. It is quite possible that there was so much information provided to Dr. Bennett that some of it got lost in translation. In the end, Dr. Bennett didn't give creedence to Silveria's mental health problems and his fifty-dollar-a-day heroin habit and his attempts to seek treatment, concluding that all Silveria's murders were motivated by greed.

After plea bargaining with the defense, Moffat settled for two consecutive life sentences in prison for Silveria. Silveria pleaded guilty to the murders of Pettit and Clites, in order to avoid the death penalty and received life with no possibility for parole. A guilty plea was filed on January 30, 1998 in Lane County and another guilty plea was entered February 17, 1998 in Marion County. Thus, Silveria's fate was sealed in Oregon.

While Silveria appeared outwardly calm in the courtroom, his dissatisfaction was reflected in letters to his second wife. On February 22, five days after the last plea was filed in Oregon, his comments about his situation revealed his deep frustration:

"I don't think anyone is doing any on-going investigations like they're leading me to believe. I know I'm stuck in this place till I die. And if I could have told my side of the story, at least I wouldn't have had to lie to the courts when I made my plea agreement and had to admit to the charges just so the state would drop the death penalty... The TV show never explained that I had told numerous stories to crimes that never really happened, because I couldn't be in two places at the same time... Never once was the reason I gave police all those confessions exposed and that bothers me. It bothers me the police lied in court to Judge Rhodes and my attorney never did anything about it." He closed with, "I hope I didn't disappoint you. I need you there."

On May 20, 1998, Silveria was extradited to Kansas to stand trial for the murder of Charles Boyd. His court-appointed attorney, working closely with Tom Bostwick, made a similar plea bargain to the one in Oregon. Once again, Silveria waived his preliminary examination in return for a twenty-five year "boxcar" sentence, which meant that Silveria would have to serve out his Oregon sentences before he would serve in Kansas. Boyd's daughter was in the courtroom to witness Silveria's sentencing, but did not speak in court. When the presiding judge, the Honorable Barry A. Bennington of the District Court of Ellsworth County, asked Silveria if he had anything to say after he was sentenced, Silveria said, "Yes, Your Honor. I would like to apologize to the victim's families for the hardship that this has created for them. I know it's a very tragic situation to be caught in and I do apologize to them."

At this point, Silveria was "on loan" to Kansas from Oregon. His next stop would be Tallahassee, Florida. He had already signed papers back in Oregon to be extradited from Kansas after his trial. There was a general consensus among many cops that Silveria would get the death penalty in Florida. Silveria shared the same outlook and was worried.

However, in Florida Tom Bostwick worked with the public defender's office on Silveria's behalf. Florida law gives the option to the prosecutor to seek the death penalty. This falls under what is called "prosecutorial discretion." Silveria changed his plea from not guilty to guilty to the charge of first-degree murder and armed robbery, with the understanding that he would receive a life sentence on each of these counts. The two sentences were scheduled to run concurrently with each other, but consecutive to the existing sentences in Oregon and Kansas.

Salt Lake City decided not to prosecute Silveria for the

death of James Lee Bowman, a.k.a. Hooter, when it became too difficult and costly to try to locate their one witness, who moved around a lot. However, the department was able to find and notify Bowman's wife, the mother of his child, regarding Hooter's death.

Silveria soon began to declare his innocence. In his letter to his second wife, he gave totally different accounts from those he directed to Schlichting. Silveria writes:

"Sometimes I feel like Job from the Bible. He suffered a lot like Christ did when he carried the cross... the pain, he too, had to suffer for crimes he didn't do...I wrote my family after I ended the fighting...thinking I'd be on death row. That's a very painful experience to suffer for as long as I did... I know that God has helped me to know the difference between right and wrong."

Silveria had begun to see himself as much a victim as the men he brutally killed. In his mind, the rage that fed on heroin and death and the savage world he lived in *forced* him to kill or be killed. He felt, in his position as an enforcer, that he could not let his guard down.

I asked myself what had generated such hate and rage. Was it something Silveria saw in his victims, an arrogance or pride that reminded him of others who had hurt him? Or was it something of himself he thought he saw — an evil that should be destroyed so it would not be allowed to fester and become malignant as it had within him?

By this time, his religious fervor had reached its apex and Silveria saw himself as an avenger, doing God's will. He wrote:

"As a Christian, I want to tell you the time is now near when Satan and his cohorts will be no more. The world, including its demon rulers, are passing away (read the newspaper, watch the news. It's all there, facts. The Bible assures 'he' that does the will of God, remains forever. (John 2:17). What a relief it will be to have that evil influence removed. May we therefore be among those who do God's Will and enjoy God's righteous new world. (Psalm 37: 9, 11, 29 and 2 Peter 3:13. Revelation 21:3, 4)."

22

Learning More about the FTRA

"Just because I didn't have a bed or a toilet doesn't mean I was homeless...
Only in your world."

Robert Joseph Silveria, Jr.

Almost two years had passed since Robert Silveria's incarceration in the Oregon State Penitentiary. When a police patch show was scheduled in Roseville, I took a couple of vacation days to drive up there. I would be able to do some visiting with the guys I knew and it would also give me the opportunity to see if I could reconnect with Forty-Pounder and Soda Pop to find out if anything had changed since Silveria's arrest.

Walking under a bridge by Washington Avenue on a crisp, sun-touched November day, I saw a hobo and recognized him to be an FTRA member. He wasn't wearing a bandanna or concho. He didn't even have a back pack or a roll, but by then I had

287

learned to recognize them among the other transients and home-less by a certain quality of toughness in their demeanor. I pulled my car alongside the street, climbed out of it and walked towards the man, lighting up the cigar I had brought with me.

He said his name was Swabi. It turned out that during the Viet Nam War, this FTRA member was in the Navy, as I was. That gave me a start, because I recognized his signature and name from the flag I had bought from Forty-Pounder. He told me Soda Pop was rubber tramping in southern California and was no longer riding rails. Forty-Pounder was in intensive care in a county hos-pital dying of cancer. "Riding the rails is tougher," he complained. "There are more bulls on the line now and they're not giving tick-ets anymore. They're hauling everyone into jail, but it's not the old timers stirring up the shit. It's these Flintstone kids."

"Flintstone kids?" I cupped my ear while puffing on my cigar. It's a little trick I picked up in training so the individual will repeat, in order to confirm his statement.

"Yeah, those damn kids you see around with earrings and button rings pierced in their noses and anything else they can pierce," Swabi snickered, but his agitation was highly visible. "They're wearing red rags and talking shit and tearing things up, making it hard on everyone. Me, Cannon Dave, Little Hose and Spitz took some cans and found them sleeping under a bridge one night. We kicked their asses and took their rags and camos. We left them running around bare in their shinnies." Swabi grinned proudly.

I asked Swabi if there were other FTRA members to whom I could talk. I was still interested in finding out about the group. It would give me more insight into the mind of Silveria. He agreed to meet me by a bridge next to the rail yard. "That's where a bunch of them are," he said.

"I'll be there in about twenty minutes." I stopped at a mar-ket and got a case of beer and a bottle of whiskey. When I arrived at the meeting place, I realized it was the same campground in which Juan Lara's body was found more than five years earlier.

Cannon Dave, California Kid and Bill the Young Rider, a group of young transients, were waiting to catch out to Vancouver that night. What stuck in my mind after the visit was the stench of feces and urine that was hard to shake for days after leaving the site. It didn't seem to bother the three FTRA riders. They were smoking reefers and drinking their own beer when I joined them with a new supply of refreshments. Later on, Uncle Ernie joined us after Cannon Dave went down deep into an area where the creek lay hidden underneath a spread of thick layers of bushes and trees and woke him up. The two men returned to camp with Cannon Dave carrying Uncle Ernie's roll, while Uncle Ernie dragged his feet, his eyes still half-closed. Cannon Dave explained that in case he got too drunk, he wanted Uncle Ernie with him so that he wouldn't be left behind when the time came to jump a box car. Uncle Ernie, another Viet Nam veteran, tilted his head, eyeing me up and down. "You look pretty strong. You wanna arm wrestle me for a hundred dollars? Do you got a hundred dollars?"

"Maybe," I grinned back, looking up and down his emaciated frame, evident in spite of the thick down jacket covering it. I wondered if Uncle Ernie was testing to see how much cash I had on me. The others I noticed were quiet, just listening.

"I used to be in the Wrecking Crew," Uncle Ernie said, still smiling with droopy eyes. Suddenly, Cannon Dave shot back.

"Don't listen to him. He doesn't know what he's talking about. He's never been in the Wrecking Crew. Those guys are killers. I've seen them beat up one guy just sitting there, doing nothing but reading a Bible. He's never been in the Wrecking Crew."

"Yes, I was." Uncle Ernie looked, puzzled, at Cannon Dave.

"No you weren't," Cannon Dave gave him a firm look.

Uncle Ernie stood there for a minute or two. I wasn't sure if he was trying to see if he could maintain his balance or to decide which one of them was right. Finally, he shrugged his shoulders.

"Okay. I wasn't. Did I hear someone mention cocktails here?"

"I brought beer and whisky," I said.

"That'll do," he replied.

I spent more time with them than I thought I would. I decided I would not tell them I was a cop. I didn't have a gun on me and that revelation could be dangerous. The night air grew chillier. While they were dressed for a colder climate up north, I wore only a black t-shirt and jeans. We talked about train hopping and they invited me to come with them.

"You gotta come with us to understand," said California Kid, C.K. for short. "Come with us tonight. We'll show you what we mean. You can travel anywhere you want to and it's free. You don't pay anything for moving around. You got freedom and you don't have to pay for it. It's free." I studied him for a few seconds. His blond hair was pulled back into a long ponytail. With the exception of a couple of small open sores on his face, his complexion was rosy and his eyes a clear blue. His army-style camouflage jacket, unlike his jeans, looked surprisingly clean, almost new. There was a black bandanna strapped around his neck. It was held together not by the traditional concho, the type found on saddles or western bolo ties that the FTRA members wear, but a silver wing nut. I asked him why he wasn't wearing his concho.

"No way man," California Kid shook his head. "It's a giveaway to the cops. I don't want to bring heat on. They see you with that and you go straight to prison."

Cannon Dave pulled out a small chain with nail clippers and dangling from it was his concho. He also displayed his toothless grin again. "I ragged him," Cannon Dave proudly pointed to California Kid.

"How do you get ragged?"

"Three members rag you. They choose your name and they piss on the rag that you wear from then on around your neck," Cannon Dave chuckled sheepishly.

"I'm just a greenhorn. I'm not there yet, but these guys are. Listen to them, man," Bill the Young Rider cut in, pointing towards California Kid and Cannon Dave. "I'm just a greenhorn, but I respect their ways. I'm learning. Know what I mean?"

I wanted to ignore him but he pushed too hard for attention. Finally, I said, "Okay. How did you get involved?"

"California Kid found me. I got divorced and I had no family. He taught me to ride the rails. I still have a lot to learn. He took me for Thanksgiving to his parents' house this year, because I have no family. My parents are dead. I have no brothers or sisters. I got no family. I got California Kid. He's teaching me."

"You ride together?"

"I ride alone," California Kid broke in. "I don't ride with no one in the box car." He paused and gave Bill the Young Rider a stern look.

I looked at Young Rider to catch his reaction, but his eyes were turned away. It appeared he got the message.

"You ride alone?" I watched for clues in his expression. I knew Silveria frequently rode alone. California Kid raised his brows.

"Yeah, I don't take any chances. I was riding down with a guy from Alaska one time. I was teaching him about riding rails. I had $5,000 that I made up there. When he thought I was asleep, he tried to rob me. I grabbed my goon stick, my peacemaker as I call it, and let him have it. I threw him off a train that was going about forty miles an hour. I taught him a lesson. No one is going to mess with me. I ride alone," said California Kid firmly. I noticed he threw a glance at Bill the Young Rider again. Then he added, "If I ever see that guy again, he'll know I mean business." I nodded, thinking of the similarity between this attitude and that of Silveria, who would sometimes say that he gave the victim a last blow because he wasn't sure that his victim was dead. For a split second I felt divided as to which way to go. How many men did this guy throw off trains? Had he killed in other ways? I quickly decided I would stay, but a second line of questioning was safer.

"Your goon stick?" I was still trying to picture how a man could survive a fall from a train at forty miles an hour and the force of a goon stick. Again, a flashback struck me of Robert Silveria telling me about his goon stick with Sidetrack, his FTRA moniker, neatly carved on the side of it. I knew from what happened to McLean that a goon stick was a powerful weapon in the wrong hands. I thought of all the times Silveria had cracked the heads of his victims with one. A photo I had seen of the huge hole in Pettit's head flashed through my mind. I wondered if I had made a serious mistake not bringing my gun with me. More doubt surfaced a moment later when California Kid pulled out an axe handle.

"Here, see? I have 'peace' carved on it," California Kid snickered. "That's how I get it."

"You wanna see my peacemaker?" Cannon Dave's voice rang out. Before anyone could answer him, he swiftly strode over to his backpack and pulled out several flares.

"These are my peacemakers. And look at this," he said, pulling a small match box out of his jacket's pocket."

"Oh, man. You're gonna show those off?" California Kid shook his head in amusement.

"Don't they look like corn dogs?" Cannon Dave opened up a long matchstick box and pulled out an odd shaped matchstick.

"These will light up under any weather conditions, even in rain. No one messes with my peacemaker," he chuckled, showing off his wide gap of missing teeth.

"What do you guys fight about?" I looked around at the mostly young faces, with the exception of Uncle Ernie, who quietly settled down on the ground drinking the whisky.

"Respect. We fight for respect." All three of them nodded in unison. It's the same thing cops hear from street gangs all the time. They're always fighting for respect. I thought of the times Silveria felt he fought for respect in a murderous rage. These young guys all knew Silveria and traveled the same route he did. I was wondering whether it would be safe to ask about him. I still had not admitted to being a cop, although I was tempted to. But I wondered if I should take the chance, especially without a gun. I was outnumbered and fighting was a way of life for these FTRA guys. Finally, I decided I had to ask them about Silveria. Immediately, the mood changed dramatically.

Cannon Dave appeared most upset by the mention of Sidetrack's name. He walked away and stood several yards away, starring down a hill where trash filled the opened areas between bushes and trees. His posture and his silence made it clear he did not want to talk about Robert Silveria.

"Hey," I called to him, "what's the matter? You're not going to use one of your flares on me?" I chuckled nervously.

"It was a terrible thing he did," said Uncle Ernie, with a solemn face. "He killed people for nothing more than their food stamps. He brought sorrow to his parents." Bill the Young Rider from Vancouver moved away, too. He sat down on his roll with his back to everyone. From then on, he kept to himself with his back turned to the rest of us, gesturing with his arms, talking mostly to himself.

California Kid, I felt, was in better shape to handle my questions. Or maybe enforcers act at being mellow, in order to catch their potential victims off guard when they strike, thereby giving them the advantage of the element of surprise. Robert Silveria had that easygoing charm about him, too, I recalled during the sudden moment of silence that fell over the camp. Then again, I hoped, maybe California Kid was not in a fighting mood that day, having been in trouble with the Roseville Police Department only a day earlier over a fight with a man wearing an FTRA rag, which the Kid claimed he couldn't prove he earned. Suddenly, I lucked out when California Kid noticed a blond female rail rider heading towards town.

"Hey, Gayle, wait," California Kid shouted, walking in the direction of the woman's campsite, past the men's hideout. He ran up to her and they hugged. Curious, I approached them. Up close, Gayle's face was prematurely lined, but otherwise she had fine features. Her body looked firm and youthful beneath her black jeans and white tailored blouse. I felt a great sense of relief that the cold, icy atmosphere had not turned violent.

Surveying the scene around me, I shook my head. How strange, I thought. Here we were in the new millennium, with the Internet, cyberspace and a booming frequency of air travel, but the old American folk tradition built around trains and train hopping still lingered. Yet up close, I thought, this folklore had a different perspective. The reality was a smelly campsite strewn with trash and garbage occupied by men who relinquished the names they were born with to take on monikers given to them by other hobos whose power over them is based on the number of miles traveled on rails.

Although I had gotten to know a couple of FTRA men in Albany, the following year I returned to Roseville. Soon I ran into some of the same guys and met new ones. I learned Canon Dave had been struck by a vehicle crossing the street and was seriously hurt. California Kid had been arrested and locked up in the county jail with his group of FTRA friends after they attacked and beat up a rail rider who had made a lewd comment about a female they all knew who was bathing naked in a creek. Of course, I also learned that they had all been drinking a lot of beer and it's my guess that common sense did not prevail over their so-called chivalry.

Some six months later, I was in Roseville again and ran into Cannon Dave and Swabi. Cannon Dave had just gotten out of the hospital the day before and came straight to Roseville to look for Swabi. He wouldn't be riding rails for a while, because his right leg was still in a cast. He wanted to find a friend to hang out with. Swabi had not ridden the rails much himself lately. He hung around Roseville getting drunk every day. I drank a beer with the men under a bridge by a busy boulevard. When it got dark, we moved to a bar that accepted transients as customers. We drank some more beer and talked about the FTRA, their lifestyle and how they got there. Soon it was time for me to leave. It was raining hard and very cold outside. I just didn't feel right leaving them to sleep under the bridge. I drove them to a hotel and put their room on my credit card. The grateful expression on their faces and the prayers they said before I left will be with me forever.

Maybe someone else would say their lifestyle is their choice. At one time I might have even agreed with the comment. Now I think of what Silveria said when Mike Quakenbush asked him why Mike, as a taxpayer, should support the food scams that guys like Silveria used. And wasn't it a scam when guys like him stood at freeway entrances to fly their cardboards? Mike went on to ask why people should give them any money. The whole thing was a scam, the food stamps, the cardboard signs asking for work. Silveria looked at Mike with troubled eyes.

"Those people really needed help. And if some church-going person can find it in their hearts to help, they should do what they can," Silveria voice was solemn.

You wouldn't think a killer could soften a cop's heart and give him more compassion for fellow human beings who are destitute. But thanks to Silveria, I began to have a different perspective on the homeless and the train hoppers. This solidified as I continued to go back to the camps, missions and their places under the bridge.

The story Jenny told me explained their irrational world best. I thought of how she described the night when she was still living out of her car and was headed towards a 24-hour market to buy cigarettes. Suddenly, she was attacked by a neatly dressed man. She managed to break away, running towards the rails and screaming as loud as she could. "Today," she said, interrupting her story, "there is a fence around the area, but then it wasn't closed off." Her assailant caught her and held a knife against her throat, telling her to shut up. She didn't know what he was planning to do next and began screaming. Maybe, she thought, he would throw her on the ground and rape her or just kill her for fun. She never found out his plans, because suddenly three rail riders appeared, seemingly out of nowhere. She found out later that they had been sleeping in a nearby boxcar when they heard her cries for help. The tallest one of them, she recalled, stood in front of the others. "I think the little lady wants you to let her go," he said, eyeing the attacker through darkness.

"Yeah, what the mother-fuck you gonna do about it if I don't?" the assailant shot back. There was a pause. For Jenny, time itself had frozen.

"I'm going to kill you." The rail rider's voice was calm and confident. Jenny said she could feel her assailant's muscles tightening around her. Suddenly, the man who had accosted her released his grip. He turned and fled. Jenny hugged the man who had saved her, thanking him and the others. He said he was an FTRA rail rider, but when she asked the stranger his name, he told her he couldn't give it out, because he was wanted for murder. He explained he was just passing through and didn't want it to be known that he was in town.

Jenny saw the stranger again several times in Roseville and spoke with him on one occasion when he came up to her in a mission. "Hi, remember me?" he said. "I'm the one who saved you that night." The last time Jenny and I spoke she claimed she still hasn't learned his name since he still said he was running from the law. Then, out for a drive in her car, she saw him one last time, walking near the rail yard with his traveling companions. She honked the horn and he waved to her. I heard her in my mind again, saying, "I've never been afraid of an FTRA member and I'd be lying if I said I was afraid of Silveria for even a second."

Afterword

I made an appointment to visit Robert Silveria at the Oregon State Penitentiary on St. Patrick's Day, March 17, 2004. It's not an easy task to visit an inmate. You have to first deal with bureaucracy and the paperwork. After the appropriate forms are filled out, the papers go through a chain of command for approval, among them the inmate himself. I knew beforehand that in case of an unforeseeable, violent uprising of the prison inmates, there would be no hostage negotiations for visitors. Should trouble arise and the prisoners somehow capture you, the prison authority will not bail you out.

I did not receive notice from Silveria's prison counsel that I was approved to see him until a few days before the visit. The approval was lucky for me, because I had already purchased a non-refundable ticket, made arrangements to fly to Portland and reserved a rental car to drive to Salem. They informed me that no jewelry could be worn, which meant my St. Christopher medal was not allowed. There were lockers provided on premises where for a quarter a visitor could store items not permitted inside the compound.

There are two time slots allowed for visitors. I picked the first one that starts at 7:30 in the morning. This would also give me enough time to head back to the Bay Area the same day. Prisoners are allowed twenty-four points a year with each point representing one person per visit.

When I arrived in Portland, I did a trial run to be sure I knew the exact location of the penitentiary. It's a good thing I did, because I took a wrong turn, being unfamiliar with the area. When I adjusted my directions, I passed a Salem police officer frisking a man who, by his dress and roll, appeared to be an aging rail rider. Finally, I saw the penitentiary. It looked like a large fort with towers and barbed wire. Visible behind the fence were less than a dozen inmates gardening.

The Oregon State Penitentiary, O.S.P., is the state's oldest maximum security institution. It is basically a self-contained city with two dormitories, several types of industries, five vocational training schools, a physical plant with ten shops, education department, a library, counselors, infirmary, canteen, dining room, kitchen and two recreation areas. The main structure is a yellowish painted brick building that from the distance looks like a nineteenth century imitation of a medieval castle. It was built in 1880 and because of its age, has been having problems with its underground water system. Large projects have been undertaken to correct the problem, which could impact the health of inmates and employees alike.

In terms of prison history, O.S.P. is probably best known for the shackle that was put on prisoners during transport, named the "Oregon Boot" or the "Gardner Shackle," which was created by

O.S.P. Warden, J.C. Gardner. The shackles were manufactured at the penitentiary by prisoners. Wearing the shackle for extended periods of time caused physical damage to inmates, who would become bedridden for weeks at a time with extreme pain. As a result, The Gardner Shackle became nicknamed "man-killer." The subsequent superintendent discontinued the use of the shackle, although they are still commonly used in transporting inmates.

On the day of my trial run, I drove into the compound and asked one of the tower guards where I should park and which entrance I should use the following day when I would be visiting an inmate. Talking through a loudspeaker while watching me on his monitor high in the tower, he explained the procedure and instructed me where to park. Afterward, I turned and drove around the perimeter of the prison. I was amazed by its size — twenty-two acres. Here 2,200 inmates are housed. A vast field on one side has a "No Trespassing" sign. I noticed this didn't stop a couple of male transients from sleeping by the side of a fence on the property grounds. A supermarket cart was parked nearby, loaded with piles of objects that only a homeless person would prize.

After attempting to circle the vast grounds of the penitentiary, I headed downtown to look for the Salem Police Department. That in itself was an interesting experience. One minute I'm traveling through what looks like a lovely country village and then, suddenly, I'm downtown in a small city.

To my disappointment, when I called him I found out that Mike Quakenbush had court that day. I was annoyed at myself for not letting him know that I was coming. I hadn't wanted to bother Mike until I knew for sure that I would be there. From my own personal experience, I know how valuable a detective's time is. After leaving a message for Mike, telling him where I was staying in Salem and giving the phone number of the hotel and my pager, I headed down to the Marion Court House to do some research of my own. I was crossing the street when suddenly I heard some one shout, "Hey, Bill. Bill Palmini." I turned around and saw Mike walking towards me. "I got your message. I'd recognize you anywhere," he said. "You haven't changed."

Despite his very busy schedule, Mike managed to spend some time with me. We headed back to the station, where he dug out some old files on Silveria and we sat outside the station under the warmth of the bright sun, surrounded by early blooming spring buds. Later, Mike came over to the place where I was staying and we walked over to the hotel's lounge.

"I never asked him to come into my life," Mike said as we sat at the bar. His words echoed through the lifeless lounge. Things were so slow in Salem that night that Mike and I noticed a couple seated in a booth next to us, craning their necks, obviously listening to our conversation. Soon they decided to join us without asking our permission. Pulling two nearby chairs up to our table, they introduced themselves. Then they settled down so that they wouldn't have to stretch their necks while they followed our every word. Mike and I ignored their intrusion and continued our conversation.

"You know why I went after him?" Mike turned with a challenging gaze. Without waiting for my reply, he said, "He bugged me. He really bugged me. I hate it when some dipshit thinks he can outsmart me. That's all that it's about. I don't like these dipshits thinking they can outsmart me. It's that simple." Mike's negative reaction to Silveria was different from my own and the other cops to whom I had talked. One of them even showed me a scrapbook he had made of Silveria's case.

"He told me you reminded him of his younger brother," I said, waiting for Mike's response. For a moment, I saw a surprised look on Mike's face, but then he shrugged and took a gulp of his drink.

There was not much I could add. Mike knew I was there to keep my appointment the next day with Robert Silveria at the Oregon State Penitentiary.

The next morning I got up while it was still dark. I wanted to arrive well before visiting hours at the penitentiary. I didn't dress in the Elvis outfit Silveria liked, but in one of my better business suits. I even wore a tie. I figured that, for once, I would look presentable. Anyway, no jeans were permitted for visitors, because that's what the inmates wore. Besides, this was an important meeting to me.

"I saw Silveria on Court TV. Did you see that show?" A blond female guard behind the counter looked at me as she ran my identification through the computer.

"Actually, no," I said, shaking my head. "But a lot of people have told me about it."

"Oh, it was good, but I can't imagine him being like that from what I've seen of him around here. He's so different from the way they showed him on TV. Know what I mean? Here, he's very easygoing, the quiet type. I'd never picture him committing horrible acts in a million years." She handed me back my identification.

That morning there were only a handful of people waiting to get inside to visit an inmate. Most were women, dressed in what looked like their Sunday best; a couple of them were heavily made up. One perky young woman who looked to me like she couldn't have been more than nineteen years old, took it upon herself to explain the system of going through a metal detector. She said it was very similar to the ones used in airports, except this one appeared to be far more sensitive.

Once on the other side of the metal detectors, we were told to wait in a small hallway. We stood there while one of the female guards walked past, giving us a final check with her glance. A member of our group didn't pass the test and the guard ordered the woman to turn back, because she was wearing a wraparound skirt. "Unless you change your outfit, you can't come in. If you change, you can still make the next visiting session."

"What's wrong with the outfit she's wearing?" I leaned down towards the nineteen-year-old self-appointed guide.

"They don't allow that because of the way she can sit. That kind of skirt can rise up high very easily," she said with a knowing grin. "No hanky-panky," she added.

Next, we were led into another short hallway where heavy steel doors closed behind us and, shortly afterwards, another set of doors opened.

We walked into a general area where waiting inmates, sitting on lounge-type chairs, met with their visitors. One of the guards, as a professional courtesy, led me to a semi-private room with three walls to wait for Silveria.

"He'll be right down. I'll call up there," the guard said.

Settling down on one of the chairs, I made myself as comfortable as I could, downplaying the anticipation of the meeting and the tinge of excitement I felt. The wait was longer than I expected. I couldn't help but notice that the visitors who came in with me in the large hall were immediately reunited with the waiting inmates. I wondered why Silveria wasn't there. He knew I was coming.

I waited and waited. Doubt began to set in. Where was Silveria? I kept glancing at my watch, thinking of the time I was losing from the amount allocated for each visiting slot. Almost half an hour passed.

"Why isn't he here?" I wondered.

Then, finally, I saw Silveria being led by a guard. He was looking over into the glass-wall room where I was waiting, before checking in with the guard at the desk, who had initially greeted me. I rose from my chair and watched as Silveria walked in looking confident, casual.

"Somehow, I knew I'd see you again," he said and we shook hands. Suddenly, we were alone in a tiny glass alcove, separated from the guards, the other visitors and inmates. I don't know what I expected, but I was surprised by how well he looked. There was some new gray around his temples, but the rest of his hair, which was cropped short, still was blonde. His complexion looked smooth but pale and his eyes alert. The tattoo of the word "freedom" on his neck was still noticeable.

"So how are you doing?" I couldn't think of anything cleverer to say. The initial awkwardness I felt the first time I saw him seized me again.

"I've got hepatitis. It's from all the needles I was using when I was on drugs," he pointed with his right forefinger to his left arm. "But so far it hasn't killed me. I'm hanging in there. I'm fine. I feel strong, even though I haven't taken any medication for it. I'm just hanging in there."

"Yeah, I saw that photo of you lifting weights. How much can you lift?" He seemed to me, as I studied him, to have worked out.

"545 pounds." Silveria grinned.

I blew a whistle. "What's the top here?" I looked at him in disbelief.

"680 pounds." Silveria smiled.

Then Silveria changed the subject. "I have a photo of you in an Elvis outfit hanging on my cell wall that someone sent me." I nodded and knew immediately the picture he was talking about. Barry Galloway took that photo when I was performing for some Albany teenagers. It's also one of the rare photographs of the project coordinator on the stage with me at the same time — my female Colonel Parker. Then we both reflected on the time that Silveria did the Elvis imitation in the holding cell.

"I saved that article about me singing in the cell," he chuckled. "I held on to it for years." He shook his head and then shrugged. "I don't know what happened to it. It just disappeared." I made a mental note to send him a copy that I still had.

"You know," I said, leaning forward. "To this day I don't know how it got into the press."

"Um, really?" He grinned noncommittally.

"Seriously, I don't know how it got in the press." I shook my head.

I took out some photos that I wanted Silveria to look at so he could explain their significance. Suddenly, he got nervous. He looked up and around for any hidden cameras.

"Look, I don't want any trouble. It took me seven years to get off gang status to qualify for special privileges." The so-called FTRA Brotherhood held a gang status in prison. Nevertheless, Silveria was helpful in explaining major points in the details of the photos.

"So what's your setup like?" I changed topics to ease up on him for a while.

Silveria said that there were only two of them in the cell and the other guy was a cook.

"I never go hungry." He patted his stomach, grinning sheepishly. "Put on a few pounds, too." His grin grew wider.

"I saw some guys out there tending a garden. Do you do that?"

"No, I don't go out much, but I mop the floors here." Silveria also described time spent mostly drawing and painting. He said he took some classes in cognitive psychology, which he felt helped him understand perceptions better.

I glanced at my watch. I had prepared a long list of questions to ask him and time was running out. I began to follow up on things I wanted to know before we parted. One was the matter of Schlichting's words about him.

"Schlichting, Schlichting." Silveria shook his head. "Most of those things he wrote, that list he made with the questions and answers, he got that from TV." Silveria looked frustrated.

"But come on, Robert, there were those other letters," I prompted, watching to see if I jarred his memory. He was silent.

We switched to the murder of Charles Boyd in Kansas.
"Okay. I did hit him with the rock," he admitted, "but Arkansas
Bobcat was the one who hit him with the axe. We picked Arkansas
Bobcat up at a mission in Albuquerque."

"But Robert, Boyd's daughter was a witness, remember?
You went to her house in Kansas and then left. She saw only you
and Boyd."

"That's because Arkansas Bobcat was dropped off to look
for drugs. Later on we met up with him and picked him up. Boyd
didn't like him and wouldn't let him come into the tent with us.
He let me come in, but not him. They argued the night before."
Then Silveria paused. "I was pressured into pleading guilty in
Kansas. I was there and I was responsible for hitting Boyd with the
rock. I mean, I am responsible for participating in the killing, but
I didn't hit him with the axe. It was Arkansas Bobcat's fingerprints
on that check that was deposited [at the campground], not mine."

I had to move on. Although I wanted to remind him what
he said about going around deliberately touching all the objects at
the camp, I decided not to.

I especially wanted to hear what he had to say about his
family to check out what I'd read. "What about that psychological
report?" I watched Silveria as he leaned forward, his elbows on his
knees, his hands clasped together.

"I don't know where that came from about me and my dad.
He was a regular dad who used to take us camping. He gave us what
he could." Silveria shook his head as if in disbelief.

"What about the bat story, the one where your dad wanted
you to fight with those boys in the park, one on one?"

"Oh, that one," Silveria sat up again. "My uncle was there,
too. He was egging my dad on. He's the one who used to give me
drugs all the time. I had him hold some money for me one time
and he just took it and kept it and wouldn't give it back. He said I

owed him because of the drugs he gave me." I decided not to pursue the story behind Silveria's uncle. As far as I was concerned, he was pretty shallow. Besides, from what I had heard, most of Silveria's family was on the outs with him since he made a big splash with the media, which the family felt was at their expense.

Finally, I turned to the fateful day when Silveria was stopped and arrested in Roseville.

"You could have easily gotten away, you know." I watched for his reaction.

"Oh, I know. The guard didn't even have the right to stop me, because I was on public property, not on railroad property." Silveria shrugged. "But I was planning to turn myself in anyway. It was as good a time as any. I knew they were looking for me. I saw the flyers. Bam-Bam even showed me one. I wanted to give myself up." He said he felt that he deserved to be locked up, where he could straighten out his head, but at the same time, he doesn't feel that justice was served in the court of law. "I don't care, but I didn't deserve what I got. I was forced to plea bargain to avoid going on trial and getting a death sentence."

Silveria's family still feels that the glare of the media is obtrusive in their lives and this bothers Robert Silveria. His mother is convinced that Silveria plea-bargained, rather than go to trial, in order to protect them from the embarrassment and the focus that a long trial would bring to them.

"William Pettit and Mikey Clites — were they FTRA?" The question had been on my mind a long time.

"Yes," Silveria nodded. "They were."

There was no way I was going to leave without touching on the Arizona derailment that had plagued law enforcement for so long. I wanted to confirm the suspicions I held.

"Yeah," Silveria grinned, nodding. "Dogman Tony did know how to do it. There was that one time near Big Spring, Texas, when a bunch of us were sitting around a campfire drinking, and Dogman Tony said, 'I'm gonna go and steal an engine.' We all said, 'Yeah, sure.' We didn't believe him, but he got up and went over to the yard in a drunken stupor and got inside a parked freight train engine and got it moving. He also managed to get it derailed." Silveria explained how he did it, which further showed me that he also knew how to derail trains. They all probably did. FTRA guys are very knowledgeable when it comes to trains. They are so knowledgeable that they could be working for the rail companies instead of illegally train hopping. Silveria also knew the spot where the derailment occurred, the one a snitch accused Dogman Tony of perpetrating. Yet Silveria would not come out and point fingers. Everything he said was carefully worded so that I knew the story, but it wouldn't hold up in court.

"You could drive down there in a car and see the spot where the derailment happened." He motioned with his hands to show a downward motion.

I got an eerie feeling when Silveria said this. I thought back to his confession of killing the drug dealer in Arizona. Silveria hinted to us in his confessions that he knew something about the Arizona derailment, but I guess we were so overwhelmed with everything else he had to say that this one slipped through. There is probably a lot we can still learn from Silveria. With the new threats of terror, it would be wise to have someone as knowledgeable as him point out the weak spots along America's rail system.

I told Silveria what was happening to some of the people we both knew. "I have Forty-Pounder's flag, the one you signed the last time you were at the Roseville safe house. I had it framed." I also told him that she had passed away a couple of years before. Soda Pop, I told Silveria, moved to southern California and gave up rail riding. I told him that Angel and TNT said "Hi."

Silveria looked pleased at the mention of the last two names. "Why don't they write to me? Angel and I had our fingers cut in the same initiation. Baby Girl was there and so was Forty-

Pounder. Tell TNT and Angel to write." When he finished, I also
told him that Jenny said she still prays for him and thinks of him.
He nodded and said, "Thank you."

Soon it became apparent the time had come for me to leave.
But before I left, there was one more question I wanted to ask.

"What about the FTRA? What would you describe the
FTRA as?" I held my breath.

"The FTRA? I'll tell you about FTRA in one word: fear.
That's what the organization is. It's based on fear."

I was taken back by the insight he showed in his comment.

Leaving the penitentiary, I felt conflicted. How does a man
fall into such a deep, dark hole? I wondered. I thought of Silveria's victims, especially about Michael Ari Garfinkle and Quincy
Dear. After all, they were just kids who wanted to hop trains and
ended up in the proverbial wrong place at the wrong time. I
thought of James McLean, trying to recall if I ever noticed him
riding on his bike. Did our paths ever cross? Did he ever see me
perform at the annual Solano Berkeley Albany Stroll? I wondered
what difference it might have made if I knew him as well when he
was alive as I came to know him after his death.

As I walked to my car, I felt a great sense of sadness. While
I remembered all that Silveria had done and all the horrible crimes
he committed, in spite of this I felt compassion for the man. We
shared many interests and insights. If his life had been different, I
could picture the two of us sitting in my den on leather chairs,
drinking brandy, smoking cigars and talking about collectibles,
memorabilia and the untold stories of the FTRA.

Suddenly, I wondered, how and when did I cross over the
line of a cop's detachment? We're supposed to be society's
garbagemen, hired to clean up the streets and throw the human
trash behind bars. But sometimes it's hard not to notice the souls
crying out in cases where the line between the victim and perpetrator blurs. Then I thought about whether others saw our similarities first, recalling that two years earlier, two separate teams filmed

documentaries that were aired even in Germany and Hungary on the "Elvis Cop and the Boxcar Serial Killer." I thought about how Silveria pushed Schlichting to tell me to write a book. I wondered, is that why he held on to the article about him singing the Elvis song in the holding cell? Was that one of the ways he tried to get me to get his story out? The irony of it all would be that, eight years later, I actually was writing the book about him.

Then I thought about what Silveria said about fear and how much it had also been part of my life. It's a battle that many of us carry inside. If you stop to analyze it, fear is a guiding force behind so many things: anger, power, jealousy, pettiness and even murder.

Silveria, I had come to realize, long after my investigations into McLean's murder, is just a tip of an iceberg. There is a world of drugs, violence and madness out there that turns lives that could be ordinary into hellish ones. The rails offer them an escape route, while one aspect of the FTRA brotherhood helps them survive and the other, governed by fear, destroys them. At some point, Silveria made a choice as to which fork in the road he wanted to take. In the end, Silveria, had he not been wanting in some part of himself to be caught, could still be riding the rails and nobody who knew him would have turned him in. The open cases would have grown cold and forgotten.

A letter Silveria wrote to his second wife came to my mind. In it, he stated, "The sadness just won't go away." He wrote that he wanted to come clean and put all the past "foggy dreams" behind, but the horrific consequences of those dreams remain with him. I couldn't help but notice that the sense of sadness still hung over him.

I know that while Robert Silveria is locked up, with every war and economic downturn there is a burgeoning of rail riders. Silveria is among the second generation trained by Vietnam veterans, whose minds and bodies did not recover from the traumas they experienced in Southeast Asia.

As I drove that day towards Portland to catch a flight back to Oakland, I wondered how many more future generations of

Robert Silverias might be created by the violence, brutality and horrors of the Afghanistan and Iraqi wars. I asked myself, what can we do to change that? What can we do to stop the proliferation of serial killers that our own faulty laws, ghastly wars and broken systems help to create?